Commonsense methods for children with special needs

WITHDRAWN

It is now common practice for many students who experience difficulties in learning or who have disabilities, to be placed in ordinary schools and, where practicable, to receive their education in the mainstream. This situation presents a challenge to regular class teachers who must develop confidence and competence in dealing with the personal, social and educational needs of such students, and who often feel inadequate when faced with students with special needs.

This text is based on the premise that there is actually very little which is unique or 'special' about the teaching required by students with mild to moderate difficulties. Most so-called special techniques or special methods are just good basic teaching procedures applied with intensity and precision. The ideas presented throughout the book seek to illustrate this point by giving practical advice which can be incorporated into the mainstream programme in order to cater more effectively for a wide range of student ability. By adding some or all of the strategies described in the book to their normal repertoire of skills, teachers should become more versatile and adaptable in their approach to *all* children.

This new, revised and enlarged edition provides a wealth of useful advice for the busy teacher and for the student teacher in training. Issues of self-management and self-regulation are central to the book's detailed coverage of behaviour problems, learning difficulties and social skills development. Six chapters are devoted to basic academic skill improvement, and attention is given to ways in which the regular curriculum can be adapted to enable students with learning difficulties to experience some measure of success. Advisers and co-ordinators of special services will also find advice on school-based and regional support service operation highly relevant to their work.

Peter Westwood is Senior Lecturer in Special Education at Flinders University, Adelaide. His distinguished career in special education spans more than thirty years, and includes experience as a teacher, educational psychologist, college and university lecturer and administrator. He has written more than forty articles for professional journals, three books for teachers and six books for children.

Commonsense methods for children with special needs

Strategies for the regular classroom

Third edition

Peter Westwood

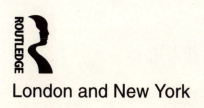

London and New York

First published 1997
by Routledge
11 New Fetter Lane, London EC4P 4EE

Simultaneously published in the USA and Canada
by Routledge
29 West 35th Street, New York, NY 10001

© 1993, 1997 Peter Westwood

Typeset in Times by
Ponting–Green Publishing Services, Chesham,
Buckinghamshire
Printed and bound in Great Britain by
T.J. International Ltd, Padstow, Cornwall

British Library Cataloguing in Publication Data
A catalogue record for this book is available from the
British Library

Library of Congress Cataloging in Publication Data
Westwood, Peter S.
    Commonsense methods for children with special needs : strategies
for the regular classroom / Peter Westwood. – 3rd ed.
        p.   cm.
    Includes bibliographical references (p.) and index.
    1. Handicapped children–Education.
    2. Mainstreaming in   education. I. Title.
LC4015.W44   1996
371.91–dc20   96–35396
                                              CIP

ISBN   0–415–15623–8 (pbk)

Contents

Introduction

Since the publication of the first and second editions of this book much has changed in the overlapping fields of special and regular education. In particular, special education has moved closer to a merger with regular education, driven in this direction by the current philosophy of 'inclusive schooling' (Sebba and Ainscow 1996). The inclusive schooling movement, building upon the earlier trend toward mainstream integration of students with disabilities, presents the view that *all* children have the right to be educated in regular schools and to have an equal opportunity to participate in the mainstream curriculum.

The 1970s and 1980s saw a gradual increase in the number of students with milder forms of disability and learning difficulties retained in regular classrooms. Since that time there has been active campaigning to have students with more significant disabilities also receive their education in the mainstream. Extreme advocates of 'full inclusion' (e.g. Lipsky and Gartner 1989; Stainback and Stainback and Stefanich 1996) argue that any form of segregation of students with special needs is socially unjust and a denial of their rights to be exposed to the same broad range of learning experiences enjoyed by all other students. They wish to see students with even the most severe forms of disability placed in regular schools and receiving any special services they need in that setting. Less extreme supporters of inclusion suggest that the needs of students with significant disabilities are best served by retaining the full range of placement options, including special schools and special classes for those who need them. Special services should be organized in such a way that students with severe and multiple disabilities can more easily join with mainstream students on a frequent and regular basis (e.g. Fuchs and Fuchs 1995; Smelter, Rasch and Yudewitz 1994).

There is an obvious commitment now in most developed countries to move toward a policy of inclusive schooling. To this end, effective ways of including students with moderate to severe disabilities are being investigated and evaluated at school and classroom level (Farlow 1996). In reality, catering for such a diverse range of students in the regular classroom is far from easy, and requires very careful planning, gradual implementation and close monitoring to identify beneficial practices which might be replicated in other settings (Barton 1995; Williams and Fox 1996). It has already become evident that close collaboration among different schools and different teachers, and between teachers, other professionals and parents, is one necessary component in the move to make regular education 'special' (Dyson 1994). Another essential feature is the ability to apply the principles of differentiation in curriculum planning and in teaching approach (Lewis 1992; Bearne 1996). These issues are discussed in Chapter 13.

The practice of inclusion brings with it an increasing necessity for regular class teachers in primary schools, and subject specialists in secondary schools, to increase their range of teaching and organizational strategies to meet the needs of a very diverse group of students. This book attempts to provide teachers with practical advice which will help them to respond to this challenge. The target group of students is not small. It is estimated that some 20 per cent of the school population will have special educational needs at some time during their school careers (Department for Education 1994).

This text is based on the belief that students with special educational needs benefit most from carefully structured, explicit teaching methods. The use of unstructured, child-centred enquiry methods tends to make too many unrealistic assumptions concerning children's motivation and their ability to teach themselves. It is important, as we move toward more inclusive practices, that we do not ignore explicit teaching approaches which have proved to be extremely effective with all students.

This third edition of *Commonsense Methods for Children with Special Needs* has been expanded and updated. Two new chapters have been added to the book, one dealing with early recognition and intervention for learning difficulties, and the other presenting practical strategies for improving children's spelling skills. All other sections have been significantly revised to include recent developments in the field.

Acknowledgements

I wish to thank the following individuals for permission to quote from or reproduce sections of their work in this book.

Merrill Jackson, for permission to describe his 'visuo-thematic' approach for remedial reading. It is taken from his text *Reading Disability: Experiment, Innovation and Individual Therapy* (1972).

William McCormick, State Supervisor for Elementary Education, Dover, Delaware, for permission to quote from his article 'Teachers can learn to teach more effectively', in the journal *Educational Leadership* (1979).

Geoff Rogers, Principal of Heathfield Primary School, for permission to reproduce a section from his rebus reading programme *Truckin' with Kenny* (1982).

Peter Westwood
Flinders University
South Australia

Chapter 1

Learning difficulties and learning disabilities

Students who have a learning difficulty do not form a homogeneous group. They have a wide variety of characteristics, ranging from academic difficulties to cognitive and social-emotional problems.

(Van Kraayenoord and Elkins 1994: 244)

The term 'learning difficulties' is a very general one, used widely and without much precision to refer to the general problems in learning experienced by some 10 to 16 per cent of the school population (National Health and Medical Research Council 1990). Usually the term is applied to students whose difficulties are not directly related to a specific intellectual, physical or sensory disability, although students with disabilities often do experience problems in learning and in social adjustment. Students who have, in the past, been referred to as 'slow learners', 'low achievers' or simply 'the hard to teach', certainly fall within the category 'learning difficulties'. So too do the children described as specifically *learning disabled* (LD); those of at least average intelligence who, for no obvious reason, experience great difficulty in learning the basic academic skills (American Psychiatric Association 1994). It seems likely that only approximately 3 per cent of the school population should be regarded as specifically learning disabled (Frost and Emery 1996) and their unique problems will be addressed later in the chapter.

It is important to realize that students with general and specific learning difficulties comprise by far the largest group of students with special educational needs. These students require some measure of additional support and special consideration if they are to achieve success in regular classrooms.

PLACEMENT

Increasingly over the past decade students with learning difficulties have been retained in mainstream classes, rather than segregated or withdrawn into special groups. They have been joined, too, by students with intellectual, physical and sensory disabilities and those with emotional or behavioural problems, many of whom would previously have had to attend special school.

This move toward inclusion of children with special needs in regular classes, which began in the 1970s and gained momentum in the late 1980s and early 1990s, has changed dramatically the nature of special educational provision. It has also had a major impact on the role of the regular class teacher, who is now required to cater for the needs of an increasingly diverse group of students (Fuchs and Fuchs 1994; McCoy 1995). Originally termed 'integration' or 'mainstreaming', the policy of placing children with special needs in regular classes is now referred to as 'inclusion'. Inclusion has become one of the more contentious issues in the field of education today (Banerji and Dailey 1995; Barton 1995; Brucker 1995).

It has been said that, 'The goal of inclusion is not to erase differences, but to enable all students to belong within an educational community that validates and values their individuality' (Stainback *et al.* 1994: 489). The notion that it is the right of each and every child, if at all possible, to be educated in the regular classroom has been adopted in most developed countries. It has certainly influenced policy-making in the United States, Canada, Britain, Australia, New Zealand and much of Europe, where inclusion is now the accepted placement model for students with special needs (Ashman and Elkins 1994; Gross and Gipps 1987; Murray-Seegert 1992).

Policies which advocate the inclusion of *all* students with disabilities in regular classes are not without their critics, with some educators arguing that regular class placement is not necessarily the least restrictive learning environment for some children (Smelter, Rasch and Yudewitz 1994; Putnam, Spiegel and Bruininks 1995). For this reason, it is also argued that the full range of placement options, including special schools and special classes, should be retained, allowing for responsible choices to be made concerning the most appropriate educational setting for each individual with a disability (Vaughn and Schumm 1995).

The practical problems surrounding inclusion are most obvious in the case of individuals with severe and multiple disabilities, since many of these students require a high degree of physical care and management over and above their special educational needs. However, there is evidence to suggest that where schools are prepared to accept the challenge of full inclusion, it is indeed possible to provide appropriate programmes for these students (Clark 1994; Farlow 1996; LeRoy and Simpson 1996).

By comparison, the inclusion of students with milder forms of disability and with general learning difficulties, in theory at least, presents fewer problems. It is believed that regular class teachers can be helped to adopt teaching approaches which are more flexible and adaptive to the specific needs of such students (Andrews and Lupart 1993; Koop and Minchinton 1995). On the other hand, some doubt has been expressed that children with specific learning disability (LD) can benefit from total inclusion (Roberts and Mather 1995). These children, who have major problems in acquiring basic academic skills, usually need at least one period per day when they are withdrawn from class and taught individually. Within the regular classroom it is virtually impossible to provide remedial instruction of the intensity, frequency and duration required by these students. The same is probably true of other students with special instructional or therapeutic needs.

INCLUSIVE PRACTICES

Research is really only just beginning to determine which school and classroom practices result in the most effective inclusion (Hollowood *et al.* 1995; Giangreco 1996). However, it seems that the following ingredients are certainly required if students with significant learning or adjustment problems are to be successfully included in the regular classroom, with appropriate access to the general curriculum:

- strong leadership on the part of the school principal;
- the development of a whole-school policy supportive of inclusion;
- the development of positive attitudes toward students with disabilities;
- a commitment on the part of all staff to work collaboratively and to share problems, responsibilities and expertise;
- the development of support networks among staff, and links with outside agencies and services;
- adequate resourcing in terms of materials and personnel;
- regular training and professional development for staff;
- close liaison with parents;
- adaptation of curriculum and teaching methods (differentiation).

It is beyond the scope of this chapter to elaborate here on each and every point in the list above. Several of the key issues are taken up in later chapters. Here it will only be mentioned that several educators have addressed the final point in the list, the issue of teaching methods, by suggesting that student-centred, process approaches have most to offer children with disabilities (Goddard 1995; MacInnis and Hemming 1995). These process approaches, which often seem to emphasize personal and social development rather than mastery of curriculum content, are thought to be more accommodating of student differences. However, there is some evidence to suggest that process approaches do not meet the learning needs of all students, and in particular are not necessarily the optimum way of developing the basic academic skills for students with learning problems (Harris and Graham 1996). Care must be taken to ensure that a process approach as an example of inclusive practice is not simply a soft option which allows students with disabilities and learning difficulties to fade into the background without being unduly challenged and without really making progress through the curriculum. To be effective, inclusion should result in much more than simply minor gains in social development.

The viewpoint expressed in this book is that enquiry-based, process or discovery learning methods should certainly be used frequently with children, but should be reserved for the types of learning and stages of learning where they have most to contribute. For example, the development of higher-order cognitive skills and problem-solving strategies will certainly necessitate an enquiry approach. So too will the more advanced application of explicitly taught strategies and skills to new situations, in order to facilitate generalization and transfer of learning. However, this type of enquiry approach is usually inappropriate for the beginning stages of learning something as important as basic literacy and numeracy skills. It is this writer's belief that the early stages of learning basic academic skills and mastering core curriculum content are best accomplished by explicit forms of teaching (Westwood 1995a).

Evidence suggests that students with disabilities and learning problems most frequently do best in structured programmes where effective direct teaching methods are employed. In particular, students with behaviour problems, or with some degree of emotional disturbance, require an environment which is well organized and predictable, and a programme which is presented clearly and with abundant opportunities for success (Lloyd 1988; Gow and Ward 1991; Kauffman *et al.* 1995).

EFFECTIVE INSTRUCTION

In the first edition of this book, information from McCormick (1979) was presented in support of the view that clear, effective teaching not only raises the attainment level of all students but also reduces very significantly the prevalence of learning failure. More recent evidence fully supports this viewpoint (Rosenshine 1995; Creemers 1994; Phillips *et al.* 1996). Effective teaching also serves as an obvious first step toward creating an inclusive classroom (Barry 1995).

Effective teaching practices are those which provide students with the maximum opportunity to learn. These practices increase student achievement levels through maintaining on-task behaviour. The term 'academic engaged time' is often used to describe such on-task behaviour. Academic engaged time refers to the proportion of instructional time in which students are actively involved in their work. This active involvement includes attending to instruction from the teacher, working independently or with a group on assigned academic tasks, and applying previously acquired knowledge and skills. Studies have shown that students who are receiving instruction directly from the teacher spend more time attending to the content of the lesson than students who are expected to find out for themselves. Effective lessons, particularly those covering basic academic skills, tend to have a clear structure.

Effective classroom lessons which maintain high levels of academic focus tend to contain the following elements:

- daily review of previous day's work;
- clear presentation of new skills and concepts, with much modelling by the teacher;
- guided student practice, with high success rates and with feedback to individual students;
- independent student practice, applying the new knowledge and skills appropriately;
- systematic cumulative revision of work previously covered.

It is particularly important that *all* students experience a high success rate during the guided practice phase of the lesson. The teacher must be expert in monitoring performance at the level of each student in the class as corrective feedback is then geared to individual needs and learning rate.

McCormick's guidelines for more effective teaching

McCormick (1979) identified a number of characteristics of teachers who helped children to achieve at better-than-expected levels. His summary provides a valuable framework against which to design effective programmes to meet the needs of children with and without disabilities. His advice is as valid now as it was in 1979.

In schools where students achieve better results than expected, teachers demonstrated a greater understanding of the structure and substance of the content being taught. In particular they:

- were more specific about lesson objectives;
- were better able to judge accurately the time needed to accomplish these objectives;
- made more frequent use of structuring comments as instruction proceeded;
- successfully broke the lessons into manageable and logical sequences;
- more ably anticipated problems in reaching the objectives and made accommodations for them.

Teachers also demonstrated a greater understanding of the special characteristics of their students. In particular they:

- more often modified instruction on the basis of student responses;
- used a vocabulary, oral and written, more appropriate for the age or ability level;
- adjusted the level of questions for different ability levels in the class;
- presented materials at an appropriate level of difficulty.

Furthermore, the teachers demonstrated a greater understanding of the principles of learning. They:

- made frequent use of opportunities to create and maintain an appropriate mind-set for pupils;

- frequently encouraged students to set appropriate and realistic goals for themselves;
- spent time and effort in creating an atmosphere of concern about the importance of learning the lesson content;
- more often provided opportunities for learner success;
- more often provided immediate feedback to learners;
- more often checked the level of mastery being achieved (and proceeded only if an acceptable level of learning was evident);
- gave more appropriate consideration to the length and spacing of practice;
- in general provided more meaningful and coherent presentations.

(Based on McCormick 1979: 60, and reproduced with permission.)

Explicit teaching

Closely allied to the notion of effective instruction is that of 'explicit teaching'. Explicit teaching is the term used to describe a very direct way of instructing children in important skill and content areas of the curriculum. Explicit teaching does not leave learning to chance. For example, in basic skill subjects such as reading, writing and mathematics children are taught thoroughly the knowledge, skills and strategies they need, rather than expecting them to acquire these essentials through incidental learning.

The terms 'direct teaching' and 'active teaching' are frequently used to mean the same as explicit teaching (Kindsvatter, Wilen and Ishler 1992). As the term 'explicit' implies, the children are given very clear instructions, demonstrations, explanations, practice and corrective feedback for each new step in learning.

Explicit teaching typically embodies the following key elements:

- analysis of the learning task into easy steps;
- direct teaching of task-approach strategies (how to go about the particular learning task);
- clear modelling, demonstrating and 'thinking aloud' by the teacher;
- provision of much guided practice with corrective feedback;
- use of strategies to keep children on task and academically engaged;
- close monitoring of each child's progress;
- reteaching to individuals where necessary;
- provision of successful practice and application of new knowledge and skills;
- frequent revision of previously taught knowledge and skills;
- optimum use made of available instructional time.

Where explicit teaching is used, students with learning difficulties appear to make much better progress, and they later become more confident and effective learners. The use of explicit teaching methods in the early stages of learning something new in no way precludes the student from ultimately developing independence in learning: quite the contrary (Pressley and McCormick 1995).

PERSONALIZATION AND INCLUSIVE PRACTICES

In addition to explicit teaching, teachers are also often advised that the solution to special needs in the regular classroom is 'individualized programming'. There are potential problems if this advice is misinterpreted. When teachers are urged to cater for students' individual differences, including those of students with significant disabilities and learning problems, it should not be taken to mean that each and every child must be given an individual work programme for most of the school day (Good and Brophy 1994). Such an arrangement is both unworkable and unnecessary. Group work and whole class activities can be used frequently, provided that different outcomes are expected for different students. For example, within a whole class lesson one child may write three pages of his or her own thoughts unaided; another may manage only three sentences with much help from the teacher; yet another may manage only a picture. All these responses are acceptable. A classroom activity is 'inclusive' if it allows every child to make an attempt, and to achieve some degree of success alongside others. The integration of students with special needs into regular classes must involve inclusive curricula rather than, or in addition to, individual programming. Where individual educational plans (IEPs) are required they should indicate quite clearly not only what the student needs to do which is different from the rest of the class, but also the areas of the curriculum where he or she can be counted in with the others. Ideally such inclusion in the mainstream programme will be for most of the school day.

Even within whole class or group sessions teachers can and do 'personalize' their approach. For example, when questioning a group the teacher directs a straightforward and simple question to Child A in the expectation that he or she will manage to respond to it. A more searching question is directed at Child B. Similarly, when a teacher provides additional work at the same level for one child in order to help that child master the topic, while at the same time setting something different and more complex for another child, that teacher is personalizing the approach. Other examples of personalization, which reflect a thorough knowledge of the students in the class, include waiting longer for certain students to respond to a question; praising specific students; drawing upon the interests and abilities of individuals when discussing a topic; delegating responsibilities within the group; modifying short-term goals; providing more (or less) direct assistance; revising topics more frequently for some students; and selecting or developing alternative resource materials.

Effective instruction, combined with personalization and the use of inclusive activities, will reduce the frequency with which a teacher needs to devise separate programmes for students with disabilities or learning difficulties. In addition to knowing their students extremely well, teachers also need to be aware of the factors which may cause or exacerbate learning difficulties. In particular, they need to recognize the factors over which they have most control.

FACTORS ASSOCIATED WITH LEARNING DIFFICULTY

In their chapter titled 'Dimensions of learning problems', Wallace and Kauffman (1986) support the view that seldom is a *single* cause found for a particular student's learning problem; and they also stress that sometimes it is impossible to identify *any* predisposing or precipitating factors. Certainly diagnosis of learning difficulties remains a very inexact science.

Over to you: *Possible causes of learning difficulty*

- Before moving to the next section you are asked to prepare a list of possible reasons why students may develop learning difficulties. For example, 'difficulty with English as a second language', 'hearing impairment', 'school absence', etc.

- Now move to the categories below and analyse your list. Place a tick against the appropriate category for each item on your list. For example, 'difficulty with English as a second language' would score a tick against 'family background'. 'Hearing impairment' would score a tick against 'within the student'. Some items may need a tick in more than one category.

Within the student.
Within the family background or culture.
Within the peer group.
Within the curriculum.
Within the teaching approach.
Within the student–teacher relationship.
Within the school/classroom environment.
Other.

The results of your analysis above will probably show far more ticks in the 'within the student' category than in any other. A common reaction when faced with a student who is failing is to look for problems or 'deficits' within the learner, rather than elsewhere (Westwood 1995b; Bearne 1996). 'What's *wrong* with him (or her)?' we ask. Yet such a question is unlikely to yield a useful answer, since at best it will give only a partial explanation for the problem. Even parents tend to assume that there is something 'wrong' with their children if school progress is unsatisfactory, and it is common to find such children referred to educational psychologists and general practitioners for evaluation or diagnosis. However, it is usually much more productive to examine factors outside the child, such as quality and type of instruction given, teacher expectations, relevance of the work set, classroom environment, interpersonal dynamics within the class social group and rapport with the teacher. These factors are much more amenable to modification than are factors within the child or within the family background or culture. In particular, the learning difficulties exhibited by some students may well reflect inappropriate curriculum content and poor quality instruction. Elliott and Garnett (1994: 6) refer to such students as 'curriculum disabled'. They are bored by a programme of work that fails to meet their interests or match their learning characteristics. Many of them reject school, particularly in the secondary years, and school in turn virtually rejects them (Rees and Young 1995).

An 'ecological perspective' on this situation recognizes that a learning problem is almost always due to a complex combination of interacting factors, all of which merit attention when seeking to provide additional help for the student concerned. If teachers do not consider these factors, and if they do not seek to teach effectively and personalize their approach, they may easily precipitate a child's entry into a failure cycle.

The failure cycle

The basic message of the failure cycle is, 'If at first you don't succeed, you don't succeed!'

Observation of young children suggests that, even at an early age, children begin to regard themselves as 'failures' in given learning situations. If, for whatever reason, a child finds that he or she cannot do something which other children are doing easily, there is a loss of confidence. This loss of confidence leads to deliberate avoidance of the type of activity associated with the failure; and sometimes even avoidance of any new or challenging situation. Avoidance leads to lack of practice. Lack of practice ensures that the individual does not gain in proficiency or confidence, while other children forge ahead. Constant failure results in poor self-esteem and lowered motivation.

The effects of early failure are thus cumulative and probably account for many instances of learning difficulty in particular school subjects. While there are almost certainly different thresholds of tolerance for failure among any group of students, it must be acknowledged that failure is not a pleasing experience, and given sufficient exposure to it almost any student will

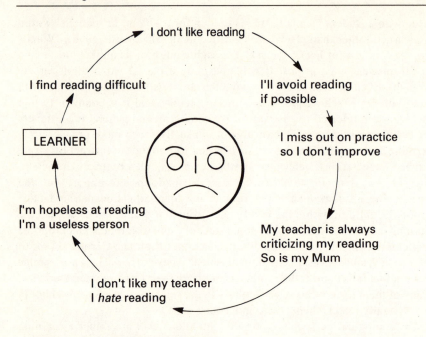

I don't like reading

I find reading difficult

LEARNER

I'll avoid reading
if possible

I miss out on practice
so I don't improve

I'm hopeless at reading
I'm a useless person

My teacher is always
criticizing my reading
So is my Mum

I don't like my teacher
I *hate* reading

Figure 1 The failure cycle: an example

develop avoidance strategies. It must be noted too, that the failure cycle is not confined to early school experiences, but can be established at any time in life.

The implications of the failure cycle for the teacher are twofold. First, it is evident that to reduce the possibility of early failure in a new learning situation, teachers must prepare and present new tasks very clearly indeed, with as much direct guidance and support as necessary to ensure success. It is here that explicit teaching has a major role to play. Second, the only way of breaking the failure cycle is to devise some way of providing successful practice in which the learner recognizes that he or she is improving. Strategies for achieving this goal, and for helping the learner to become more independent in his or her learning, are presented in the following chapters.

Students who are most likely to have learning problems and to experience frequent failure are those often described in the past as 'slow learners'. The term 'slow learner' has given way now to the more general description 'student with learning difficulties' as, like many labels used to describe students, the term 'slow learner' acquired its own odium over the years. Dyer (1991) suggested that it should be abolished as it was a derogatory term and it tended to colour the attitudes of teachers. It also implied that such students should be 'taught slowly', quite the reverse of their actual need. In this context, Brandt (1985) cautioned teachers that allowing students to progress slowly actually creates an ever-widening gap between the able and the less-able learners.

Certainly, the evidence is that students with learning difficulties and learning disabilities fall increasingly behind and experience fewer and fewer successes if they are not given special consideration. In terms of teaching approach, 'special consideration' should mean more rapidly-paced, effective instruction which teaches students more, not less, in the time available.

Students with general learning difficulties

Two viewpoints have emerged concerning students with learning difficulties: the Deficit Model and the Inefficient Learner Model.

The Deficit Model

A number of writers have attempted to summarize the characteristics of students with learning difficulties. The following list represents a compilation from those sources.

It is argued that students with learning difficulties experience problems because they have:

- below average intelligence;
- poor concentration span;
- poor powers of retention for knowledge and skills;
- underdeveloped listening skills;
- difficulties in understanding complex language structures;
- a meagre vocabulary;
- a lack of ability to generalize and transfer new learning;
- little desire to go beyond the information given in any lesson at school;
- an inability to use reading as a means of acquiring information, extending knowledge and for enjoyment;
- major problems in written language;
- poor self-esteem;
- a lack of self-management skills;
- behavioural and emotional reactions to failure.

It is easy to see why the list tends to be described as a 'Deficit Model': all the comments are negative and pessimistic. There is a danger that teachers may shrug their shoulders and feel that such students are impossible to teach. However, it can be argued that if a teacher is aware of these areas of difficulty experienced by the student he or she can take account of them when preparing classroom work. Each of the above so-called 'deficits' has an immediate implication for *what* we teach and *how* we teach it to students with learning difficulties.

Many years ago Gulliford made a comment which is as true now as we approach the year 2000 as it was then: 'Though slow learners and the socially disadvantaged often appear to have less to offer, this is a measure of their need rather than an indication of their limits' (Gulliford 1969: 48).

The Inefficient Learner Model

The second viewpoint on students with learning difficulties attributes their problems to inefficiency in their approach to learning. Some students are observed to have very poor task-approach skills. They do not have effective ways of attempting new tasks but rather employ hit-and-miss strategies which produce high failure rates. They do not plan ahead or monitor their own performance. Frequently they become locked into a failure cycle, even in the first year at school; and their problem is exacerbated by the rapid development of behaviour patterns detrimental to good learning. Early failure undermines confidence and the child develops avoidance strategies which further reduce the opportunity to learn. Stott, whose work in the 1970s gave the first insights into these problems, suggested that many students regarded as mildly intellectually disabled, or specifically learning disabled, are not lacking in potential ability. He considered that their poor approach to learning prevents them from attending to or working at anything for very long. They need to 'learn *how* to learn' (Stott 1978; Stott, Green and Francis 1983). The evidence is that students *can* be helped in this direction (Bechtol and Sorenson 1993; Butler 1995).

The 'inefficient learner' perspective presented by Stott certainly strengthens the argument that students with learning difficulties benefit most from explicit teaching of new concepts, skills and strategies. They need to be placed in well-managed classrooms, with clear, active teaching and where students spend productive time on-task, experiencing successful practice and knowing that they are reaching mastery. These students also require relevant and motivating curricula. When activities are appropriately geared to their interests, and when the programme combines direct teaching in class with challenging and realistic out-of-class experiences, it is clear that these students improve in attitude, behaviour and achievement (Young and Rees 1995).

LEARNING DISABILITIES

Learning disability is the term applied to students whose difficulties cannot be traced easily to any lack of intelligence, to sensory impairment, to cultural or linguistic disadvantage or to inadequate teaching (Brock 1995). This small group, perhaps no more than 3 per cent of the school population, exhibits chronic problems in learning, particularly within the academic skill areas of reading, writing, spelling and mathematics.

Although the field of 'learning disabilities' is often said to date back only to the 1960s, with the name Samuel Kirk mainly associated with pioneering work in identification and classification of students with learning problems, the initial recognition of unusual learning difficulties actually began well before the turn of the century (Richardson 1992). Since those early days, the field of learning disabilities has represented something of a growth industry, with more research, more publications and more public interest generated than in almost any other field of education. Nevertheless, learning disability remains a controversial issue. Some educators deny that there *is* a form of learning difficulty distinct from the general learning problems which are known to impede the progress of some students (Franklyn 1987). Other experts argue strongly that a form of learning disability does exist which is qualitatively and etiologically different from the more general forms of academic failure, often referred to in the literature as 'garden variety' (Badian 1996). Even after many decades of research no final consensus has been reached concerning a precise and unambiguous definition of learning disability (Kavale, Forness and Lorsbach 1991; Shaw *et al.* 1995).

The best known form of specific learning disability is, of course, dyslexia. This form of reading problem is thought to be present in approximately 1 per cent of the school population (although some reports place the prevalence rate much higher). It is often defined as a disorder manifested by difficulty in learning to read despite conventional instruction, adequate intelligence and sociocultural opportunity. Other forms of learning disability have been identified as dysgraphia (problems with writing), dysorthographia (problems with spelling) and dyscalculia (problems with arithmetical calculation). However, such quasi-medical terms are not at all helpful in educational decision-making related to placement and teaching of the students concerned.

Some authorities in the learning disability field tend to attribute the learning problem to neurological or constitutional deficiencies within the student (Brock 1995). For example, Adelman and Taylor (1987) devote several pages to a discussion of possible neurological dysfunction as a causal factor. They suggest that the LD student may have sustained very minor, subclinical brain damage before or during birth; or may have a nervous system which is maturing at a slower rate than is normal (maturational delay theory) or which exhibits biochemical irregularities. However, even if some of these factors do apply in a particular student's case, two comments must be made. First, the diagnosis does not provide useful information for educational intervention: it doesn't tell us what we should do. Second, it is most unlikely that such a factor can operate alone to cause the learning difficulty.

Although much emphasis has been placed upon the 'organic or biological' causes of learning disability, and interest has also been shown in possible 'genetic' factors in some cases, recent studies have suggested other possible causes. In particular, attention has been directed toward learning style (Bradshaw 1995). In many cases of learning disability the children exhibit very inefficient learning styles, for example, not approaching a task such as word recognition or phonic decoding or arithmetical computation with any adequate system. The important thing to note is that the current evidence suggests that these children can be taught more efficient strategies and can then function at a significantly higher level (Sullivan, Mastropieri and Scruggs 1995).

Another factor considered to cause the learning problems typical of students with a specific reading disability is weakness in processing oral language. This is most evident in their inability to deal effectively with the phonological (sound) aspects of oral language. This problem is reflected in their poor performance in word recognition and spelling, two areas where efficiency in mapping speech sounds to letters or letter clusters is required (Wimmer 1996). It must be pointed out, however, that poor phonological skills are also evident in most students with so-called 'garden variety' reading problems.

One of the major difficulties which has been evident in the learning disabilities field for some years is that of accurate identification. Any list of symptoms used to describe the learning disability syndrome creates problems. It has been asked 'How can child A be described as a learning disabled child (or more specifically, perhaps, a dyslexic child) when he or she shows only three of the so-called symptoms?' The inability to identify a list of characteristics which were 'always present' in cases of specific learning disability was one of the main factors which weakened the argument for the existence of a particular form of learning difficulty which is different from a general learning problem. To some extent this confusion was reconciled when it was proposed in the late 1960s that subtypes of dyslexia exist. More recent studies have confirmed the existence of subtypes (McKinney 1988; Flynn *et al.* 1992). It was found that the symptoms or characteristics presented by dyslexic children tended to cluster into syndromes or patterns of difficulty. For example, subtypes with major phonological and linguistic problems, or with visuo-spatial difficulties or with emotional blocks to learning.

Characteristics of students with learning disability

Over the years, children with learning disabilities have been described as having, in addition to the problems with reading, writing, spelling and arithmetic, some of the following difficulties:

• a history of late speech development (and continuing immaturities in articulation and syntax);
• visual perception problems (frequent reversal of letters and numerals; and some individuals reporting distortion or blurring of print when reading);
• auditory perception problems (including difficulties in phonemic awareness, which involves identifying sounds within words and blending sounds into words);
• poor integration of sensory information (for example, the student can't easily learn to associate and remember sound–symbols relationships);

- difficulty in recalling words; or quickly naming familiar objects (dys-nomia);
- weak lateralization (for example, underdeveloped hand–eye preferences; directional sense confusion);
- soft signs of neurological dysfunction;
- hyperactivity and/or attention deficits;
- weak sequencing skills (as reflected in jumbled letter sequences in spelling or in word-attack skills in reading);
- poor motor co-ordination;
- low level of motivation;
- secondary emotional problems due to learning failure and poor school progress.

Studies have tended to show that far more LD students have phonological and language problems (approximately 60 to 70 per cent) than have problems with visual perception and motor skills (approximately 10 per cent); and some students have mixed difficulties or no obvious difficulties in either area.

It has become clear that accurate diagnosis of any type of specific learning disability is very difficult in young children. For example, it may not be possible to differentiate between 'garden variety' reading problems and dyslexia until a student is at least 8 years old (Badian 1996). Also, some students who show early signs of difficulty in learning later make good progress. This is not to suggest that one should wait to see if a child 'grows out' of early learning problems without taking action. It will be made very clear in the next chapter that early intervention is crucial, regardless of the possible causes of a learning problem.

Teaching approaches for students with learning disabilities

General advice on methods and approaches for LD children will be found in later chapters dealing with literacy and numeracy. Here it is only necessary to state the main principles which emerge from the literature on teaching learning disabled children.

- Reading, writing, spelling and maths skills should be explicitly taught, leaving nothing to chance.

- At the same time the skills must be utilized in a meaningful way so that reading and writing and arithmetic are used for a real purpose, not merely as drill exercises.

- More attention must be given to phonic skill development than is currently the case in contemporary approaches to the teaching of reading. However, in a few cases, a predominantly phonic approach may be contraindicated if the child has significant auditory problems. As a generalization, training in phonological awareness is now regarded as an essential component of remedial teaching in the literacy area.

• Metacognitive and self-monitoring strategies, such as those described in later chapters, must be used alongside skill-building and practice.

• Ideally, special tuition will be provided, perhaps by withdrawing the child from the regular class for brief, intensive sessions. Where this is not possible, individual help should be given daily within the classroom setting. Parents often make use of tutors who work with children after school hours. It is unrealistic to expect a child with a learning disability to make optimum progress if not given individual tutorial help. This is one situation where full-time inclusion of a student with a disability is not in that student's best interests.

• There is little evidence to support the view that identifying subtypes of learning disability will easily lead to the selection of a particular method of instruction for a specific type. This aptitude-treatment approach has yet to prove itself (Snider 1992).

• The use of any training programme which claims to improve visual perception has been discredited in recent years (Connor 1994). Such training appears not to result in improved achievement levels in reading, writing or spelling.

• In dealing with learning difficulties in mathematics, most of the experts recommend an approach which uses apparatus and visual aids to the full, and demonstrates clearly the steps required in recording and carrying out basic processes (Chinn and Ashcroft 1993; Thornton and Bley 1994). It is also essential that students be explicitly taught effective strategies for dealing with word problems. For students with learning disabilities, note also the advice contained in Chapter 12, dealing with the development of numeracy skills.

SUMMARY

This chapter has presented an overview of the problems encountered by students with general and specific learning difficulties. It is suggested that, rather than concentrating solely upon so-called deficits within the learner, it is more productive to identify other factors over which a teacher can exert much greater influence, such as curriculum and teaching methods, when planning an educational programme. Attention was given to exploring what is meant by effective instruction and explicit teaching, and to notions of a personalized approach within an inclusive curriculum.

A conclusion can be reached that within the whole class context, students with general learning difficulties and those with specific learning disabilities need to be taught more effective ways of managing themselves and regulating their own learning. These issues are addressed fully in later chapters of the book.

Discussion points

- Finding topics and activities within the daily programme which are 'inclusive' of all children across a wide ability range presents a real challenge. Discuss some examples of inclusive activities from your own experience.

- How might a teacher break in to the 'failure cycle' and help a student to improve?

- What needs in common do students with general learning difficulties and students with learning disabilities share?

- Refer to the 'Deficit Model'. Discuss the teaching implications for each item in the list said to be typical characteristics of a student with learning difficulties.

Further reading

Andrews, J. and Lupart, J. (1993) *The Inclusive Classroom: Educating Exceptional Children*, Scarborough, Ontario: Nelson.

Ashman, A. and Elkins, J. (eds) (1994) *Educating Children with Special Needs* (2nd edn), Sydney: Prentice Hall.

Bender, W. (1995) *Learning Disabilities: Characteristics, Identification and Teaching Strategies*, Boston: Allyn and Bacon.

Burden, P.R. and Byrd, D.M. (1994) *Methods for Effective Teaching*, Boston: Allyn and Bacon.

Casey, K. (1994) *Teaching Children with Special Needs*, Sydney: Social Sciences Press.

Cunningham, P.M. and Allington, R.L. (1994) *Classrooms that Work: They Can all Read and Write*, New York: Harper Collins.

Falvey, M.A. (1995) *Inclusive and Heterogeneous Schooling*, Baltimore: Brookes.

Jones, K. and Carlton, T. (eds)(1993) *Learning Difficulties in Primary Classrooms*, London: Routledge.

McCoy, K.M. (1995) *Teaching Special Learners in the General Classroom* (2nd edn), Denver: Love.

Scruggs, T.E. and Wong, B.Y. (1990) *Intervention Research in Learning Disabilities*, New York: Springer Verlag.

Young, R.M. and Savage, H.H. (1990) *How to Help Students Overcome Learning Problems and Learning Disabilities*, Danville: Interstate Publishers.

Chapter 2

Early identification and intervention

> Early recognition is important because the child's learning difficulty does need to be understood and steps taken to organise educational assistance.
>
> (Brock 1995: 22)

Almost all children with significant physical, sensory or intellectual disabilities, and those with communication disorders, will have been recognized during their preschool years. The identification process has improved in recent years (Bennett 1993), with increasing use being made of 'at risk registers', in which are recorded those children whose status immediately after birth or during the first year of life gives cause for concern. In an ideal situation, these children can be followed up on a regular basis and their development monitored closely. Their needs can be assessed from an early age and appropriate interventions, such as parent guidance and structured preschool programmes can be implemented (Kemp 1992). There is evidence to support the view that early intervention in the preschool period can have extremely beneficial outcomes in terms of higher success rates when the children begin formal schooling (Campbell and Ramey 1994; Wasik and Karweit 1994).

The early identification of children with milder forms of disability, or with potential learning difficulties, is much less certain, and many of these children remain undetected until they enter school and for the first time begin to fail. Because the long-term impact of early school failure can be devastating for the children concerned, it is important that procedures be improved for identifying children at risk (Talay-Ongan 1994). This chapter examines some of the issues related to the early recognition of young children who may go on to experience general or specific learning problems in schools.

For many years attempts have been made to identify specific signs within the developmental pattern or the overall performance of the preschool child which might be predictive of later learning difficulties. The main approaches to this problem have included screening procedures, readiness tests and direct observation by kindergarten teachers.

SCREENING PROCEDURES

Several researchers have looked for performance indicators which might be used to identify 'at-risk' children in the preschool years. The most common research design involved the assessment of kindergarten children on a range of different tasks which the researcher felt might reflect specific traits, skills or knowledge important for early learning. Results from these measures were then correlated with the children's later school achievement, most usually in reading. Measures which correlated moderately to highly with later achievement were then regarded as good predictor variables. If a child was found to be weak in performance over a number of these variables his or her 'at-risk' factor increased. Some promising work in the prediction field was carried out in the 1960s by de Hirsch, Jansky and Langford (1966), and in the 1970s by Paul Satz and his collegues (e.g. Satz and Friel 1974; Satz et al. 1978). More recent studies of the same type have been reflected in the work of Horn and Packard (1985), Badian (1988) and Felton (1992).

Before examining some of the variables thought to be of potential value for the early detection of learning problems, it is important to state that accurate prediction of future learning difficulties is very difficult. No matter how good the design of a predictive screening test is it will not pick up *all* at-risk children, and it will pick up some who will eventually have no problems (Mantzicopoulos and Morrison 1994). While most predictive test batteries do detect children who will either be extremely good performers or will be extremely poor performers, they are much less accurate in identifying children who will have mild forms of learning difficulty (Jansky 1978; Badian 1988). Unfortunately, unless detected and remedied early, mild forms of learning difficulty commonly become much more serious as the child gets older.

Although there are obviously some problems in the accurate interpretation of results from early screening procedures, this does not mean that we should therefore abandon all attempts at early screening for learning difficulties (Talay-Ongan 1994). Rather, we should combine the results from early screening measures with reliable information from other sources, including parents' and teachers' observations of the child's development and progress. Supplementary information of this type has been shown to improve significantly the process of identifying young children at risk of educational failure (Mantzicopoulos and Morrison 1994).

In the 1990s there appears to be a renewed interest in the development of screening procedures for early learning. For example, The National Foundation for Educational Research in England has produced three new screening instruments, *Early Years Easy Screen* (EYES), the *Middle Infant Screening Test (MIST)* and the *LARR Test of Emergent Literacy*. In America, the *Early Screening Profiles* have been designed for children aged from 2 to 7 years. These instruments are also available in Australia and New Zealand through their respective Councils for Educational Research (ACER and NZCER).

The principal features of these screening tests are summarized below.

Early Years Easy Screen (EYES) (Clerehugh 1991)

This material can be used during a child's first term in school at age 5-plus. The tests allow the teacher to assess a child's pencil skills, active body skills, number skills, oral language skills, visual skills such as word matching and letter matching, and auditory skills such as auditory sequential memory. The information collected in the screening test is designed to help teachers not only to detect at-risk children but also to identify teaching priorities for an intervention programme.

Middle Infant Screening Test (MIST) (Hannavy 1993)

MIST can be used with children who have been in school for five terms. The materials assess children's listening skills, letter knowledge, word knowledge and written vocabulary. Associated with MIST is a follow-up programme for teachers and parents. With the help of parents at home, children at risk of developing learning problems work through an activity book called *Forward Together*. The parents attend workshop sessions at school to assist them in working on the programme with their child.

LARR Test of Emergent Literacy (Downing, Schaefer and Ayres 1993)

This test is suitable for the age range 4 years to 5 years. The letters LARR stand for 'linguistic awareness related to reading'. The test explores children's concepts about books and reading, and checks for their understanding of some of the language associated with early literacy instruction. To some extent it covers the same ground as Marie Clay's (1985) *Concepts about Print* test, but it has the advantage of being a relatively brief assessment and is designed for small group administration.

Early Screening Profiles (ESP) (American Guidance Service 1991)

ESP allows early childhood teachers and psychologists to assess a child's cognitive, language, motor, self-help and social skills development. The material also surveys the child's home environment, health history and behaviour. All information collected can be used in decision-making about the child's educational placement and instructional needs.

READINESS TESTING

Before developmental screening tests arrived on the scene, one of the earliest approaches to the problem of potential learning difficulties was 'readiness testing'. In the late 1930s and 1940s Monroe (1935) devised screening tests to detect young children who lacked the skills necessary for learning to read.

Her work led to a growing interest in the notion of 'reading readiness', and even to 'school readiness' (Ilg and Ames 1964). Paper-and-pencil tests were designed to help determine whether or not a kindergarten child had the knowledge and skills thought at that time to be important for beginning to learn to read. The tests usually assessed a child's ability in such areas as listening comprehension, following instructions, hand–eye co-ordination, visual discrimination, auditory discrimination, sound blending, letter recognition and word identification. The underlying belief was that if certain children were identified as not being ready for formal instruction in reading, such instruction could be delayed to avoid placing the children in a failure situation. In most cases it was also suggested that the children be given specific 'readiness training' activities to hasten their acquisition of these important prereading skills.

By the end of the 1960s the whole notion of readiness was being openly challenged. For example, the idea that children needed a mental age of $6\frac{1}{2}$ years to begin reading was rejected as many young children with mental ages well below 6 were already reading (Downing 1966). Reading readiness seemed to have much more to do with motivation, early language experience, exposure to books in the home and the quality of early teaching, rather than being in possession of specific perceptual or motor skills. It was increasingly believed that many important skills, such as visual discrimination, auditory discrimination and letter recognition, could most usefully be developed in young children as an integral part of their beginning reading and writing experience, rather than being taught separately and out of context.

Reading readiness tests were never widely used in Britain or Australia, and by the early 1970s they had all but vanished from the scene. Even in the United States their use declined. However, interest in the notion of readiness for number work continued, and several instruments for assessing prenumber skills and concepts were devised in the 1970s and 1980s (e.g. Weimer and Weimer 1977; Burton 1985).

It is interesting to note that the key components in the recent screening tests previously described are very similar indeed to the activities included in the older readiness tests. While the notion of readiness has been abandoned, for good reason, it is clear that our beliefs about the subskills necessary for successful early learning have not changed. Most task analyses of early learning in literacy and numeracy identify such essential prerequisite skills as oral language, visual discrimination, phonemic awareness, letter knowledge, symbol recognition and hand–eye co-ordination.

TEACHER AS OBSERVER

It has been acknowledged for many years that early childhood teachers are reasonably skilled in noting when young children are experiencing learning problems (Salvesen and Undheim 1994). Indeed, in many ways they are at the cutting edge of the early identification process. More than twenty years ago, in a text on the prevention of learning problems, Jansky and de Hirsch (1972) highlighted the importance of a teacher's observations. They stated that the preschool or first grade teacher should take into account such things as the child's ability to work at a table for relatively long periods, capacity for independent work, persistence despite frustrations, ability to listen for sustained periods of time, use of oral language, interest in reading and obvious efforts to try to learn to read and write. The contribution of these observations to the identification of at-risk children is quite as important as any results from more formal testing or assessment (Manzicopoulos and Morrison 1994). What else should teachers look for as signs of potential learning difficulty?

SOME EARLY AT-RISK INDICATORS

The following list describes some aspects of a young child's performance which are worth observing, since poor performance in these simple skills has proved to be significantly correlated with later progress in school. The items in the list, and the additional pointers below it, have been gleaned from the work of Jansky and de Hirsch (1972), Horn and Packard (1985), Badian (1988), Walker et al. (1994), Stuart (1995) and Majsterek and Ellenwood (1995). Most of the items in the list represent observable behaviours or responses to set tasks.

- *Pencil grasp*: Can the child hold a pencil or drawing instrument in an appropriate manner in order to make marks on paper?

- *Copying shapes*: Can the child copy such shapes as a circle, a square, a triangle and a diamond?

- *Use of scissors*: Can the child cut paper with some degree of control?

- *Expressive language**: Can the child retell a familiar story from memory, or describe in detail a picture placed in front of him or her?

- *Vocabulary**: In speech, does the child use a reasonably wide range of different words?

- *Repeating sentences**: Can the child repeat dictated sentences of increasing length?

- *Writing own name*: Can the child write own first name unaided?

- *Auditory discrimination**: Can the child detect whether two words presented orally are the same or different?

- *Phonemic awareness**: Can the child detect rhyming words and alliteration?
   Can the child identify the initial sound in a word?
   Can the child blend sounds to make words?
   Can the child segment words into their component sounds?

- *Word matching*: Can the child match two identical words on cards?

- *Letter naming*: Can the child recognize and name (or sound) some of the letters of the alphabet? (Capital and lower case)

- *Naming five shapes and naming five colours*: The child is shown objects of different shapes and colours.

- *Immediate learning and recall of words*: This is assessed by teaching the child two new words on flashcards for a few minutes, then testing recall immediately. Recall is also checked later in the lesson. A variation of this procedure is to place the two cards on the table and ask the child to point to the word you pronounce (recognition memory). Then the cards are put on the table and the child is asked to say the one you point to (recall). Finally, the cards are removed and the child is asked to write the two words from memory.

One particular aspect of oral-aural language which has proved to be a powerful predictor of later success in reading and spelling is phonological awareness. This includes such skills as detecting alliteration and rhyme, segmenting a word into its separate sounds and blending sounds to make words, which have been found to be very important predictors of early reading and spelling ability (Mann 1993; Torgesen, Wagner and Rashotte 1994). The results from a large number of studies strongly support the notion that children's awareness of the phonemic properties of the words they hear and say is very closely related to their early acquisition of literacy (ERIC Digest # E540 1996). This matter will be discussed fully in the later chapters dealing with literacy acquisition.

Screening procedures for phonological awareness do not have to be lengthy or complex. For example, Bradley (1990) found that children's rhyming ability predicted both reading and spelling progress. Working with kindergarten children, Felton (1992) found that their ability to discriminate beginning sounds in words and to rapidly name letters of the alphabet predicted their later reading ability.

Note: At least five of the indicators in the list above, indicated by asterisks, might be regarded as aspects of aural and oral language (listening and speaking), thus confirming the importance of language development for beginning reading. For example, it has been reported by Walker *et al.* (1994) that differences in preschool children's language related to differences in socioeconomic status are highly predictive of the children's subsequent verbal ability and school achievement.

Additional at-risk indicators

Some studies (e.g. Silver 1978; Badian 1988; Talay-Ongan 1994) have indicated that the following general factors can also be predictive of later learning problems:

It is essential, however, to point out that some children with these particular problems actually settle down well in school and do not experience learning difficulties.

- speech delay;
- below average intelligence;
- limited concentration span;
- distractibility;
- low threshold for frustration;
- hyperactivity;
- birth difficulties;
- low birth weight;
- family history of learning difficulties.

Over to you: Teacher as observer

- From the information in the section headed 'some early at-risk indicators', devise an observation schedule for classroom use.

- Apply the schedule to two quite different children in preschool or in their first year of schooling. One child should be considered 'advanced' by the teacher and the other child possibly 'at-risk'.

- How many differences between the two children are revealed by your observations?

- How many so-called 'at-risk' indicators are evident in the child who is making good progress?

- What are your conclusions?

EARLY INTERVENTION

It is already widely acknowledged that the impact of early failure can be devastating on a child's self-esteem, confidence, motivation and overall progress in school (Stanovich 1986; Beck and Juel 1992; Kameenui 1993). It is also recognized that intervention, if it is to be successful, must occur earlier rather than later in the child's school life (Pikulski 1994; Wasik and

Slavin 1993). Having identified some children as being at risk of experiencing early learning failure, what can be done?

In the past few years researchers have found out much more about the important ingredients for successful intervention than was previously known. In particular, the reviews by Pikulski (1994), Wasik and Slavin (1993), Pinnell and associates (1994), Ashman, van Kraayenoord and Elkins (1992) and Hiebert and Taylor (1994) have identified the following important features of effective early intervention:

• Children who are experiencing difficulties in learning must spend con- siderably more time receiving help and guidance from teachers and parents: frequent successful practice is essential. Daily instruction will achieve much more than twice-weekly intervention.

• In intervention settings the instruction must be of a very high quality and intensity, not merely 'more of the same'.

• As well as attempting to improve basic academic skills, early intervention must also focus on the correction of negative behaviours, such as disruptive tendencies, poor attention to task and task avoidance.

• At-risk children will need to be taught individually for at least part of the time, graduating later to small groups and to in-class support, before independent progress in the regular class is viable.

• Although withdrawal for individual and small group work can achieve a great deal, it is essential that the regular classroom programme is also adjusted to allow at-risk children a greater degree of success in that setting. Failure to adapt the regular class programme frequently results in loss of achievement gains when the student no longer receives assistance.

• In the case of literacy intervention, the texts to be used with at-risk children must be carefully selected to ensure a very high success rate. Repetitive and predictable texts are particularly helpful in the early stages; and repeated reading of the same text seems to increase fluency and build confidence. Children should be provided with books that they can read successfully at home.

• It is essential that, in literacy interventions, training is provided in phonemic awareness, letter knowledge and decoding.

• Children should be explicitly taught the knowledge, skills and strategies necessary for identifying words, extracting meaning from text, spelling and writing.

• Writing should feature as much as reading in early literacy interventions. Concepts about print can be acquired through writing; and a great deal of phonic knowledge can be developed through helping children to work out the sounds they need in order to spell words.

• The use of other tutors (aides, volunteers, peers, parents, etc.) can be very helpful, but these individuals need to be taught how to function in the tutor–supporter role. For example, this writer has observed that parents frequently use texts which produce high error rates and frustrate the child. They also tend to be too critical of the child's performance, rather than being encouraging and supportive.

• Maximum progress occurs when parents or other adults can provide the child with additional support and practice outside school hours.

Teaching procedures in successful intervention programmes tend to draw upon what is known about effective teaching, as discussed in Chapter 1. Effective teaching involves:

• the creation of a friendly, supportive learning environment;
• the presentation of the learning task in easy steps;
• resource materials at an appropriate readability level;
• direct teaching of task-approach strategies (how to go about the task);
• clear modelling and demonstrations by the teacher or other adult;
• provision for much guided practice with feedback;
• efficient use of available time;
• close monitoring of the child's progress;
• reteaching particular skills where necessary;
• provision for successful independent practice and application;
• frequent revision of previously taught knowledge and skills.

Virtually all the surveys indicate that specific literacy intervention programmes, (for example, Reading Recovery, 'Early intervention in reading' and 'Success for all'), do serve a very useful function in preventing the onset of reading failure (Pikulski 1994; Shanahan and Barr 1995; Slavin 1996). For example, Clay (1990) reported that only 1 per cent of children undertaking her Reading Recovery programme fail to make significant progress and require remedial assistance higher up in the primary school. A reduction in the number of children having to repeat first grade and fewer referrals for special education services are reported as positive outcomes from the 'Success for all' programme in the United States (Wasik and Slavin 1993). However, some writers have questioned whether the gains made in the programmes are maintained once children cease to receive the same amount of intensive support (Chapman and Tunmer 1991; Wheldall, Center and Freeman 1993). It is certainly essential to ensure that children returning from early intervention programmes encounter high-quality literacy instruction in the regular classroom, and are matched appropriately to books at the correct level of difficulty to ensure success. It is also vital to continue to monitor the progress of such children and to provide on-going support where necessary.

In terms of preventing reading problems beginning in the school years, evidence suggests that teaching children to read in the preschool is of lasting benefit. A study by Hanson and Farrell (1995) indicated that the advantages of having been taught to read in kindergarten were still evident when the students were in high school. It is perhaps unfortunate that the philosophy which guides much of early childhood education tends to be critical of formal attempts to instruct children in the preschool years.

SUMMARY

In this chapter you have explored some of the ways in which children with potential learning problems may be identified either before school or very early in their school lives. Particular attention was given to screening tests and to teacher observation. The similarity between the content of some recent screening tests and the content of the much older 'readiness tests' was pointed out. From several different sources a list of possible 'at-risk' indicators was presented. This list may be useful to teachers working in early childhood settings. The final section of the chapter provided an overview of the key components of effective early intervention programmes, with particular reference to the development of early literacy skills.

Discussion points

• Accurate record-keeping is considered to be an important part of any teacher's job. Discuss how record-keeping might be of value in the early identification of learning difficulties.

• What are some of the problems involved at school level in trying to implement effective early intervention programmes?

• It was said that the regular class literacy programme would need to be adjusted in order for gains to be maintained by children returning from intervention programmes. Discuss some possible changes or adaptations that might be necessary in the regular programme.

Further reading

Bagnato, S.J. and Neisworth, J.T. (1991) *Assessment for Early Intervention*, New York: Guilford Press.

Hiebert, E.H. and Taylor, B.M. (1994) *Getting Reading Right from the Start*, Boston: Allyn and Bacon.

Masland, R.L. and Masland, D. (eds) (1988) *Preschool Prevention of Reading Failure*, Parkton: York Press.

Slavin, R.E., Karweit, N.L. and Wasik, B.A. (1994) *Preventing Early School Failure*, Boston: Allyn and Bacon.

Trethowan, V., Harvey, D. and Fraser, C. (1996) 'Reading Recovery: comparison between its efficacy and normal classroom instruction', *Australian Journal of Language and Literacy* 19, 1: 29–37.

Watson, A. and Badenhop, A. (eds) (1992) *Prevention of Reading Failure*, Sydney: Ashton Scholastic.

Chapter 3

Helping children develop self-management skills

> . . . children need to be taught self-management skills for planning and carrying out learning experiences with increased independence just as they need to be taught to read
>
> (Wang 1981: 201)

The term 'self-management' refers in this chapter to the child's ability to function independently in any given learning environment (Vincent 1995). In the classroom it relates to such behaviours as knowing how to organize one's materials, knowing what to do when work is completed, knowing how and when to seek help from the teacher or a peer, how to check one's own work for careless errors, how to maintain attention to task without constant supervision or reassurance, how to observe the well-established routines in the class such as ordering lunch, having sports equipment or books ready for a specific lesson, knowing when a change of lesson or room is to occur, and so on. According to Good and Brophy (1994), from an early age students should assume as much responsibility for self-management as they can handle.

The actual self-management skills required by a child will tend to differ slightly from classroom to classroom according to a particular teacher's management style, routines and expectations. For example, in some classrooms a premium is placed upon passive listening, note-taking and sustained on-task behaviour, while in other classrooms initiative, group-working skills and co-operation with other children are essential prerequisites for success. The self-management skills required in an informal setting tend to be different from those needed in a more formal or highly structured setting. Knowing how to respond to the demands and constraints of different lessons or settings is an important aspect of self-management.

Evidence exists to show that the type of classroom learning environment created by the teacher, and the instructional approach used, can both markedly influence the development of self-management and independence in children. Teaching approach and learning environment determine how effectively available learning time is used by the children to increase their independence (Wang and Zollers 1990). Some teachers seem to operate with students with special needs in ways which foster their *dependence* rather than their independence. For example, they may offer too much help and guidance for these children in an attempt to prevent possible difficulties and failures. They may virtually spoon-feed the child using an individual worksheet programme which offers few challenges and calls for no initiative on the child's part. Too much of this type of approach is not what inclusion of special-needs students should be about. Not only does it not foster independence, it may well operate in such a way as to segregate the child from the mainstream curriculum and from the peer group for too much of the day.

SELF-MANAGEMENT IS CRUCIAL FOR INCLUSION

Why are self-management skills important and why have they been given priority early in this book? The reason is simple: the possession of self-management skills by a child with a disability or a learning problem seems to be one of the most important factors contributing to the successful inclusion of that child in a regular classroom (Choate 1993; Salend 1994). It is essential that students with special needs, whether placed in special settings or in the regular classroom, be helped to develop adequate levels of independence in their work habits, self-control, social skills and readiness for basic academic learning.

Self-management is closely allied to a much broader phenomenon, that of adaptive behaviour. It also shares much in common with what psychologists term 'self-efficacy' (Pressley and McCormick 1995).

The concept of adaptive behaviour

Adaptive behaviour has been defined by Butler (1990: 707) as 'The individual person's skill in adjusting to the environment at adequate levels of independence and responsibility through maturation, learning and social adjustment'.

Adaptive behaviour manifests itself in at least three ways:

- as the acquisition of age-appropriate self-help skills to permit independent functioning;
- as the development of patterns or codes of behaviour which are appropriate for different social contexts;
- as the ability to benefit and learn from direct personal experiences.

The extent to which an individual's behaviour is appropriately adaptive in any given situation is gauged by the degree to which the behaviour is compatible with the standards of personal and social responsibility and self-sufficiency expected in a person of that age and within that culture (Baroff 1991).

Some students, for example those with intellectual disability, or with social, emotional or psychological disorders, frequently exhibit poor adaptive behaviour (Thurman and Widerstrom 1990). Indeed, impairment in adaptive behaviour, combined with subaverage general intelligence, is still used as a criterion in identifying individuals with an intellectual disability (Grossman 1983). Knight (1992) has commented that the failure of many students with intellectual disability to develop adequate skills in adaptive behaviour can negatively affect their self-esteem, and can seriously limit their academic performance and their social relationships. One of the major goals of intervention with such students is to increase their independence by improving their skills in self-management. Even students with milder forms of disability or learning difficulty often display ineffective self-management and need positive help to become more independent learners (Weinstein 1989; Cole and Chan 1990).

SELF-MANAGEMENT CAN BE TAUGHT

Evidence is accumulating to support the view that deliberate training in self-management can be effective in promoting students' independence (Hughes, Korinek and Gorman 1991; Lovitt 1991; Knight 1994). What can be done to teach self-management? First, teachers must believe that such teaching is important and that it is possible to teach self-management skills to children who lack them. Second, teachers need to consider precisely which skills or behaviours are required by their students in order to function independently in their particular classrooms.

Let us examine a very simple example of teaching self-management in a regular classroom. Obviously the routine involved, the amount of modelling and specific direction, and the complexity of the language used, will be adapted to the age and ability of the class.

Teaching students what to do when a piece of work is completed

Establish attention. Call upon specific students for responses, particularly those known to be lacking in self-management and initiative.

> 'Let's make sure that we all know what we do when we finish a piece of work in this class. Perhaps you finish your maths assignment, or you complete your first draft of a story and you don't need to see me to check it at once. This is what you do. First, you read through the work carefully yourself.'

Write on blackboard: 'READ YOUR OWN WORK CAREFULLY'.

> 'Why do we do that Allan?'
> 'Good! To check that we have the heading and date and your name. I'll write that on the blackboard.'

Write: 'CHECK HEADING, DATE AND NAME.' Perhaps have the class read this aloud.

'Good. Any other reasons, Karen?'
'Yes, to check for careless mistakes.'

Write: 'CORRECT ANY ERRORS.'

'Now that you have checked those things you place your work in this tray on my desk. So, what do I write about that on the blackboard?'

Write: 'PLACE IN Mr. W's TRAY.'

'Good.'
'Then you go back to your desk and you can do one of these things.'

Write: 'MOVE ON TO THE NEXT EXERCISE, OR COMPLETE ANY UNFINISHED WORK FROM PREVIOUS LESSON, OR FIND A BOOK TO READ SILENTLY, OR TAKE A PUZZLE SHEET, OR MOVE TO THE COMPUTER AREA'

Review:
'Let's read those rules through together; then we'll start our writing lesson. When you've finished I want you to do exactly what it says on the blackboard without me needing to remind you. Sally, come out and point to each one of our rules as we read them together once more.'

When a child fails to do the correct thing after completing work you are now in a position to refer him or her to the routine previously established.

For students with special needs Salend (1994) devised a six-step programme to teach self-management. The steps are:

- *explanation*: discussing why the particular behaviour or skill is important;
- *identification*: helping the child to recognize examples of the behaviour;
- *demonstration*: the teacher or a peer models the skill or behaviour;
- *differentiation*: the child is taught to tell appropriate from inappropriate examples of the behaviour;
- *role play*: the student practises the behaviour with feedback;
- *assessment*: checks are made at regular intervals to ensure that the child has acquired and maintained the skill or behaviour over time.

Teaching a student the appropriate way to manage himself or herself in the classroom links closely with the establishment of general classroom rules. This matter is discussed further in the later chapter on managing behaviour.

In some situations a teacher might employ a 'star chart' or other visual recording system to reward at regular intervals all those students who demonstrate the specific self-management skills expected of them. Rewarding would be most frequent immediately after the teaching of the rule (as above, for example), but would not be phased out totally even after several weeks for those who are generally lacking in initiative.

It is important to establish the idea of maintaining the appropriate

performance *without prompting*. Remember, when you are constantly remind-
ing the class of what to do you are maintaining the students' dependence.
You may need to remind the children with special needs more frequently than
the others to begin with, and reward more frequently their correct responses;
but your long-term aim is to help these children to function independently.
When they *do* function independently you have helped them to become more
like other children in the class, and that is a goal of inclusion.

Over to you: *Self-management in your classroom*

- Consider your own class setting (preschool, primary, middle or senior
  school) and the subjects you cover within the curriculum. Write down
  a comprehensive list of the knowledge and skills needed by a child
  to function independently in your setting. The examples provided in
  the first paragraph of this chapter may serve as a starting point.

- Write down the steps and procedures you might use in teaching any
  two of the skills needed for self-management in your list above.

LOCUS OF CONTROL

The whole issue of self-management and initiative in children links closely
with the personality construct known in psychology as locus of control. To
explain locus of control one needs to understand that individuals attribute
what happens to them in a particular situation either to internal factors (e.g.
their own efforts or actions) or to external factors (e.g. luck, chance, things
outside their control). The children with an internal locus of control recognize
that they can influence events by their own actions, that they do to some extent
control their own destiny. Or to bring it down to classroom level, that when
they concentrate and try hard they get better results. Knowing that one's fate
is under one's personal control to a significant extent is also referred to as
'self-efficacy' (Pressley and McCormick 1995).

Self-efficacy skills and the internalization of locus of control (i.e. the
development of responsibility and self-reliance) usually increase rapidly with
age if a child experiences normal satisfaction and reinforcement from his
or her efforts and responses. However, it has been found that many children
with learning problems, and with negative school experiences, may remain
markedly external in their locus of control, feeling that their efforts have
little impact on their progress, and that what happens to them in learning
tasks is unrelated to their own actions (Cole 1995). In its extreme form
the externality is usually described as 'learned helplessness', where the

individual anticipates failure immediately any new situation occurs and cannot conceive of being able to change this outcome (Schunk 1989; McLeod 1992).

The child who remains largely external is likely to be the child who fails to assume normal self-management in class and is prepared to be managed or controlled by 'powerful others' such as the teacher, parent, teacher's aide or more confident peers. There exists a vicious circle wherein the child feels inadequate, is not prepared to take a risk, seems to require support and encouragement, gets it and develops even more dependence upon others. The teacher's task is one of breaking into this circle and quite deliberately causing the child to recognize the extent to which he or she has control over events and can influence outcomes. It is natural for a teacher to wish to help and support a child with special needs; but it should not be to the extent that all challenge and possibility of failure are totally eliminated. Failure must be possible and children must be helped to see the causal relationship between their own efforts and the outcomes, and to accept responsibility for both. Children will become more internal in their locus of control when they really recognize that effort and persistence can overcome failure (Lovitt 1991).

Strategies for increasing internality

Much of the research on matching teaching style or learning environment to a child's perceived or measured locus of control suggests that children who are markedly external respond best at first in a highly structured, predictable, teacher-directed setting, particularly for the learning of basic academic skills. It also suggests that strongly internal students are able to cope well with open or child-centred programmes (Bendell, Tollefson and Fine 1980). Regardless of this, teachers must recognize that for some children with a markedly external locus of control there is a need to help them develop greater internality (Knight 1994). This development is likely to be a gradual process, therefore such strategies as suddenly placing external children in a very open, child-centred teaching environment may only increase the number of occasions when they fail and develop an even greater feeling of helplessness and lack of ability. There is a need to work slowly toward the children assuming slightly more responsibility for their work and effort over a period of time. Consideration should be given to the fact that a structured teaching approach, which itself does little to increase internality, may be necessary for a while before a child can become independent enough in school work and study to survive in an open situation. For example, a very teacher-directed programme may be needed initially in order to raise the child's level in basic academic skills. Evidence suggests that such an approach is certainly required by students with behaviour problems if they are to be integrated successfully into regular classes (Conway 1990).

Wang and Stiles (1976) first experimented with a system whereby 7- to

8-year-old children were gradually encouraged to plan more and more of their own work (including how long to spend on each task) within the constraints of available classroom resources and timetable. Their conclusion was that the self-scheduling system was effective in developing the children's abilities to take increased responsibility for school learning. It also increased their perceptions of personal responsibility for achievement and success. In other words, the gradual increase in the use of self-directed learning may increase the self-management skills and internality of locus of control. This is certainly one of the underlying principles embodied in the Adaptive Learning Environments Model (ALEM) developed by Wang and her colleagues as a system for integrating students with special needs in regular classrooms (Wang and Zollers 1990). It is also evident in the emphasis now placed upon encouraging students to work collaboratively (Holmes 1990; Grenot-Scheyer *et al.* 1995; Lyle 1996).

What are some of the strategies a teacher might use to increase internality? The following list may provide a few ideas.

- Individual 'contracts' between teacher and child can be introduced in a fairly simple form. These may specify the tasks assigned for a two-hour period or for a morning, but allow the child to decide in what order to tackle the work, how long to spend on each section and when to seek assistance.

- The use of self-instructing material (e.g. programmed kits or computer programs) may also help a child to gain an awareness of the extent to which his or her own efforts result in progress and achievement.

- Situations may be contrived where children are given a range of graded tasks, some of which will be a little beyond them. When they begin to fail on these tasks they can be shown that with a little more effort on their part, and if they seek help when necessary, they can complete the work successfully. The children are taught how to try, rather than to give up.

- Teachers who provide only direct correction for school work (i.e. simply marking responses right or wrong without giving feedback and extra practice) are merely establishing a feeling of lack of ability in the child. Feedback to children should be corrective when possible and they should be given the opportunity to prove that they can solve similar items to those that were initially incorrect. Teachers should plan to provide corrective feedback in such daily activities as mental arithmetic or spelling if they want the lower achievers to improve in these areas. Too much testing without follow-up teaching may increase externality.

- If at some time it is necessary to punish a child for some misdemeanour the punishment should be given immediately following the incident and the child must fully understand the reasons for it. Punishment which is divorced in time and place from the event is likely to exacerbate feelings of helplessness. The child should also be given the earliest opportunity to act appropriately in a similar situation and be rewarded and specifically praised for doing so.

- While every opportunity should be taken to praise or reward a slower or poorly motivated learner for genuine progress, teachers must avoid rewarding success if no real effort was required.

- Employ the notion of 'wait time' when orally questioning the less-able students within a class lesson. Too frequently a teacher moves quickly from the less-able student, probably to avoid embarrassment when he or she does not immediately answer. This can create a feeling of frustration and uselessness in the students; and after a time they don't make any effort to reply. Studies have shown that if teachers wait only a few seconds longer many of these students will make a response which can be accepted and praised (Rowe 1986).

Praise

The whole issue of teachers' praise merits fuller comment. Teachers' use of praise has been well researched, but its overall effects are still somewhat uncertain. It appears to have a differential effect according to the characteristics of the children being praised. Good and Brophy (1994) have reviewed studies in this area and concluded that praise does seem important for low-ability, anxious, dependent students, provided that it is genuine and deserved and praiseworthy aspects of the performance are specified. A child should know precisely why he or she is being praised if appropriate connections are to be made in the child's mind between effort and outcome. Trivial or redundant praise is very quickly detected by children and serves no useful purpose. Descriptive praise, however, can be extremely helpful:

'That's good work, Leanne. I really like the way you have taken care to keep your letters all the same size.'
'Good, David! Those lines are really straight today because you pressed hard on the ruler.'
'I'm very glad you asked me that question Sara. It shows you are really listening very carefully to the story.'

Thompson, White and Morgan (1982) carried out observations in third grade classrooms and noted that high-achieving students received significantly more praise than less able or difficult students. For example they received up to 50 per cent more praise than children with behaviour problems. These researchers also made the telling observation that *all* children received far more neutral comment, criticism and warnings than they did praise. They state that teachers were far more disapproving than approving and tended therefore to create a negative classroom climate which was not conducive to learning or self-esteem.

Attributional retraining

It is important to recognize the negative impact which an external locus of control can have upon a student's motivation to persist in learning. It is easier for the child to give up and develop avoidance strategies rather than persist if the expectation of failure is high. In the instructional approach known as 'attributional retraining' (Dohrn and Tanis 1994; Cole 1995) students are taught to appraise carefully the results of their own efforts when a task is completed. They are taught to verbalize their conclusions aloud. 'I did that well because I took my time and read the questions twice'; 'I listened carefully and I asked myself questions'; or 'I didn't get that problem correct because I didn't check the example in the book. Now I can do it. It's easy!'

The main purpose in getting the students to verbalize such attribution statements is to change their perceptions of the cause of their successes or failures in school work. It helps to focus their attention on the real relationship between their efforts and the observed outcomes.

Attributional retraining seems to have maximum value when it is combined with the direct teaching of effective task-approach strategies to use in a particular task. This strategy training is discussed fully in the chapter dealing with self-regulation in learning.

Assessing locus of control

Questionnaires exist for the assessment of locus of control in children of various ages and with various disabilities (e.g. Knight 1992), but it is usually possible to recognize from classroom observation those children with a markedly external locus. Teachers should be on the lookout for such children and attempt to intervene to improve the situation.

Lawrence and Winschel (1975) have concluded that children with intellectual disability being considered for inclusion into regular settings should demonstrate an internality for both success and failure which is not less than the average level in the regular class. While such judgement may need to be made rather subjectively, locus of control is certainly one learner characteristic which does need to be taken into account. It may need specific attention once the student with a disability is integrated (Rogers and Saklofske 1985; Salend 1994).

SUMMARY

This chapter stressed the importance of teaching all children the most effective ways to manage themselves in the regular classroom, to show initiative and to become self-reliant. These attributes are of particular importance in the case of children with disabilities since self-management appears to be a crucial prerequisite to successful inclusion in the mainstream.

Helping children develop self-management skills also involves assisting them to develop a more internal locus of control and to recognize the extent to which their own actions influence their successes and failures. Techniques for fostering this development were discussed.

Everything which has been said in this chapter applies across all categories of disability and across all ability levels. For example, the vision-impaired student with above average intelligence needs specific self-management skills quite as much as the sighted child with some degree of hearing loss. Appraisal of each individual's level of self-management should be a starting point for assisting children with special needs to cope more adequately in regular settings.

In the next chapter the notion of self-management is extended to include the even more important issue of self-regulation in the actual process of learning.

Discussion point

Jason is 12 years old. He has been assessed as moderately intellectually disabled and he spends most of his time at a special school. However, on two mornings each week he attends a regular class in the local school, with some assistance provided in the form of a teacher aide. The intention is, that over a period of time, Jason will be included in the regular school programme on a more permanent basis.

At the moment, Jason has difficulty in coping with the demands of the regular school and clearly needs help in adjusting to the routines and expectations there. He is a friendly boy and has no emotional or behavioural problems. His family is very supportive.

Consider some of the actions you might take in order to maximize his chances of success when fully included in the regular school setting.

Further reading

Cohen, S. and de Bettencourt, L. (1983) 'Teaching children to be independent learners', *Focus on Exceptional Children* 16, 3: 1–12.

Fisher, J.B., Schumaker, J.B. and Deshler, D.D. (1995) 'Searching for validated inclusive practices: a review of the literature', *Focus on Exceptional Children* 28, 4: 1–20.

Flores, D.M., Schloss, P.J. and Alper, S. (1995) 'The use of a daily calendar to increase responsibilities fulfilled by secondary students with special needs', *Remedial and Special Education* 16, 1: 38–43.

Hughes, C.A., Korinek, L. and Gorman, J. (1991) 'Self-management for students with mental retardation in public school settings', *Education and Training in Mental Retardation* 26, 3: 271–91.

Kern, L., Dunlap, G., Childs, K. and Clarke, S. (1994) 'Use of a classwide self-management program to improve the behavior of students with emotional and behavioral disorders', *Education and Treatment of Children* 17, 3: 445–58.

Lambert, N., Nihira, K. and Leland, H. (1993) *Adaptive Behaviour Scales* (School edition), Camberwell: ACER.

Licht, B.G., Kistner, J.A., Ozkaragoz, T., Shapiro, S. and Clausen, L. (1985) 'Causal attributes of learning disabled children', *Journal of Educational Psychology* 77, 2: 208–16.

Mangello, R.E. (1994) 'Time management instruction for older students with learning disabilities', *Teaching Exceptional Children* 26, 2: 60–2.

Notari-Syverson, A., Cole, K., Osborn, J. and Sherwood, D. (1996) 'What is this? What did we just do? How did you do that?: teaching cognitive and social strategies to young children with disabilities in integrated settings', *Teaching Exceptional Children* 28, 2: 12–16.

Nowicki, S. and Strickland, B.R. (1973) 'A locus of control scale for children', *Journal of Consulting and Clinical Psychology* 40, 1: 148–54.

Wang, M.C. (1992) *Adaptive Education Strategies*, Baltimore: Brookes.

Zeitlin, S. and Williamson, G.G. (1994) *Coping in Young Children: Early Intervention Practices to Enhance Adaptive Behaviour*, Baltimore: Brookes.

Chapter 4

The development of self-regulation in learning

> Strategy instruction refers to the process of helping students become self-regulated learners, individuals who have knowledge of how to learn as well as knowledge of how to effectively use what they have learned.
>
> (Fisher, Schumaker and Deshler 1995: 14)

In Chapter 3 attention was given to the development of basic self-management skills in children. Self-management was defined as the child's ability to function independently in any given learning environment. Discussion in that chapter focused mainly upon the importance of teaching students how to organize themselves, physically and mentally, for classroom learning. In particular, work habits, attention, on-task behaviour, self-control and initiative were stressed as vitally important prerequisites if a student is to benefit fully from an educational programme. Self-management in organizational practices helps a student to become a more independent learner (Bowd 1990).

SELF-REGULATION IN LEARNING

In this chapter the term self-management is expanded to include not only the elements above, but also the learner's ability to regulate his or her own thinking processes while involved in a learning task. Such self-regulation requires that the students play an active role and monitor closely the effects of various actions they take and decisions they make while learning. This involves the capacity to think about one's own thinking (metacognition) and to apply appropriate cognitive strategies necessary for tackling the particular learning task.

One of the common observations concerning many students with learning problems is that they have become 'passive' learners (or even non-learners). They show little confidence in their own ability to control learning events in the classroom, or to bring about improvement through their own efforts or initiative. Teaching a student how to learn and how to regulate and monitor his or her own performance in the classroom, how to become a more self-regulated learner, must be a major focus in any intervention programme.

It is pertinent for teachers to ask, 'Can we teach students how to learn? When a student lacks effective learning strategies can we provide instruction which will develop such strategies?' These questions are answered, at least in part, by the mainly positive results which have emerged from research into self-regulated learning (Zimmerman and Schunk 1989; Pressley and McCormick 1995), metacognitive training (Chan 1991; Cole 1995) and cognitive behaviour modification (Paris and Winograd 1990; Polloway and Patton 1993). These approaches will be discussed in this chapter, and their practical applications for students with learning difficulties will be explored.

METACOGNITIVE INSTRUCTION

'Metacognition' can best be described as 'understanding and controlling one's own thinking'. It refers to an individual's capacity to monitor and regulate his or her mental processes while approaching a new learning task or solving a problem (Ashman and Conway 1989). Metacognition has two main components: an awareness of the skills needed to perform a specific task effectively (i.e. a knowledge of the appropriate attack-strategies to use); and the ability to use self-regulation to ensure successful completion of the task (i.e. planning one's moves, evaluating the effectiveness of one's actions, checking progress), and coping with any difficulties as they arise (Cornoldi 1990).

It is considered that metacognition helps a learner to recognize that he or she is either doing well, or is having difficulty learning or understanding something. A learner who is monitoring his or her own on-going performance will detect the need to pause, to double-check, perhaps begin again before moving on, to weigh up possible alternatives or to seek outside help. In this respect, metacognitive strategies are an essential part of what are traditionally referred to as independent study skills. But metacognition also enters into many areas of classroom performance, and the conscious use of appropriate self-monitoring strategies makes for more effective learning. 'Metacognitive strategies are plans we use to direct our own learning and include setting objectives, listing resources needed, planning a sequence of actions, and using an appropriate yardstick to judge success' (Bowd 1990: 41).

The view is now widely held that many learning problems that students exhibit are related to inefficient use of metacognition, that is, the learners lack the ability to use effective strategies when faced with a learning task, and cannot monitor or regulate their responses appropriately. Some students undoubtedly develop their own efficient strategies without assistance; others do not. Pressley and McCormick (1995) have observed that often cognitive strategies are not taught explicitly in classrooms and may remain obscure or totally misunderstood by many students. Quite clearly, some teachers don't make their instruction explicit enough for these students. They add to the students' learning problems by failing to demonstrate effective ways of approaching a new task. A teacher needs to provide clear modelling of the most appropriate strategies to use to minimize the chances of failure and to maximize the chances of early success. A teacher who says, 'This is how I do it, and this is what I ask myself as I do it. Watch and listen', is providing the learner with a sound starting point. The teacher who says, 'See if you can find out how to . . .', is often providing an invitation to failure and frustration. Perhaps a useful example to consider here is that of teaching early hand-writing skills to young children. This is one area where teachers do provide modelling, verbal cues and corrective feedback, and do invite the students to monitor their own performance. Few teachers would invite beginning writers to discover efficient letter-formation for themselves. Similar direct in-struction should also be provided in such skills as mathematical problem-solving, reading comprehension, spelling and story writing.

It is important to indicate that there is a difference between cognitive instruction and metacognitive instruction. Cognitive instruction involves teaching the student the specific steps to follow and the skills to use when tackling a particular task, for example, the exchanging rule in subtraction, the 'look-cover-write-check' method of learning to spell an irregular word, or the appropriate way to read a six-figure reference to locate a point on a map. This type of instruction embodies what is often called training in 'task-approach skills'. Metacognitive instruction goes beyond this, focusing on techniques which require the learner to monitor the appropriateness of his or her responses and to weigh up whether or not a particular strategy needs to be applied in full, in part, or not at all in a given situation. For example, to recognize that there is no need to use the exchanging rule in a particular subtraction problem because there is obviously a short-cut solution; or recognizing that the application of the 'look-cover-write-check' method to learn a simple phonetically-regular word is unnecessary. Most teachers tend to focus almost entirely upon cognitive training, which is a necessary but insufficient procedure in itself to ensure independence in learning. It is essential that teachers realize the need to devote time and effort to encourage students to think about their own thinking in a variety of learning situations. In particular, students need to be shown how to use what Conway and Gow (1990) refer to as 'self-interrogation' and 'self-checking'. They need to be taught appropriate questions to ask themselves as they carry out a specific task and monitor their own progress.

According to several authorities a variety of intellectual tasks can be more easily accomplished if students use metacognitive skills and are provided with instruction in how to do so (Ellis 1993; Salend 1994; Butler 1995; Dole,

Brown and Trathen 1996). The curriculum areas of reading and mathematics are often cited as examples of academic skills which can be improved by metacognitive strategy training. Students should be taught how to approach these areas 'strategically' and then given abundant opportunity to practise the application of these key strategies.

The PQRS strategy described below provides an appropriate example of a step-by-step plan of action a student might adopt when faced with a reading assignment. In later chapters dealing with literacy and numeracy, examples will be provided of other strategies for planning and writing stories, improving spelling and for problem-solving in mathematics.

The PQRS reading comprehension strategy

P = Preview   Scan the chapter or paragraph, attending to headings, sub-headings, diagrams and illustrations. Gain a very general impression of what the text is likely to cover. Ask yourself, 'What do I know about this already?'

Q = Question   Generate some questions for yourself. 'What do I expect to find out?' 'Will it tell me how to make the object?' 'Will it tell me how to use it?' 'Will I need to read this very carefully or can I skip this part?'

R = Read   Read the passage or chapter for information. 'Are my questions answered?' 'What else did I learn?' 'Am I understanding this?' 'Do I need to read this again?' 'What does that word mean?'

S = Summarize   Briefly state in your own words what the text is saying. 'What was the main idea?' 'Does my statement sound correct?' 'Do I need to add anything else?' 'What reaction am I getting from the person who is listening to me?'

The teacher models good application of the PQRS approach, demonstrating how to focus on important points in the passage, how to check on one's own understanding, how to back-track or scan to gain contextual cues. This modelling assists students to internalize particular strategies and self-questioning techniques. They are then helped to apply the same approach, with corrective feedback from the teacher. Strategies of this type are best taught through dialogue between teacher and students working together to extract meaning from the text. Peers can facilitate each other's learning in small groups. This dialogue approach has also been termed 'reciprocal teaching'. Dialogues allow students and teachers to share their thoughts about the process of learning, and to learn from the successful strategies used by others. Dialogues also serve a diagnostic purpose by allowing teachers to appraise students' levels of understanding and their unaided use of certain strategies.

Over to you: A comprehension strategy

- Read again the PQRS strategy described above.
- Which of the questions are metacognitive, rather than simply cognitive?
- Generate a few more metacognitive questions for that example.

Generalization of the application of a particular strategy to a new situation can be a problem. This fact needs to be recognized and transfer of training needs to be planned for, rather than assumed. Chan (1991) has recommended that teachers ensure that specific strategies taught are actually needed in the daily curriculum to facilitate immediate application. It is also necessary to provide a variety of new contexts (e.g. different texts, different problems) over a period of time and to discuss fully with students the various situations in which a particular strategy can be used effectively.

Research studies seem to provide the following tentative conclusions:

- Metacognition is developmental in nature. As children grow older they become involved more actively in their own learning. Children following normal developmental patterns develop strategies to facilitate their learning and become able to monitor the effects of their own efforts.
- Metacognitive training can assist students with learning problems to develop appropriate strategies in given contexts.
- The effects of metacognitive training are often task-specific, especially with low-ability students. Provision must be made for training to be applied across a variety of tasks to aid generalization.
- Cognitive and metacognitive training has been effective in improving aspects of performance in mathematics such as computation and problem-solving, in improving reading comprehension and recall of information from texts, in the writing of summaries, in preparing essays and in spelling.

Over to you: Designing a strategy

- Identify the strategies needed when a student is required to prepare and write a concise factual report following a simple science experiment.
- Taking Conway and Gow's (1990) point that metacognition involves self-checking and self-interrogation while completing a task, write down some questions which students might ask themselves while writing this report.

COGNITIVE BEHAVIOUR MODIFICATION

Cognitive behaviour modification, or verbal self-instruction, is a closely related approach to metacognitive training (Polloway and Patton 1993). It involves the application of a set of procedures designed to teach the students to gain better personal control over a learning situation by use of 'self-talk' or directions which guide their thinking and actions. The students are taught an 'action plan' in which they talk themselves through a task in order to control their performance and monitor their results. 'Inner language' is seen as very important for both cognitive and metacognitive development, and the learner is taught to use language to control his or her own responses.

Cognitive behaviour modification: basic principles

The training procedure for a typical cognitive behaviour modification pro-gramme usually follows this sequence:

Modelling   The teacher performs the task or carries out the new procedure while 'thinking aloud'. This modelling involves the teacher asking questions, giving directions, making overt decisions and evaluating the results.

Overt external guidance   The student copies the teacher's model and completes the task with the teacher still providing verbal directions and exercising control.

Overt self-guidance   The learner repeats the performance while using verbal self-instruction as modelled by the teacher.

Faded self-guidance   The learner repeats the performance while whispering the instructions.

Covert self-instruction   The learner performs the task while guiding his or her responses and decisions using inner speech.

Typical covert questions and directions a student might use would include: What do I have to do? Where do I start? I will have to think carefully about this. I must look at only one problem at a time. Don't rush. That's good. I know that answer is correct. I'll need to come back and check this part. Does this make sense? I think I made a mistake here, but I can come back and work it again. I can correct it.

These self-questions and directions cover problem definition, focusing attention, planning, checking, self-reinforcement, self-appraisal, error de-tection and self-correction. They are applicable across a fairly wide range of academic tasks. Sometimes the instructions, cue words or symbols to represent each step in the procedure may be printed on a prompt card displayed on the student's desk while the lesson is in progress.

Training in self-instruction techniques of this type is considered to be particularly useful for students with mild intellectual disability as part of their improvement in self-management (Conway and Gow 1990). The application of cognitive behaviour modification to cases of chronic behaviour disorder is discussed in the next chapter.

Over to you: *Applying the principles*

- Construct a set of self-instructions which a student might use when copying a diagram from a textbook.

- Devise a sequence of instructions which a student could use when reading a chapter from a novel which he or she must later summarize.

- How might cognitive behaviour modification be used to slow down the performance tempo of a student who is impulsive?

SUMMARY

Students with learning difficulties are often perceived as passive, powerless, incompetent and without motivation to succeed. In this chapter a case has been put for changing this situation by placing students more actively in control of their own learning processes. Research has shown that students can be taught to become self-regulated learners, capable of taking the initiative and controlling their own responses more effectively.

The teacher's role involves the explicit modelling of effective ways of approaching a learning task or solving a problem. Students must be helped to internalize appropriate task-approach strategies and must be given abundant opportunity to practise and master these across a wide range of new concepts. The aim is to ensure that students learn how to learn. The value of metacognitive instruction and cognitive behaviour modification in achieving this goal has been discussed in this chapter.

Self-regulated learning can build the confidence of a student and thereby increase motivation and self-esteem, as well as producing higher achievement within the curriculum. As Harris and Pressley (1991: 401) have said, 'Used appropriately, cognitive strategy instruction is an exciting and viable contribution to the special educator's repertoire'.

Discussion point

Given that the methods used in the early years of schooling have tended to become less structured and more child-centred in the mainstream of education, how might the specific strategy training advocated in this chapter be included in general classroom practice?

Further reading

Ashman, A. and Conway, R. (1989) *Cognitive Strategies for Special Education*, London: Routledge.

Ashman, A. and Conway, R. (1992) *Using Cognitive Methods in the Classroom*, London: Routledge.

Chan, L. (1991) 'Metacognition and remedial education', *Australian Journal of Remedial Education* 23, 1: 4–10.

Cole, P. and Chan, L. (1990) *Methods and Strategies for Special Education*, Sydney: Prentice Hall.

Droscoll, M.P. (1994) *Psychology of Learning for Instruction*, Boston: Allyn and Bacon.

Evans, G. (ed.) (1995) *Learning and Teaching Cognitive Skills*, Camberwell: ACER.

Meltzer, L.J. (ed.) (1993) *Strategy Assessment and Instruction for Students with Learning Disabilities*, Austin: Pro-Ed.

Pressley, M. and McCormick, C.B. (1995) *Advanced Educational Psychology*, New York: Harper Collins.

Chapter 5

The management of behaviour

Effective behaviour management is essential to the smooth running of a school and in the creation of an environment where everyone's rights and responsibilities are addressed. A balance between fundamental rights and responsibilities is at the heart of behaviour management.

(Rogers 1995: 12)

Many teachers report that one of their main concerns in the regular classroom is the child who disrupts lessons, seeks too much attention from the teacher or peers and who fails to co-operate when attempts are made to provide extra help. In other words, the teachers feel that although they may know what the child needs in terms of basic instruction it is impossible to deliver the service because the child is totally unreceptive. Some writers suggest that the inclusion of students with emotional and behavioural disorders in regular classes will present an almost impossible challenge to teachers unless adequate support is made available to them (Branson and Miller 1991).

CLASSROOM BEHAVIOUR

While it is true that some students exhibit behavioural problems in school which are a reflection of stresses or difficulties outside school (e.g. in the family), it is also evident that in some school situations disruptive behaviour and apparent social maladjustment result directly from factors within the learning environment. Large classes can contribute to problem behaviour. Research has shown that smaller classes seem to have fewer discipline problems, are friendlier and produce higher achievement in the students (Achilles 1996). Even the seating arrangement in classrooms seems to influence both behaviour and achievement. For example, Hastings and Schwieso (1995) report that on-task behaviour is significantly better and students are more productive when they are seated in rows rather than grouped; yet the common practice in most primary schools is to have children seated in groups to facilitate co-operative learning. The most effective ways of using group work is discussed fully in the next chapter.

Any student who is bored by work which is trivial and lacks challenge may well become troublesome (King 1995). The atmosphere in some schools and the approach of some teachers, tend to alienate certain students; and therefore maladjustment and the development of poor self-image can be caused by factors within the system rather than within the child (Young and Rees 1995). Unfortunately, as Conway (1990) suggests, teachers are more likely to see the problem as lying within the student and his or her background than within the school curriculum or the methods used.

When cases of disruptive or what is now termed 'challenging' behaviour are reported, particularly in high schools, it is important to consult with other teachers to discover whether the student is also a problem when in their classes. All teachers who have contact with the maladjusted student will usually need to get together to agree upon a common approach to be used in dealing with the problem behaviour. One of the factors which can add to a maladjusted student's problems in high school is the frequent change of teachers for different subjects. Within the course of one day a student may encounter quite different treatment, ranging from the authoritarian to the permissive. This lack of consistency needs to be minimized. It is one of the reasons why some large schools have established 'subschools' with a smaller but consistent pool of teachers to cater for specific groups of students through in-class support at a more personal level. With younger children the problem of inconsistent management is minimized since most of the curriculum is planned and implemented by one teacher who gets to know the children well. In senior schools many more difficulties can arise.

Occasionally of course it is necessary to seek expert advice when a child's behaviour does not respond to consistent forms of management set out below; but in many cases behaviour can be modified successfully within the school setting. All teachers need to adopt a proactive, rather than a reactive approach to classroom control (Bishop and Jubala 1995). A sound starting point is the establishment of good classroom rules.

CLASSROOM RULES

Classroom rules are essential for the smooth running of any lesson and should be formulated by the children and the teacher together very early in the year. The application of rules should be consistent and should recognize both the rights and responsibilities of the students and the teacher (Grossman 1995). Rules should be few in number, clearly expressed, displayed where they can be seen by all, and expressed in positive terms (what the students *will do*, rather than *must not do*). Students must understand why the rules are necessary and must know exactly what will happen if a rule is broken (Calf 1990).

Classroom-based research on the management style of teachers has yielded a clear indication that the most effective teachers establish rules and procedures as a top priority at the beginning of the year (King 1995). They discuss the rules with the students, and apply them systematically and fairly. Such teachers were also more vigilant in the classroom, used more eye contact, were more proactive to prevent behaviour problems rather than reactive, set appropriate tasks for students to attempt successfully, avoided 'dead spots' in lessons, kept track of student progress, checked work regularly and provided feedback to the whole class and to individuals (McManus 1989; Lovitt 1991).

William Rogers (1989a, b, 1995) suggests that all teachers should develop their own discipline plan to enable them to know in advance what to do when classroom behaviour is disruptive. The plan gives a teacher confidence when the pressure is on. Corrective actions which a teacher can decide to use might include:

- tactical ignoring of the student and the behaviour (low level disruptions);
- simple directions ('Ann, get back to your work please');
- positive reinforcement ('Good, Ann');
- question and feedback ('What are you doing, Mark? I'll come and help you');
- rule reminders ('David, you know our rule about noise. Please work quietly');
- simple choices ('Excuse me Joanne. You can either work quietly here, or I'll have to ask you to work at the corral. OK?');
- isolation from peers (take the student aside and discuss the problem, then place him or her in a quiet area with work to do);
- removal from class (time out in a different room, under supervision, may sometimes be needed).

Teachers may also use strategies such as deflection and defusion to take the heat out of a potential conflict or confrontation. Teacher: 'Sally, I can see you're upset. Cool off now and we'll talk about it later; but I want you to start work please.' The judicious use of humour, without sarcasm, can also help to defuse a situation, without putting the student down (Grossman 1995).

Classroom rules, rights and responsibilities

Valuable advice is given by Rogers (1989a, b) in his programme called 'Decisive discipline' and in his book 'Making a Discipline Plan'. He suggests that the goals of discipline in school should be to assist students to do the following:

- accept responsibility for their own behaviour;
- exercise self-control;
- respect the rights of others;
- adopt the principles of fairness and honesty;
- face the logical consequences of their own behaviour.

Clear, consistent rules must be democratically established by all members of the class, based on the rights of others and on personal responsibility. Respect for the rights of others includes the right of other students to learn and the right of the teacher to teach.

Rogers illustrates well the principle that, while the actual rights and the rules which protect them are important, the process by which they are developed is just as important. Classroom discussion, early in the first week of a new term, should focus upon rights, rules and responsibilities. There must also be open discussion of the consequences for breaking a rule. Rules should include matters like communication (e.g. hand up and wait), and treatment of others' ideas (e.g. listening and praising), movement in the room, noise levels, safety, personal property, school equipment. Rules should be stated in positive terms, what the students *will do*, not in negative *must not* terms. Students should feel ownership for rules through contributing to their formulation.

In Roger's approach three steps are taken when any problem arises:

- give a warning in the form of a rule reminder;
- give time out for five minutes;
- student gives an apology to the class.

When it is not possible to find an appropriate consequence for a particular disruptive behaviour the students should be encouraged to write about the behaviour. They must say what they did, what they should have done and what they are going to do to fix it up.

CHANGING BEHAVIOUR: AN OVERVIEW

In order to change undesirable behaviour in a specific student it is usually necessary to consider all factors which may be supporting the behaviour both directly and indirectly. For example, a girl who openly defies a teacher's request to work quietly on an assignment and not disturb those around her may actually be seeking peer group approval for provoking and standing up to the teacher. She may also be successfully avoiding a situation where she is forced to admit that she cannot do the work which has been set. She may later gain more attention, albeit criticism, from her parents if a letter of complaint is sent home from school. These factors combine to reinforce the status quo. In addition, the girl may be preoccupied with the outcome of some confrontation she had with another teacher in the previous lesson or with another student at lunchtime. Finally, if the work appears to her to have no real significance there is little motivation to attempt it. In order to bring about change here the teacher must work to ameliorate the various influences of as many of the factors as possible. This type of global attack on the problem, an attempt to manipulate variables within the total context in which the child operates, has been termed the 'ecological approach' by Hallahan and Kauffman (1994).

A somewhat different approach, but one which is commonly used in conjunction with the ecological for maximum impact is the 'behavioural approach', more often referred to as 'behaviour modification'.

In this approach three assumptions are made:

- all behaviour is learned;
- behaviour can be changed by altering its consequences;
- factors in the environment (in this case the classroom) can be engineered to determine which behaviours will be rewarded and which will be ignored or punished.

Typically a problem behaviour is targeted for change. The factors which are maintaining it are identified. A programme is devised to reshape this behaviour into something more acceptable or more productive through a consistent system of reward, reinforcement or punishment. Attention must also be given to improving the student's own self-monitoring and decision-making in order to increase self-control relative to the problem behaviour (Grossman 1995).

Rather emotional criticism is sometimes levelled at behaviour modification programmes. It is suggested that the manipulation of the individual's behaviour and reactions is somehow impersonal and thus out of keeping with humanistic views on the value of interpersonal relationships. However, the precise planning and management of a behaviour modification programme requires very careful observation of how the child, the teacher and other children are interacting with each other and influencing each other's behaviour. Far from being 'impersonal' the techniques used to bring about and maintain change are highly interpersonal.

Some teachers are also deterred from attempting behaviour change programmes because they have been told that very accurate record-keeping and charting of frequency and duration of particular behaviours will be required. While data sheets and accurate monitoring of responses are of definite value in clinical settings or where an aide or paraprofessional assistant is available, it is usually unrealistic to expect the busy classroom teacher to maintain such detailed records.

Some examples of behaviour modification techniques will be presented in the following sections of the chapter, together with suggestions for manipulation of the classroom environment to achieve specific results. First it is timely to quote Hallahan and Kauffman's comment to place such strategies in context:

Good behaviour management for disturbed children has a lot in common with good behaviour management for all children. The best preventive action any teacher can take is to make sure that the classroom is a happy place where children take pride in their work and learn to treat others with respect

(Hallahan and Kauffman 1986: 184)

IDENTIFYING THE PROBLEM

As previously stated, teachers are often troubled by the child who is constantly seeking attention, interrupting the flow of a lesson and distracting other children. Naturally, many teachers feel threatened by the child who is a constant challenge to their discipline. That feeling of threat causes the situation to get out of hand and the teacher is trapped into confrontations with the child and an on-going war is waged rather than possible solutions sought.

All too often one observes the teacher reacting overtly to undesirable behaviour and at once reinforcing it. Many behaviour problems in the classroom, particularly disruptive and attention-seeking behaviours, have been rewarded by the adult's constant reaction to them (King 1995). For example, the teacher who spends a lot of time shouting at children or threatening them, is in fact giving them a lot of individual attention at a time when they are behaving in a deviant manner. This is a misapplication of 'social reinforcement' and the teacher unintentionally encourages what he or she is trying to prevent. Some control techniques used by teachers (e.g. public rebuke or punishment) can have the effect of strengthening a child's tough self-image and status in the peer group.

If you have a child who is presenting problems to you in terms of control and behaviour it would be useful if you took the necessary time to analyse the possible reasons for this within your classroom setting. These questions may be helpful when attempting to draw up a complete picture of disruptive behaviour.

- In which lesson is the behaviour less frequent (e.g. the more highly structured sessions or the freer activities)?
- At what time of day does the behaviour tend to occur (a.m. or p.m.)?
- What is the noise level like in the room before the problem arises?
- How is the class organized at the time (groups, individual assignments, etc.)?
- What am I (the teacher) doing at the time?
- How is the child in question occupied at the time?
- What is my immediate response to the behaviour?
- What is the child's initial reaction to my response?
- How do other children respond to the situation?
- When I have successfully dealt with the problem in the past what strategies have I used?

Notice that the analysis deals with issues which are immediately observable in the classroom. Behaviour analysis does not need to examine the child's past history or search for deep-seated psychological problems as causal explanations for the child's behaviour.

Sparzo and Poteet (1993) present a nine-step plan for setting up a behaviour change intervention. They point out that in many cases it is not necessary to

apply all nine steps; often it is sufficient merely to specify the target
behaviour to be changed, apply an appropriate change strategy and assess the
outcome. The nine steps in Sparzo and Poteet's programme are listed below:

- define the target behaviour to be changed;
- observe and record the current frequency and duration of the behaviour;
- set attainable goals, involving the student in this process if possible;
- identify potential reinforcers by observing what this student finds rewarding;
- select teaching procedures, such as modelling, prompting, role play, etc.;
- plan to have the child rehearse the target behaviour;
- implement the programme over time, providing feedback to the child;
- monitor the programme through on-going observation, and by comparing
  frequency and duration measures with those evident before the intervention;
- once the change in behaviour has occurred make sure it is maintained, and
  take every opportunity to help the child generalize the behaviour to
  different settings and contexts.

STRATEGIES FOR REDUCING DISRUPTIVE BEHAVIOUR

Sometimes changes as simple as restructuring the working groups, changing
seating arrangements, reducing noise level in general and closer monitoring
of work in progress will significantly reduce the occurrence of disruptive
behaviour. The following strategies are also recommended.

Deliberate ignoring

Ignoring the child is an approach which can be used far more frequently than
most teachers are prepared to accept. If a child begins some form of disruptive
behaviour (e.g. calling out to gain attention) the teacher ignores completely
that child's response by turning away and giving attention to another student
who is responding appropriately (King 1995). If the peer group can also be
taught to ignore a disruptive student and not reinforce the behaviour by
acknowledging it and reacting to it, the planned ignoring technique will be
even more successful. This technique is frequently sufficient on its own to
modify the behaviour of, for example, a child with an intellectual disability
in a regular class who is merely acting out in ways typical of a younger child.

Clearly it is not sufficient merely to ignore disruptive or inappropriate
behaviour. It is essential that planned ignoring be combined with a deliberate
effort to praise and reinforce that child for appropriate behaviours at other
times in the lesson (McCoy 1995). While it is common to view the frequency
of undesirable behaviour in a child as something to reduce, it is more positive

to regard the 'non-disruptive' or appropriate behaviours as something to reward and thus increase. It is a useful rule of thumb to be more positive and encouraging than to be critical and negative in your interactions with students.

A teacher cannot ignore extremely disruptive behaviour when there is a danger that someone will be hurt or damage will be done. Nor can a teacher go on ignoring disruptive behaviour if it is putting other children at educational risk through lost learning time. The teacher must intervene to prevent physical danger but should do so quickly, quietly and privately. Private reprimands coupled if necessary with 'time out' are less likely to bring the inappropriate behaviour to the attention and approval of other children.

Reinforcement and rewards

In order to modify behaviour, particularly in young or immature children, it may be necessary to introduce a reward system. If social reinforcers like praise, smiles, approval are not effective it will be necessary to recognize and cater for individual differences. If possible find several reinforcers which may be used to provide variety over a period of time. It may be that the child likes a stamp, a sticker or coloured star, a chance to play a particular game on the computer, build a model, construct a puzzle, listen to a taped story on a cassette or even clean the blackboard! Some teachers use tokens. Tokens are simply a means of providing an immediate and tangible reward. Tokens are usually effective because of their immediacy and students can see them accumulating on the desk as visible evidence of achievement. Tokens can be traded later for back-up reinforcers such as time on a preferred activity, being dismissed early or a positive report to take home to parents. While not themselves sensitive to individual preferences for particular types of re-inforcement, tokens can be exchanged for what is personally reinforcing.

A token chart or star chart may be drawn up for the classroom wall and both individual and group efforts can be rewarded quickly and visibly during the day. Some teachers find the use of a points system helpful in general classroom management; e.g. rewarding the first group ready for work, the group showing high levels of self-management, the children with the highest levels of work output, the individuals working quietly, individuals who exhibit helpful behaviour to others.

Initially we need to reinforce every small step in the right direction, but the reinforcement can be reduced over a period of time. Most textbooks on behaviour modification provide some general rules for using reinforcement. It is worth repeating them here.

- First, reinforcement must be given immediately after the desired behaviour is shown and must be given at very frequent intervals.

- Second, once the desired behaviours are established, reinforcement should be given only at carefully spaced intervals after several correct responses have been made.

- Third, the teacher gradually shifts to unpredictable reinforcement so that the newly acquired behaviour can be sustained for longer and longer periods of time without continuing feedback.

Time out

'Time out' refers to the removal of a student completely from the group situation to some other part of the room or even to a separate but safe setting for short periods of isolation. While time out may appear to be directly punishing it is really an extreme form of ignoring. The procedure ensures that the child is not being socially reinforced for misbehaviour.

It is important that every instance of the child's disruptive behaviour should be followed by social isolation if the time out technique is being used. The appropriate behaviour will not be established if at times the inappropriate behaviour is tolerated, at times responded to by punishment and at other times the child is removed from the group. It is essential to be consistent.

Avoid placing a student outside the classroom if in that situation he or she gets other interesting rewards; e.g. being able to peer through the window and attract the attention of other students in the room, making contact with other students in the corridor, watching more interesting events in other parts of the school (McCoy 1995).

Explosive situations may develop with some disturbed children and a cooling-off period will be necessary. A set place should be nominated for this (e.g. a corner of the school library where worksheets may be stored for use by the student). The student will not return to that particular lesson until he or she is in a fit state to be reasoned with and some form of contract can be entered into between teacher and student. The student, should, however, be under supervision for all of the time spent out of the classroom.

Punishment

Punishment, if administered appropriately, is yet another way of eliminating undesirable behaviours; but punishment has become an emotive issue in education today. Crittenden (1991: 80) has commented, 'There seems to be a tendency to deny the legitimacy of any form of punishment as part of school discipline'. Yet, at times punishment is necessary, and the consequences do modify behaviour.

Punishment, when needed, should be given immediately the deviant behaviour is exhibited. Delayed punishment is virtually useless. Punishment is most effective if it is combined with positive reinforcement. This combination brings about more rapid and effective changes than the use of either procedure alone. The child who pushes or punches other children will learn appropriate behaviour if he or she receives positive reinforcement (praise or tokens) for friendly and co-operative behaviour as well as punishment (loss of privileges, verbal reprimand, time out) for the inappropriate behaviour.

The principal objection to punishment or 'aversive control' is that, while it may temporarily suppress certain behaviours, it may also evoke a variety of undesirable outcomes (fear, a feeling of alienation, resentment, an association between punishment and schooling, a breakdown in the relationship between teacher and student). Punishment may also suppress a child's general responsiveness in a classroom situation as well as eliminating the negative behaviour.

As has been stated previously, punishment should not be used as the sole method for modifying behaviour and controlling certain students. Punishment has as many unfortunate side effects as it has benefits.

Behavioural contracts

A behavioural contract is a written agreement signed by all parties involved in a behaviour change programme (Salend 1994). The student agrees to behave in certain ways and carry out certain obligations. The staff and parents agree to do certain things in return. For example, a student may agree to arrive on time for lessons and not disrupt the class. In return the teacher will sign the student's contract sheet indicating that he or she has met the requirement in that particular lesson, and adding positive comments where possible. The contract sheet accompanies the student to each lesson throughout the day. At the end of each day and the end of each week, progress is monitored and any necessary changes are made to the agreement. If possible, parental involvement is negotiated by the school, and the parents agree to provide some specific privileges if the contract is met for two consecutive weeks, or loss of privileges if it is broken. When behaviour contracts are to be set up it is essential that all teachers and school support staff are fully informed of the details.

The contract system is strongly advocated by Lovitt (1991) who suggests that the daily report card can specify precisely which features of behaviour are to be appraised each lesson by the teacher. A simple yes/no response column makes the recording task quick and easy for a teacher to complete at change of lesson. For example:

Arrived on time	Y	N
Had completed homework	Y	N
Followed instructions	Y	N
Stayed on task	Y	N
Did not disturb others	Y	N
Completed all work	Y	N

Lovitt (1991) also suggests sending a copy of the report home, and liaising regularly with parents by telephone or letter.

Over to you: Intervention for behaviour change

Read the following description provided by a teacher when referring a child for assessment by an educational psychologist.

> David never seems to be able to keep quiet in my lessons. He always keeps shouting out answers without thinking and he does almost anything to get the attention of other children; shows off almost non-stop. He's on the go all the time. He is a pest before school, too. Before I can get out of my car he is waiting to tell me about something that's happened and to carry my bag to the staffroom. He clings on to me when I'm on yard duty and hangs back after school to talk. I sometimes give him jobs to do just to get him out of my hair, but half the time he doesn't finish them. The thing that really annoys me is that he keeps asking me for help during quite simple activities. He doesn't need help and he stops me from attending to those who do. Then, when I do sit down with another group he deliberately does something to interrupt or to make me cross. He really never gets stuck into his work. He produces very little and I have to virtually stand over him to get him to concentrate. Of course, I can't do that all the time. He's really hopeless when we start on something new. He doesn't listen to the instructions so just jumps in and guesses wildly at what has to be done – hit or miss, he doesn't care. Some of the other kids don't like him much because he messes up their team games in the yard. He can't stand losing either! He cheats if he gets the chance. When he's in a group at lunchtime I've seen him do really stupid things. The others lead him on and he just does anything to impress them. He's even damaged another teacher's car just because the others dared him to do it.

What would *you* do to assist a boy like David?

REDUCING AGGRESSIVE BEHAVIOUR

Teachers are bothered most by aggressive behaviour in children (Church and Langley 1990). Increase in teacher stress is now considered to be closely linked with an increase in acting-out and aggressive behaviour in school (Balson 1992; King 1995).

Some professionals consider that aggression is an outcome of a combination of frustration, alienation and a feeling of hopelessness on the part of the student (Sparzo and Poteet 1993). Others believe that aggression occurs mainly because the student has not acquired alternative strategies for resolving conflict and avoiding confrontation. These two viewpoints are not mutually exclusive, and teachers need to consider both perspectives when analysing particular incidents of aggression in their own schools.

Several of the strategies suggested above for reducing generally disruptive behaviour are applicable also to the reduction of aggression. The following supplementary points may be helpful where aggression is the major concern. If episodes of aggressive behaviour continue it is essential that the teacher obtain specialist guidance, counselling or similar support services. Work with the family as well as the child may be indicated.

Prevention

Knowing that you have a potentially aggressive child in your class should make you aware of the need to control or limit situations where aggression might be provoked. Too much unstructured time, too many deadspots in lessons, too much unsupervised movement within the room, must be avoided. It may be necessary to give particular thought to the layout of the classroom to allow ease of supervision and access to desks and resources. The establishment of predictable routines and basic rules in the room will help (King 1995). The teacher, knowing the class well, should be able to anticipate and divert acting-out and aggressive behaviour by a well-timed question, a change of activity or the delegation of a small duty to the problem child.

Proximity

When a child appears to be on the point of losing control move physically closer to him or her, even invading the child's personal space, as a means of reducing or preventing the aggressive action. Quickly direct the child's attention to something new and move him or her to a different part of the room. Give the student something easy but productive to do and stay with him or her until the work is commenced. Make positive comments about the student's attention to the new task.

Provide physical outlets and other alternatives

In educational settings it is important for some children to have extra opportunities for physical exercise and movement in order to 'burn off' excess energy in acceptable ways (e.g. competitive races, circuit training). Sometimes it is useful to have some video tapes of basic aerobics or fitness programmes available to be used in the classroom or activity room when the need arises for a quick change of activity. For certain children this cathartic 'get it out of your system' strategy seems very successful although it can claim no scientific basis at the moment. The present writer found it very useful with both primary and secondary students with major behaviour problems as a strategy for preventing difficulties.

Teach children to express their anger verbally

Students who are poor communicators, perhaps through language difficulties, often don't know how to handle their own anger and aggression, and their reactions are therefore inappropriate (Froyen 1993). Part of any programme to improve behaviour and reduce the frequency of outbursts should be aimed at helping the student to verbalize the problem. Talking through a threatening situation helps the child to establish control and thus reduces impulsive acting-out behaviour. Accept the child's angry feeling but offer other suggestions for expressing them. For example say, '*Tell* her you don't like her taking your book'; '*Ask* David politely to return your paintbrush'. Then ensure that the child *does* use this approach at once. Cognitive behaviour modification programmes may also be helpful.

Assertiveness training

Assertiveness training is designed to lead children to understand that they have the right to be themselves and to express their feelings openly. Assertive responses generally are not aggressive responses but they are open and honest. Simply stated, assertive behaviour is being able to express yourself without hurting others. Bishop and Jubala (1995) suggest that students with disabilities placed in inclusive settings may often need specific training in both social skills and assertiveness.

Dissolve explosive situation through humour

A joke can help to ease a child out of a temper tantrum or outburst without losing face and can avoid placing teacher and child into confrontation (Grossman 1995). The joke or humour must not be at the child's expense and must not hint at ridicule or sarcasm.

Improving self-control in cases of conduct disorder

A cognitive behaviour modification programme developed by Wragg (1989) is proving to be very successful with some students who exhibit chronic conduct disorders. The programme, 'Talk sense to yourself', uses individual coaching and rehearsal with cue cards to establish self-instruction strategies in the student. These self-instructions are used to help the student monitor his or her own reactions to daily problems, and to control and manage such situations more effectively.

The first stage in intervention is to help the students analyse their inappropriate behaviour and to understand that what they are doing is not helping them in any way (e.g. lashing out at others, arguing with staff). Next the student is helped to establish both the desire to change and the goals to be aimed for over the next week (to stop doing this and to start doing that). An 'emotional temperature chart' provides a graphic point of reference from which the student can begin to monitor his or her level of arousal, anger or discomfort.

Over a number of sessions the student is helped to change negative thoughts and beliefs to more appropriate positive equivalents. A key ingredient in the programme is teaching the student to use *covert self-control statements* which serve to inhibit inappropriate thoughts and responses, allowing time for the substitution of more acceptable responses, for example, to be assertive but not aggressive.

The programme can be extended to improve such essential classroom behaviours as increased time on-task.

Wragg notes that school counsellors and psychologists can also use the programme with conduct disordered children in clinical settings.

Additional advice on improving students' self-control of behaviour is provided in Grossman (1995) and Vincent (1995).

HELPING WITHDRAWN OR TIMID CHILDREN

Merrett and Wheldall (1984) have indicated that teachers are much more likely to notice and respond to aggressive and disturbing behaviour than they are to quiet and withdrawn behaviour in the average classroom. The quiet, withdrawn children who cause no problem to the teacher may even be overlooked. They are likely to go unnoticed because their behaviour never disrupts the classroom routine. They annoy no one and they do not constantly come to the teacher's attention.

Teachers are becoming more aware of the significance of extreme shyness and withdrawal as signs of maladjustment. However, quiet children are not necessarily emotionally disturbed and may have no problems at all. For example, children reared in families where parents are quiet and reflective are themselves likely to learn similar patterns of behaviour. Reticent and quiet children may be quite happy, and it is a questionable practice to force such children to be assertive.

If a child does have a genuine problem of withdrawal from social interaction with other children the teacher does need to intervene. This may apply particularly to children with physical or intellectual disabilities where social acceptance may be a major problem. Some of the strategies for teaching social skills described in the next chapter will be very important in such cases.

Let it suffice here to suggest that the lonely or rejected child may need to be helped to establish a friendship within the class by judicious selection of partners for specific activities (e.g. project work, painting, completion of a puzzle, etc.) and by planning frequent opportunities for the child to experience some very positive outcomes from working with another child. Sometimes the teacher can encourage the child to bring some unusual toy or game from home which can be shared with another child. Once established even a very tentative friendship must be nurtured by the teacher.

Highly formal classrooms, where much silent deskwork is expected, will do little to foster social development in children lacking these skills. Equally, highly individualized programmes for special needs children may attend to their cognitive needs at the expense of their social skills development.

When the social isolation is extreme it may be the result of an almost total lack of social skills, from a history of rejection, from childhood depression or from some combination of these. Verbal communication can be minimal with such children and even eye contact may be virtually absent. In many such extreme cases the social isolation may be maintained by negative reinforcement, that is, the behaviour is continued because it avoids unpleasant contact (e.g. ridicule) from other children. In recent years the number of students who suffer from chronic depression has increased very significantly. Some depressed students even go so far as to take their own lives. On this issue Salend (1994: 113) has urged, 'If teachers suspect that a student is depressed or suicidal they should work with other professionals and parents to help the student receive the services of mental health professionals'.

In the literature on socially isolated children it is usually suggested that careful observation be made within the classroom and in the school-yard in order to find the point at which some cautious intervention might be attempted (e.g. getting the child to engage in some parallel play alongside other children as a preliminary step to later joining the play of others, taking a turn, etc.). The teacher will need to guide, support, prompt and reinforce the child through these various stages. In almost all cases the co-operation of the peer group will need to be enlisted if the child is to become an accepted member of that group. Studies have shown that social skills training together with peer involvement can have lasting effects on improving children's social adjustment (Grossman 1995).

Studies which have focused upon the inclusion of children with disabilities into regular classes have indicated that social acceptance of these children into the peer group does not occur spontaneously (Stainback, Stainback and Wilkinson 1992; Sale and Carey 1995). Most children with disabilities need to be taught how to relate to others (how to greet them, how to talk with them, how to share things), quite as much as the students without disabilities need to be taught tolerance and understanding of those who are different from themselves.

ATTENTION DEFICIT DISORDER AND HYPERACTIVITY

Some students display severe problems in maintaining attention to any task, both in and out of school. These children have been classified as having an Attention Deficit Disorder (ADD). Often these students also exhibit hyperactive behaviour, and the term Attention Deficit Hyperactivity Disorder (ADHD) has been coined to describe this form of learning difficulty (American Psychiatric Assocation 1994). ADD and ADHD is considered to be present in approximately 3 per cent of the school population.

The terms ADD and ADHD are often misused and applied to children who are merely bored and restless, or who are placed in a class where the teacher lacks good management skills. However, there are genuine cases of attention deficit and hyperactivity where the child experiences great difficulty in controlling his or her motor responses and exhibits high levels of inappropriate activity throughout the day (Carroll 1994). Hyperactivity is also present sometimes as an additional problem in certain other forms of disability (e.g. cerebral palsy, congenital or acquired brain injury, specific learning disability).

No single cause for ADHD has been identified, although the following have all been put forward as possible explanations: central nervous system dysfunction (perhaps due to slow maturation of the motor cortex of the brain), subtle forms of brain damage too slight to be confirmed by neurological testing, allergy to specific substances (e.g. food additives), adverse reactions to environmental stimuli (e.g. fluorescent lighting), inappropriate management of the child at home, maternal alcohol consumption during pregnancy ('Foetal alcohol syndrome'). Most investigators now agree that the hyperactive syndrome encompasses a heterogeneous group of behaviour disorders having different symptom clusters and etiologies' (Cohen and Minde 1983).

ADHD children, while not necessarily below average in intelligence, usually exhibit poor achievement in most school subjects (Warren and Flynt 1995). They may also be poorly co-ordinated. Some have problems with peer relationships. The literature indicates that most hyperactivity diminishes with age even without treatment. However the impaired concentration span and restlessness associated with the condition may well have seriously impeded the child's progress during the important early years of schooling.

Four main approaches are used to treat ADD and ADHD.

Pharmacological (the use of medication)

This is perhaps the most common form of treatment, especially in America. Approximately 80 per cent of hyperactive children do seem to respond positively to drug treatment but the others do not. The main drugs used in America are Ritalin, Dexedrine and Cylert. The reduced hyperactivity which accompanies medication does not always result in increased scholastic achievement, perhaps because the child is not provided with remedial tuition to help make up the leeway. Hallahan and Kauffman (1994) reviewed a number of studies of the progress made by students with hyperactivity. They concluded that medication alone is rarely, if ever, an adequate answer. Some form of extra tuition is needed, together with one or more of the approaches described below. However, in some cases medication can significantly improve attention span. Dramatic changes in behaviour and a reduction in family stress have been reported by some parents (Keith and Engineer 1991).

Some undesirable side effects have been reported from prolonged use of drugs (slow growth rate, short stature, disturbed sleep patterns).

Nutritional (diet control)

This involves the avoidance of specific foods containing, for example, artificial colourings or preservatives. The Feingold Diet is the best known of these treatments. Its use remains somewhat controversial. Diet control certainly doesn't prove to be effective with all hyperactive children, but some parents have claimed that it has been extremely helpful in specific cases.

Catharsis ('Get it out of your system')

This is merely the application of the strategy described earlier in the chapter whereby children 'burn off' excess energy through vigorous physical activity provided at frequent intervals.

Behaviour modification

The ADHD child's on-task behaviour, attention to work, completion of assignments, reduction of disruptive outbursts, all need to be reinforced and rewarded. The overactive behaviour should be ignored where possible, or at least played down in importance. Where this is not possible, 'time out', where the child is removed from positive reinforcement, has been shown to be effective in reducing hyperactivity, and is regarded as considerably safer than medication or strict diet regimes (Boyle 1990).

Wragg (1989) advocates self-management training to improve on-task behaviour. In this 'cognitive behaviour modification approach' the child is taught to control his or her own responses and behaviour by strategies such as verbal rehearsal or verbal regulation: 'I must work for five minutes on this, then take a break for one minute.' Sometimes video recordings of a child's actions are played back to him or her to focus on and discuss what must be modified (Lovitt 1991). Cognitive behaviour modification is mainly applicable to children of at least average intelligence since they are more able to understand the method and utilize it consistently.

Owing to the possibility that hyperactivity is caused by different factors in different individuals it is not surprising to find that quite different forms of treatment are advocated, and what works for one child may not work for another. The conclusion must be that any approach to the treatment of ADHD must attend to *all* factors which may be maintaining the behaviour (Gurry 1990). Evans (1995: 210) has concluded that, 'Current best practice indicates that behaviour management principles, cognitive-behavioural strategies for self-management, and effective instruction in both academic and social skills assist these students substantially'.

SUMMARY

This chapter has presented some specific techniques for controlling and modifying children's behaviour. Particular attention has been devoted to disruptive and aggressive behaviour since this causes the most concern for teachers at all school age levels. Consideration has also been given to the difficulties encountered by shy, timid or withdrawn children, and those with ADD or ADHD.

In general a combined ecological-behavioural approach has been advocated whereby a child's problems are not treated in isolation but instead are tackled within the total context of the curriculum, the peer group, the classroom environment and the family. Many behaviour problems appear to stem in part from inadequate social skills. A more detailed coverage of social skills training is presented in the next chapter.

Discussion points

- Identify some problem behaviour which is giving you cause for concern in your present class. Write down as objectively as possible the main features of this behaviour. What are the most obvious characteristics? Why is the behaviour troublesome? Try to identify the specific situations which seem to trigger off the behaviour. What do you do when the behaviour occurs? What do the other children do when the behaviour occurs?

- Do you agree with the use of tokens to reward and modify behaviour?

- 'Teacher stress' has become a major problem in recent years. Discuss the factors which may be responsible for stress in teachers, and suggest ways in which the problem may be reduced.

- Every school should have a written and enacted policy which addresses behaviour management. What would a new member of staff hope to find in the written policy?

- 'You will never help a maladjusted student to develop appropriate behaviour by removing him or her from the class.' Is this true? Discuss.

Further reading

Alberto, P. and Troutman, A.C. (1995) *Applied Behaviour Analysis for Teachers* (4th edn), Columbus: Merrill.

Balson, M. (1992) *Understanding Classroom Behaviour (3rd edn)*, Hawthorn: ACER

Canfield, J. (1990) 'Improving students' self-esteem', *Educational Leadership* 48, 1: 48–50.

Charles, C.M. (1996) *Building Classroom Discipline: From Models to Practice* (5th edn), New York: Longman.

Froyen, L.A. (1993) *Classroom Management: The Reflective Teacher-leader*, New York: Merrill.

Grossman, H. (1995) *Classroom Behaviour Management in a Diverse Society* (2nd edn), Mountainview: Mayfield.

Lerner, J.W. and Lerner, S.R. (1991) 'Attention deficit disorder: issues and questions', *Focus on Exceptional Children*, 24, 3: 1–20.

Jackson, M. (1991) *Discipline: An Approach for Teachers and Parents*, Melbourne: Longman Cheshire.

Rogers, B. (1995) *Behaviour Management: A Whole School Approach*, Sydney: Ashton Scholastic.

Walker, J.E. and Shea, T.M. (1995) *Behaviour Management: A Practical Approach for Educators* (6th edn), New York: Merrill.

Wragg, J. (1989) *Talk Sense to Yourself*. Hawthorn: ACER.

Chapter 6

Improving social skills and peer group acceptance

> With the inclusion of students with disabilities into general education classes, the composition of classroom social networks can influence whether students with special needs make positive social gains or become entrenched in a social system that supports and maintains their problematic or deficient social characteristics.
>
> (Farmer and Farmer 1996: 432)

The quotation above from Farmer and Farmer reminds us of the need to address the vital issue of social acceptance of children with special needs when placed in a regular class. Inclusive educational settings create a situation where children with disabilities can increase their social competence. It is important to note, however, that such an increase in social competence certainly does not always occur automatically (Vincent 1995).

The results of most studies of integration and inclusion do not support the belief that merely placing a child with a disability in the mainstream spontaneously improves the social status of that child (Slavin 1991; Sale and Carey 1995). There is actually a danger that the child will be marginalized, ignored or even openly rejected by the peer group. This situation must not be allowed to occur since it is evident that poor peer relationships in early school life can have a lasting detrimental impact on social and personal competence in later years (Taffe and Smith 1993). It is for this reason that establishing good social relationships with other children has been described as one of the most important goals of education (Cooper and McEvoy 1996).

OPPORTUNITIES FOR SOCIAL INTERACTION

For positive social interaction and the establishment of friendships to occur among children with and without disabilities at least three conditions must be present (Falvey and Rosenberg 1995):

- *opportunity*: that is, being within proximity of other children frequently enough for meaningful contacts to be made;
- *continuity*: being involved with the same group of children over a relatively long period of time, for example, several consecutive years; and also seeing some of the same children in your own neighbourhood out of school hours;
- *support*: being helped to make contact with other children in order to work and play with them; and if possible being directly supported in maintaining friendships out of school, for example, by being driven to a friend's home or being allowed to sleep over at a friend's house at weekends. This is particularly important in the case of children with disabilities.

Inclusive schooling provides the opportunity for friendships to develop in terms of proximity and frequency of contact, and in terms of potential continuity. It creates the best possible chances for children with disabilities to observe and imitate the social interactions and behaviours of others (Sacks, Kekelis and Gaylord-Ross 1992). What inclusive classrooms must also provide is the necessary support for positive social interactions to occur. This is particularly important for students who are low in self-esteem and confidence and who are missing some of the basic social skills.

When students with disabilities are placed in regular settings without adequate preparation or support, three basic problems may become evident:

- disabled children, contrary to popular belief, do not automatically observe and imitate the social models which are around them;
- children without disabilities do not readily demonstrate high levels of acceptance of those with disabilities;
- some teachers do not spontaneously intervene positively to promote social interaction on the disabled child's behalf.

In relation to the last of the three points above, it seems that teachers in general are becoming much more aware of the need to intervene and assist children in establishing friendships in class (English *et al.* 1996; Lowenthal 1996). Strategies for encouraging the social development of children feature much more frequently now in training and development programmes for teachers than was the case a few years ago.

However, even with this increase in awareness of the importance of social development, some teachers still inadvertently deal with children emotionally and physically, in ways which contribute to the social exclusion of some class members. Some examples from the 'hidden curriculum' which influences attitudes and beliefs will illustrate this point.

- Teacher A always selects two team-leaders for outdoor games with the instruction to 'choose your own teams'. Guess who is always chosen last or excluded because she is poorly co-ordinated? This situation could be totally avoided by the use of a different organizational strategy.

- Teacher B always has Wayne sitting near her table so that she can more easily control his behaviour and provide help when needed. While serving to 'maintain' Wayne in the classroom, and attending to two of his educational needs, the approach inevitably isolates the boy from normal interactions with other children during deskwork time. This may not be a problem if he is programmed into group work and pair activities at other times in the day; but he may not be.

- Teacher C believes that Linda must have individual work assignments set because she can't cope with the general level of classwork (and this teacher never uses ability or friendship grouping for any purposes). The teacher spends time and effort in programming appropriate material for Linda and even provides a carrel for her to work in, away from the other children. While this is totally defensible as a method of catering for this child's academic learning needs, it must be recognized that it virtually eliminates any social interaction and highlights her 'differences' in the class setting. Is this 'inclusive practice'?

- Teacher D rarely visits the school-yard unless on duty. If Teacher D spent a little time observing David in this setting he would find that this boy is always ignored by other children at lunchtime and at morning break. He spends his time by the door waiting to come back into the classroom.

It seems that some teachers may need to develop more sensitivity to these situations, and also to recognize failures in peer relationships when they occur. They also need to be willing to implement suitable strategies to bring about improvements in children's social interaction in the classroom. Some of these identification and intervention strategies will now be discussed.

It must be clear that, although reference is made frequently here to children with disabilities, the approaches discussed here are equally applicable to any child who needs help in personal-social development.

IDENTIFICATION OF CHILDREN WITH PEER RELATIONSHIP PROBLEMS

Naturalistic observation

The most obvious strategy for identifying children with particular problems is the informal observation of social interactions within and outside the classroom (Howell, Fox and Morehead 1993). A teacher who takes the trouble to note the ways in which children play and work together will quickly identify children who are neglected by their peers or who are openly rejected and become an object of ridicule and teasing. It is very important also to try to observe the surface reasons which appear to give rise to this situation. For example, is the child in question openly obnoxious to others through aggression, hurtful comments, a tendency to spoil games or interfere with work? Or at the other extreme, does the child seem to lack motivation, confidence and skills to initiate contact with others, remaining very much on the outside of any action?

Naturalistic observation is probably the most valuable method of identification for the teacher to use since it focuses on the child within the dynamics of peer group interactions and can thus indicate a number of factors which might be modified.

Sociometric survey

Naturalistic observation tends to identify the most obvious cases of popularity or rejection. It may not pick up some of the subtleties of social interactions in the class. For this reason some teachers find it useful to carry out a whole-class survey in order to get all the children to indicate, in confidence, their main friendship choices (Serna 1993). The teacher may interview each child privately or, if the children can write, may give out slips of paper with the numerals 1 to 3 printed on them. The teacher then requests that each child write down first the name of the person he or she would most like to play with or work with as a partner in a classroom activity or at lunchtime. The teacher may then say, 'If that person was away from school who would you choose next?' and that name is listed second. A few teachers might also say, 'If there is anyone in the class you really don't like to work with or play with you can write that person's name against number 3. You don't *have* to write any name there; if you get on well with everyone, just leave it blank.' (This last procedure is sometimes criticized by teachers who fear that children may afterwards discuss what they wrote. If handled carefully this problem should not arise.) When the papers are collected the teacher calculates the score for each child on the basis of two points for a first choice and one point for a second choice. If Susan is chosen three times as the first preference by other children and twice as second preference, her total score is eight points. The results for each individual in the class can then be tabulated. Some teachers go so far as to map the choices in the form of a sociogram, showing the 'stars' (most popular), the 'isolates' (not chosen by others), mutual pairs and cliques, etc.

The information gained from a survey of this type may not only help a teacher identify children who are of low sociometric status but also to determine the composition of certain working groups in the class. It can sometimes be useful in identifying which children are named as first preference or second preference by the isolates even though the choice was not reciprocated. There may be a chance to pair these two children for some activities. However, it is often found that isolates merely name the stars in the class and the choice is not realistic. Children who are not chosen or who are listed as 'not liked' should obviously become the target for some of the intervention strategies described in this chapter.

Peer ratings

Gresham (1982) advocates the use of a peer rating scale rather than a sociometric survey since he feels that this provides a better measure of 'likeability'. Also it ensures that some children are not forgotten or overlooked as may happen with a sociometric survey of the type described above.

The children are provided with a list of the names of all children in the class and required in confidence to place a score from 1 (not liked very much) to 5 (liked a lot) against each name. Summation of the completed scores will reveal the children who are not liked by most class members as well as showing the level of acceptance of all other children. The result may sometimes correlate highly with naturalistic observation, but occasionally quite subtle positive or negative attitudes appear which are not immediately obvious to outside observation.

Mapping friendship patterns

Falvey and Rosenberg (1995) have presented the idea of using a 'Circle of friends' diagram, using three or four large concentric circles drawn on paper or on the blackboard. In the inner circle the child's name is written. In the next circle moving out from the centre are written the names of all the most important people in that child's life (parents, care-givers, closest friends, etc.). In the next circle out are written the names of all the other people the child is friendly with in his or her class or group. In the outer circle are written the names of other people the child knows and gets on with, but who are not classed as actual friends. The diagram which results from this activity presents a helpful picture of the child's network of contacts. In some cases it can even prove to the child who feels that he or she has no friends that indeed many names do go into the diagram.

It is suggested that a circle of friends diagram can be developed from a small group activity, or by working individually with a child. When working individually and in confidence the teacher might suggest that they write outside the boundary of the diagram the name of any person the child dislikes. Falvey and Rosenberg (1995) suggest that discussions emerging from the process can help to identify support networks for the child with a disability and can influence the composition of classroom work groups.

Teacher ratings

The use of checklists which specify important indicators of social competence can be helpful in providing a clear focus for teachers' observations of children (Serna 1993; Vincent 1995). The items in the checklist would normally be those responses and behaviours considered to comprise 'social skills', such as greeting, interacting with others, sharing, avoiding conflict, etc.

Parent nomination

Sometimes a child's social relationship problems at school may be brought to the teacher's attention first by the parent who says 'I'm worried about Paul. He doesn't bring any friends home and doesn't play with other children after school', or 'Marion has been coming home from school saying that the other girls are making fun of her in the yard and on the bus'. This type of information should be followed up by the teacher and treated in a sensitive manner.

Over to you: Social relationships in the classroom

- Use the sociometric survey or the rating scale procedure described above with your class. Before charting the results try to predict those children who will obtain high scores and those who will obtain low scores. How accurate was your prediction? Did your survey reveal any unexpected information? How might the results of this exercise help you in your day-to-day work with your class?

- If the activity is age-appropriate for your class, try the 'Circle of friends' procedure.

CREATING A SUPPORTIVE ENVIRONMENT

To facilitate social interaction for children with special needs in regular classrooms three conditions are necessary:

- the general attitude of the teacher and the peer group needs to be made as positive and accepting as possible;
- the environment should be arranged so that the child with a disability has the maximum opportunity to spend time socially involved in a group or pair activity, during recess and during academic work in the classroom;
- the child needs to be taught the specific skills that may enhance social contact with peers.

Influencing attitudes

Lack of previous experience with disabled children, and a lack of knowledge about disabilities, can lead children (and even teachers) to feel uncomfortable in the presence of a person with a disability. This, in turn, causes them to avoid contact where possible. Where the disabled individual has a marked speech and communication problem, has an unusual physical appearance and is poorly co-ordinated, the difficulties are greatest. Gow and Ward (1991) have noted that students with moderate intellectual disability and language problems are the most difficult to include successfully in regular classrooms. In extreme cases, ignorance concerning disability can result in quite damaging prejudice, hostility and rejection (Hickson 1990).

Fortunately, evidence is accumulating to show that attitudes can be significantly changed in teachers and in the peer group. Teachers and peers tend to become more accepting of children with disabilities when they better understand the nature of the disability. Experience has shown that a combination of information about, and direct contact with, disabled children provides the most powerful positive influence for attitude change in both teachers and in the peer group (McCoy 1995). It is also evident that attitude change tends to be a long and gradual process.

Children's attitudes are likely to be influenced most when teachers work to build a climate of concern for others in the classroom (Salisbury, *et al.* 1995). This can be achieved in part by the teacher's own example, and also by the open discussion and resolution of problems that may arise from time to time. Facilitating and encouraging peer assistance and buddy systems in the classroom can also be useful.

The following approaches, particularly when used in combination, have all been beneficial in improving attitudes toward children with disabilities. Throughout these 'awareness raising' techniques the stress should be upon 'How can we help?'; 'How would we treat someone like that in our class?'; and 'Notice how much that person can already do unaided'.

- Viewing films or videos depicting disabled children and adults with disabilities coping well and doing everyday things.
- Factual lessons and discussion about particular disabilities.
- Having disabled persons as visitors to the classroom or as guest speakers.
- Simulation activities, e.g. simulating deafness, or vision impairment or being confined to a wheelchair. (Note that unfortunately two conditions which cannot be simulated are intellectual disability and emotional disturbance. These are also the two disabilities which produce the greatest problems in terms of social isolation and rejection in the peer group.)
- Reading and discussing stories about disabled persons and their achievements.
- Regular visits as helpers to special schools or centres.

Creating opportunities

If social learning is to take place it is essential that the socially inept child has the opportunity to be truly involved in all group activities both inside and outside the classroom. If children with disabilities are to be socially integrated then group work situations and co-operative learning should be used frequently in preschool, primary and secondary settings (Slavin 1991; Honig and Wittmer 1996; Lowenthal 1996). Unfortunately, while grouping and activity methods are common in the early years of schooling they are rather less common in the middle school or upper primary school. Even less are they used in the later years when children are often faced with a rigorous academic curriculum and a fairly rigid timetable.

Much of the work which has supported the value of co-operative learning and grouping within the classroom has been carried out by two brothers, Roger and David Johnson (1991; Johnson, Johnson and Holubec 1990). They make two assumptions: that teachers create classroom environments where competition is not a dominant element; and that teachers use grouping strategies to encourage co-operation among students for at least part of each day. Regrettably both assumptions prove to be false when applied to certain classrooms. Some teachers still use too much competition among their children on a regular basis, and some make no use at all of co-operative group work. Some teachers keep the children in formal settings, all working on the same material for the same time regardless of individual differences, and may actively discourage any discussion and collaboration. The implications here are that if a teacher rarely, if ever, uses grouping as an organizational option, it is unlikely that much will be achieved in terms of social inclusion of students with special needs (Salisbury et al. 1995).

Organization for group work

The success of collaborative group work depends on classroom organization, the nature of the tasks set for the students to work on and the composition of the working groups (Lyle 1996). Too often group work begins to become chaotic because the tasks set are too vague or too complex, the students are not well versed in group-working skills and the room is not set up to facilitate easy access to resources. It is essential that all group work has a very clear structure which is understood by all. Careful planning is required if group work is to achieve the desired educational and social outcomes.

When utilizing group work as an organizational strategy it is important to consider the following basic principles.

• Merely establishing groups and setting them to work is not enough. Group members have to be taught how to work together. They must be shown the behaviours which encourage or enable co-operation, e.g. listening to the views of others, sharing, praising one another, offering to help each other. If the task involves the learning of specific content, teach the children how to rehearse and test one another on the material.

• Teachers must carefully monitor what is going on during group activities and must intervene when necessary to provide suggestions, encourage the sharing of a task, praise examples of co-operation and teamwork and model co-operative behaviour themselves. Many groups can be helped to function efficiently if the teacher (or the aide or a parent helper) works as a group member without dominating the situation.

• The way in which individual tasks are allotted has to be very carefully planned (division of labour); the way in which each child can assist another must also be made explicit, e.g. 'John, you can help Craig with his writing then he can help you with the lettering for your title board'. Contingent praise for interacting with others should be descriptive. 'Good, John. I can see your friend really appreciates you holding the saw for him.' 'Well done Sue. That's nice of you to help Sharon with that recording.'

• The size of the group is also important. Johnson and Johnson suggest a group of two or three members if the children are young or are unskilled in group work. Select the composition of the group carefully to avoid obvious incompatibility. Information from a sociometric survey may help to determine appropriate partners for less popular children.

• The choice of topic and tasks for group work is very important. Tasks have to be selected which *require* collaboration and teamwork. Lyle (1996) comments that children are often seated in groups in the classroom, but are expected to work on their individual assignments. This does not involve productive collaboration, and the arrangement often creates difficulties for the individual student in terms of not completing assignments due to distractions.

• Initially, there is some merit in having the groups of children working co-operatively on the same task at the same time. The procedure makes it much easier to prepare resources and to manage the time effectively (Lyle 1996). When each of several groups are undertaking quite different work it can become a major management problem for the teacher, unless the students concerned are already very competent and experienced in working independently.

• When groups contain some students with special needs it is vital that the specific tasks and duties to be undertaken by those students are clearly delineated. It can be useful to establish a system whereby the results of the group's efforts are rewarded not merely by what individuals produce, but also by the way in which they have worked positively and supportively together. Under this structure, group members have a vested interest in ensuring that other members learn, as the group's success depends on the achievement of all. Helping each other, sharing and tutoring within the group must all be placed at a premium.

• Talking should be encouraged during group activities. It is interesting to note that subgrouping in the class has the effect of increasing transactional talk (talk specifically directed to another person and requiring a reply) by almost three times the level present under whole-class conditions.

• Room arrangement is important. Group members should be in close proximity but still have space to work on materials without getting in each other's way.

• Group work must be used frequently enough for the children to learn the skills and routines. Infrequent group work results in children taking too long to settle down.

FACILITATING SOCIAL INTERACTION

What other strategies can be used to enhance the disabled child's chances of positive social integration?

• 'Peer tutoring', 'buddy systems' and other helping relationships have all been found effective to a greater or lesser degree; some can result in the development of genuine and lasting friendships.

• A greater use of games and play activities of a non-academic type can place the disabled child in situations where he or she can more easily fit in and work with others.

• Make a particular topic (e.g. 'Making friends' or 'Working together') the basis for class discussion. 'If you want someone to play with you at lunchtime what would you say to that person?' 'If you saw someone in the school-yard who had just started at the school today how would you greet them? How would you make them feel welcome?' Sometimes teachers prepare follow-up material in the form of worksheets with simple cartoon-type drawings and speech balloons into which the children write the appropriate greetings or comments for the various characters. Much of this can be incorporated into a total 'social education' programme.

• It is important to get the peer-group members to reinforce and maintain social interactions with disabled children. Often they are unaware of the ways in which they can help. They, too, may need to be shown how to initiate contact, how to invite the child with special needs to join in an activity, how to help the child with particular school assignments, etc.

SOCIAL SKILLS TRAINING

One of the main reasons why certain children are unpopular is that they lack appropriate social skills which might make them more acceptable. They are in a Catch-22 situation since friendless students have no opportunity to practise social skills, and those with poor social skills are unable to form friendships. As Ariel (1992: 354) has commented, 'Problems in social skills are more debilitating than academic problems and hinder the ability to succeeed in life'.

Social isolation in childhood may have serious long-term consequences in terms of mental health in adult life, so it is vital that isolated and rejected individuals are helped to overcome some of these problems as early as possible. Fortunately there is growing evidence that social behaviours which contribute to positive personal interaction with others can be taught and can have lasting effects (Grossman 1995). However, while most social skills training programmes do produce positive effects, there is always a problem with maintenance of the trained skills over time, and generalization of the skills to new settings (Taffe and Smith 1993). It must also be noted that even when children with disabilities are specifically trained in social skills, some may not find it any easier to make friends. For example, Margalit (1995) found that students with intellectual disability still reported feelings of loneliness even after successfully participating in a social skills programme.

Even given the cautionary comments above it is still a high priority in inclusive settings that students who lack specific social skills be provided with every opportunity, including specific training, in order to acquire them. When students with special needs do improve their social skills their peers relate better to them, thus reinforcing and helping to maintain the improvement to some degree (Grossman 1995). Without social skills training, children with disabilities are more likely to interact with any *adult* present in the particular setting rather than with other children (English *et al.* 1996).

What are 'social skills'?

Broadly speaking social skills are those components of behaviour that are important for persons to initiate, and then maintain, positive interactions with others. Ariel (1992) lists as many as thirty different social skills. A somewhat condensed list includes the following specific behaviours necessary for social competence.

Basic social skills

- Eye contact: being able to maintain eye contact with another person to whom you are listening or speaking for at least brief periods of time.
- Facial expression: smiling, showing interest.
- Social distance: knowing where to stand relative to others; knowing when physical contact is inappropriate.
- Quality of voice: volume, pitch, rate of speech, clarity, content.
- Greeting others: initiating contact or responding to a greeting; inviting another child to join you in some activity.
- Making conversation: age-appropriate conversational skills; expressing

your feelings; asking questions; listening; showing interest; responding to questions asked.
- Playing with others and working with others: complying with rules, sharing, compromising, helping, taking turns, complimenting others, saying thank you, saying you're sorry.
- Gaining attention and/or asking for help: using appropriate ways.
- Coping with conflict: controlling aggression, dealing with anger in self and others, accepting criticism, 'being a sport'.
- Grooming and hygiene.

The above list represents a fairly complex amalgam of non-verbal and verbal skills which all appear crucial for successful social interaction.

As well as having the appropriate social skills an individual also needs *not* to have other behavioural characteristics which prevent easy acceptance by others, e.g.: high levels of irritating behaviour (interrupting, poking, shouting etc.); impulsive and unpredictable reactions; temper tantrums; abusive language; cheating at games. In some cases these undesirable behaviours may need to be eliminated by behaviour modification or cognitive behaviour modification procedures.

Some writers find it useful to view social skills not as merely 'verbal' or 'non-verbal' but rather as being mainly either 'cognitive' or 'overt'. Cognitive functions include: knowing what to do or not to do by interpreting social cues in a situation (e.g. knowing when an adult is ready to be approached and has time to listen); empathizing with or understanding the feelings of others; and anticipating the results of your actions. Overt functions include the actual behaviours exhibited: e.g. smiling, gesturing, speaking at an appropriate volume, making eye contact, not standing too close to another person when speaking, etc. Children with intellectual disability and those with genuine emotional disturbance tend to have difficulty in acquiring the cognitive functions even after overt functions have been taught. This is to be expected since the acquisition of these functions (e.g. the concept of what constitutes 'a friend') follows a developmental sequence in all children. Children with special needs will be very much later in reaching a full understanding of such matters. In some cases the problem has been exacerbated by parents who have overprotected the child and thus reduced social involvement with others.

How are social skills taught?

Most programmes for training social skills have been based on a combination of modelling, coaching, role-playing with rehearsing, feedback and counselling. At times, video recordings have also been used to provide examples of social behaviours in action and to provide the trainee with feedback on his or her own performance or role-play.

In an individual case the first step is obviously to decide where to begin, what the priorities are for this child. Csapo (1983) suggests that teachers should observe and analyse not only what the child does and does not do already, but should also determine the specific social skills needed and valued in that particular age group or class. It is pointless to teach skills which in that particular context are not immediately functional.

The most meaningful setting in which to enhance a child's social skills are, of course, the classroom and school-yard. At times a teacher needs to intervene to assist a child to gain entry to a group activity or to work with a carefully chosen partner. The teacher must also praise and reinforce both the target child and the peer group for all instances of co-operative, helpful and friendly behaviour. However, *in situ* intervention is not always feasible, particularly in extreme cases of withdrawal or rejection. Sometimes it may be necessary for a child to be coached thoroughly in a particular skill away from the class situation before that skill can be used in the peer group setting. Franco *et al.* (1983) provide an excellent example of this from a case study of a very shy adolescent. These practitioners focused on conversational skills as being the most important to establish in this youth. In a withdrawal room they worked on four areas: asking questions of others, making reinforcing comments and acknowledging what others say, showing affective warmth, and maintaining eye contact. Sessions were held twice weekly for twenty minutes over a fifteen-week period. After explanations and demonstrations from a tutor, the youth then practised these behaviours with the tutor and applied them in a series of ten-minute conversations with different male and female partners (to aid generalization). The partners were previously instructed to be warm and friendly but to refrain from asking questions of the subject unless he asked one first. They were also told to keep their responses brief so that the onus would be on the subject to maintain the conversation. The subject was instructed to adopt the strategy of finding out as much as possible about the other person's interests and to keep the conversation going. Observations were made at intervals after the coaching sessions had finished and significant and durable improvements were reported in his classroom interactions.

Coaching in social skills: six steps

The general training pattern used in a typical social skills programme follows a sequence of steps:

Definition   Describe the skill to be taught. Discuss why this particular skill is important and how its use helps interaction to occur. The skill may be illustrated in use in a video, a picture or cartoon, a simulation using puppets or pointed out to the child by reference to activities going on in the peer group. The teacher may say 'Watch how she helps him build the wall with the blocks'; 'Look at the two girls sharing the puzzle. Tell me what they are saying to each other.'

Model the skill Break the skill down into simple components and demonstrate these clearly yourself, or get a selected child to do this.

Imitation and rehearsal The child tries out the same skill in a structured situation. For this to occur successfully the child must be motivated to perform the skill and must attend carefully and retain what has been demonstrated.

Feedback This should be informative. 'You've not quite got it yet. You need to look at her while you speak to her. Try it again.' 'That's better! You looked and smiled. Well done.' Feedback via a video recording may be appropriate in some situations.

Provide opportunity for the skill to be used Depending upon the skill just taught small group work or pair work activities may be set up to allow the skill be applied and generalized to the classroom or other natural setting.

Intermittent reinforcement Watch for instances of the child applying the skill without prompting at other times in the day and later in the week. Provide descriptive praise and reward. Aim for maintenance of the skill once acquired. To a large extent these behaviours, once established, are likely to be maintained by natural consequences, i.e. by a more satisfying interaction with peers.

Over to you: Social skills development

- Select a social skill from the list provided in this chapter (e.g. 'Working with others' or 'Gaining attention'). Plan a series of activities following the six steps above in order to teach and maintain that skill in a child.

- Some of your colleagues in school suggest that social skills should be an 'across the curriculum' responsibility and not treated as a separate topic. How do you respond to this suggestion? Is there a place for a social skills curriculum in its own right? How would it be implemented?

SUMMARY

Many children with disabilities or learning difficulties encounter problems of peer group acceptance when placed in regular classes. In addition, some students without any specific disability also experience these social difficulties. The ways in which attitudes can be improved and the environment modified to facilitate social interaction, and the teaching of specific social skills have been described in this chapter. Evidence suggests that, in the past, teachers often overlooked and therefore neglected this aspect of a child's learning and development in school, but now teachers are more aware of the issues involved. Much can be done to assist children with social and personal problems and teachers are recognizing their responsibility in this area. To be effective an inclusive classroom programme must include provision for enhancing the social acceptance of all students with special needs.

Poor scholastic achievement seems to be a factor leading to poor social acceptance, even after social skills have been taught. Unless achievement within the curriculum can also be increased, acceptance may remain a problem for some children. Attention is therefore focused on acceleration of basic academic skills in the following chapters.

Discussion points

• Anna is in Year 3 at school and is an extremely shy and timid child. She does not cause any problems in the classroom and her general bookwork is of a good standard. Her teacher has become increasingly concerned that he cannot get Anna to be more forthcoming and assertive both inside and outside the classroom setting. He feels that, if anything, Anna is becoming even more withdrawn. What should he do?

• Many emotionally disturbed children lack the social skills to enable them to relate easily to other children in regular or special classes. A significant number of such children are not only anti-social but also openly aggressive and hostile. Imagine that you have such a child in your class. Describe the steps you might take to modify this child's aggressive behaviour and make him or her more socially acceptable in the group.

Further reading

Barnes, P. (ed.) (1995) *Personal, Social and Emotional Development in Children*, Oxford: Blackwell.

Bryan, T. and Lee, J. (1990) 'Social skills training with learning disabled children and adolescents', in T.E. Scruggs, and B.Y. Wong, (eds) *Intervention Research in Learning Disabilities*, New York: Springer Verlag.

Canfield, J. and Wells, H.C. (1994) *One Hundred Ways to Enhance Self-Concept* (2nd edn), Boston: Allyn and Bacon.

Cartledge, G. and Milburn, J.F. (1995) *Teaching Social Skills to Children and Youth: Innovative Approaches* (3rd edn), Boston: Allyn and Bacon.

Johnson, D.W and Johnson, R.T. (1994) *Joining Together: Group Theory and Group Skills* (5th edn), Boston: Allyn and Bacon.

Johnson, D.W., Johnson, R.T. and Holubec, E. (1990) *Circles of Learning: Co-operation in the Classroom* (3rd edn), Edina, Minn.: Interaction Books.

McGrath, H.L. and Francey, A. (1991) *Friendly Kids, Friendly Classrooms*, Melbourne: Longman Cheshire.

Petersen, L. and Gannoni, A.F. (1992) *Teacher's Manual for Social Skills Training*, Camberwell: ACER.

Pierce, C. (1994) 'Importance of classroom climate for at-risk learners', *Journal of Educational Research* 88, 1: 37–42.

Putnam, J.W. (1993) *Cooperative Learning and Strategies for Inclusion*, Baltimore: Brookes.

Slavin, R.E. (1990) *Cooperative Learning: Theory, Research and Practice*, Englewood Cliffs: Prentice Hall.

Thousand, J., Villa, R. and Nevin, A. (1994) *Creativity and Collaborative Learning*, Baltimore: Brookes.

Chapter 7

Literacy: where to begin

Beginning readers require more direct instructional support from teachers in the early stages of learning.

(ERIC Digest #E540 1996: 79)

Learning to read is not a simple task, even for some children of average intelligence. It may be a very difficult task indeed for children with significant disabilities such as impaired hearing, cerebral palsy, visual impairment, intellectual disability or emotional disturbance. For example, hearing impairment often limits the child's general vocabulary development and restricts awareness of the phonemic structure of words. Cerebral palsy, even if not accompanied by intellectual impairment, may cause visual perceptual problems and a tendency to become fatigued quickly in tasks which require carefully controlled eye movements. Vision impairment may necessitate the use of magnification aids and enlarged print; or in the case of blindness may require the substitution of braille materials for conventional print. Intellectual disability results in a much slower learning rate; and the child will be ready to read at a much later age than is normal (Westwood 1994). In some cases, if the disability is moderate to severe, the student may never reach this stage during the school years. Emotional disturbance may cause a child to be so preoccupied that concentration is impossible and motivation is totally lacking. Yet almost all these children can be helped to master the basic skills of word recognition and comprehension of simple texts. Quite dramatic improvements can result from special coaching of even the most difficult children (Conners 1992; Swicegood and Linehan 1995; Lingard 1996).

It has been said that there is no one method, medium, approach or philosophy that holds the key to the process of learning to read. From this it follows that the greater the range and variety of methods known to teachers the more likely it is that they will feel competent to provide appropriate help for slower learners and children with specific learning difficulties. Gillet and Bernard (1989: 16) have commented: 'Research and our own experience suggests that the approach which is successful with all children with reading difficulties is one which combines features of a number of different approaches and is adapted to a child's individual needs'.

CURRENT LANGUAGE ARTS PHILOSOPHY

The whole language approach

In Britain, Australia, New Zealand and North America the contemporary approach to beginning reading instruction has been influenced greatly by the works of Smith (1978, 1992), Goodman (1967, 1989, 1994a, b), and Cambourne (1988). It is the viewpoint of these writers that literacy skills are acquired by children through 'natural learning' rather than through direct teaching. They consider that children acquire literacy skills in much the same way as they earlier learned to use speech for purposes of communication, without having to be taught the process. Learners engaging actively with print are considered capable of constructing meaning for themselves by experimenting with language, taking risks, guessing, predicting words and self-correcting when necessary. It is believed that immersion in a learning environment where reading and writing are valued pursuits will stimulate all children to want to become literate.

The approach to literacy learning advocated by Goodman *et al.* is one that is essentially child-centred, and involves providing children with daily experiences in using reading and writing for 'real' purposes, rather than engaging in decontextualized exercises. As Goodman (1989: 70) has described the situation, 'Children learn to read and write as they read and write to learn and solve problems'. This method of facilitating literacy acquisition has become known as 'whole language'. Goodman (1989) insists that 'whole language' is not a specific method or approach; but rather a philosophy of learning and teaching across the curriculum. However, for convenience of communication in this book, whole language will continue to be referred to as a teaching approach.

Principal features of whole language

The application of the whole language approach at classroom level usually embodies at least the following principles:

- reading good literature to students every day, and having 'real' literature available for students to read for themselves;
- providing time each day for sustained silent reading;
- providing daily opportunities to read and write for real purposes;
- teaching reading skills always in context, rather than in isolation;
- integrating the curriculum to allow literacy skills to be utilized across all subject areas.

While reading, the emphasis is upon making meaning from text, using all available cues to assist with the process. The three main cueing systems readers are encouraged to use are:

- the semantic (the meaning of what is being read);
- the syntactic (the logical grammatical structure of the sentences or phrases);
- the grapho-phonic (the correspondence between the symbols in print and the speech-sound values they represent).

The views of whole language enthusiasts reflect a very strong swing against the explicit teaching of specific component skills of literacy, such as letter recognition, phonic decoding and spelling. It is believed that children will develop an understanding of the alphabetic principle for themselves as they endeavour to read for meaning and write for genuine purposes of communication (Moustafa 1993).

The meaning-emphasis viewpoint of the whole language approach implies that if a reader is thinking intelligently about what he or she is reading almost all the 'guessing' of words and meaning is based in semantic and syntactic cues (the 'top-down' approach), and very rarely is it necessary or 'natural' to resort to decoding a word from its letters or syllables (the 'bottom-up' approach). For this reason attention to phonics is given a significantly lower priority than in many other traditional approaches to teaching reading.

Whole language purists insist that phonic decoding skills and spelling skills should not be taught through specific drills or exercises used in isolation. They believe that decontextualized activities of this type actually make the learning process more difficult. Advocates of the whole language approach argue that phonic skills and spelling skills *are* in fact taught within the approach, but not as ends in themselves, and are always presented in context (Newman and Church 1990; Tester and Horoch 1995). It is claimed that these specific skills are tackled with individual students at the moment when their use serves an immediate purpose, for example, when a student is needing to spell a particular word correctly or to identify a word that cannot be predicted from context.

The whole language approach often incorporates the use of literature-based programmes, using authentic texts rather than vocabulary-controlled graded books. Reading materials from other subject areas, such as mathematics, science and environmental education, are frequently used within the programme. It is believed to be important to offer the students multiple texts and different genres if reading and writing are to be used in truly relevant ways.

Exponents of the whole language approach claim that it is valuable, not only for students who learn to read and write easily, but also for students with special learning needs and adults with literacy problems (Newman and Church 1990; Crux 1991; Swicegood and Linehan 1995). However, the whole language approach is not without its critics (e.g. Pressley and Rankin 1994; Harrison, Zollner and Magill 1996). The views of the whole language advocates may hold true for children who learn to read easily – they may well acquire reading skills almost as a natural developmental process. However, teachers who have worked with students exhibiting chronic reading problems know that in the majority of cases it is essential to instruct these children in word recognition strategies, letter knowledge and decoding skills if they are to make progress. A focus on meaning is, of course, essential when teaching children to read; but without the ability to use basic word identification skills, predicting from context can be very unreliable (Merry and Peutrill 1994). As Heymsfeld (1989: 68) commented, when arguing for inclusion of explicit basic skills instruction within the whole language approach, 'We cannot depend on haphazard, amorphous lessons to teach something as critical as knowledge of the alphabetic code'.

Problems arise within an exclusively whole language approach when a child is not at all skilled in contextual guessing. Perhaps the child's experience with language, particularly the more elaborate language of books, has been very restricted, and the child's own vocabulary is limited. No teacher would deny that the purpose of reading is to make meaning, or that the more reading one does the more likely one is to become a better reader and to enjoy the activity. However, it is relevant to wonder if one can make complete meaning and read fluently without at some stage having acquired the necessary word-attack skills to employ when context clues are inadequate?

Decoding skills

The general terms 'phonics' and 'phonic decoding' relate to the reader's ability to use a knowledge of the relationship between letters in print and the speech sounds they represent in order to identify an unfamiliar word. The terms also relate to the writer's ability to use letter-to-sound correspondences in order to attempt to spell an unseen word by attending to its component sounds and syllables.

There now exists a vast body of research that supports the explicit teaching of phonic knowledge to children in the early stages of learning to read (e.g. Chall 1989; Adams 1990; Chapman and Tunmer 1991; Snider 1992; Biemiller 1994). This instruction does not replace reading for meaning or enjoyment, but rather embeds within the meaning-emphasis approach some very systematic teaching of letter–sound correspondences. Without such information, children are lacking a reliable strategy for unlocking words. In the earliest stages of learning to read, children have not yet built up a large vocabulary of words they know instantly by sight, so they must use knowledge of letters and letter clusters to help identify unfamiliar words. Children cannot really become independent readers unless they master the code.

The most basic level of phonic knowledge is that involving the common speech-sound associated with each *single* letter of the alphabet. This knowledge is useful to the beginning reader but is fairly limited in its application, since not all words follow a regular letter-to-sound correspondence. Of far more functional value to the reader and writer is the next level of phonic knowledge represented by recognition of common letter clusters, or strings of letters, such as pre-, un-, -ing, -tion, -ough, -ite, -ous, -air-, -ee-, -ie-, -ea-, etc. These units, although not necessarily having a perfectly consistent sound value in all words in which they occur, are certainly far more predictable than single letter-to-sound correspondences. When children equate strings of letters with larger units of sound, such as syllables in spoken words, many of the inconsistencies in English spelling patterns are removed.

Learners differ in the extent to which they pick up phonic principles incidentally. Many children will deduce the code and its rules for themselves, but some will not. The judgement of just how much emphasis to give the teaching of phonics needs to be made on an individual basis. As far as gaining an understanding of the grapho-phonic system is concerned, there seem to be three types of children: those who gain insight on their own, with little or no direct instruction; those who need some initial instruction and then make progress on their own; and those who will never master it on their own, knowing only as much of the system as they have been directly taught.

The present writer's experience as a remedial teacher and as a teacher of primary and secondary special classes, suggests that the vast majority of children with reading problems exhibit poorly developed phonic knowledge and inefficient word-attack skills. They benefit from a carefully structured supplementary phonic approach in order to develop the skills which they currently lack. This view is upheld by the work of Mather (1992), Gunning (1995) and Gaskins et al. (1995).

It must be stressed here that an *exclusively* phonic approach is not being advocated for any child, with or without special needs. It is being argued that within a total reading programme due attention should be given to the teaching of decoding skills for those children who need this instruction.

The whole language and literature-based programmes emphasize the importance of such matters as:

- surrounding the child with stimulating reading material;
- creating a climate where reading is an enjoyable, necessary and valued occupation;
- the teacher modelling good reading performance and attitude;
- giving abundant encouragement to any child who makes the effort to read independently.

It is argued here that these factors create a necessary *but insufficient* condition to ensure that all children will become proficient readers. It is when learning is left to chance that the child with learning problems is at risk. To reduce the possibility that some students will not become good readers the additional factors listed below must be considered when implementing the mainstream reading curriculum.

THE PRIORITY NEEDS OF STUDENTS WITH
READING DIFFICULTIES

The child who is experiencing difficulties in learning to read needs to have the following components in his or her daily literacy programme. Many of the features listed below are already incorporated in the approach known as Reading Recovery (Clay 1985), which is described in the next chapter.

- An empathic and enthusiastic teacher.

- Abundant opportunity to read for pleasure and for information.

- An understanding of what the task of reading actually involves and what purposes are served by reading.

- Successful practice, often using material which has become familiar to the student.

- An improved self-esteem through counselling, praise, encouragement, success and the recognition of personal progress.

- A carefully graded programme, which may mean the creation of much supplementary material to use alongside the mainstream programme to provide additional practice. If child-produced or teacher-made books are being used either alongside or instead of other literature they must be used in a structured rather than an informal manner in order to teach effectively.

- More time will need to be spent on early reading activities (e.g. flashcards, word-to-picture matching, simple copy-writing, sentence building, etc.).

- More time must be spent in overlearning and reviewing material at each stage.

- If graded reading books are used, careful preparation of sight vocabulary is needed before each new book is introduced to ensure success.

- Phonemic awareness training (e.g. discrimination of sounds, blending sounds into words, segmenting long words into syllables, etc.) may be needed before decoding skills are taught.

- Systematic teaching of phonic knowledge and word-building, unless contra-indicated by speech or auditory problems. The skills taught should stem from, and be applicable to, the actual reading material being used by the student.

- Daily expressive writing activities, with guidance and feedback.

- Correct letter formation (printing) and handwriting, taught alongside the reading activities.

- Finger-tracing and other multi-sensory approaches (e.g. textured letters) may be needed by a few children with disabilities to aid assimilation and retention of the material taught.

Whatever the approach being used in mainstream classes, these basic needs of the student with learning difficulties must be met. The development of literacy skills must be given very high priority for such children.

There is evidence that after swinging too far toward the excesses of an unstructured, child-centred, whole language approach, language arts teaching is now moving back to a more balanced programme (Adams 1994; Zalud, Hoag and Wood 1995). As Pressley (1994: 211) has observed, 'Experiencing more explicit instruction of reading skills and strategies in no way precludes the authentic reading and writing experiences emphasized in whole language. Rather, explicit instruction enables at-risk students to participate more fully in such literacy experiences.'

DIAGNOSTIC ASSESSMENT

In order to cater most precisely for the specific needs of students with learning difficulties, it is necessary to appraise their current skills and knowledge. The starting point for any literacy intervention should be based on the results of some form of assessment of the child's current abilities. Such an assessment need not involve the use of highly sophisticated tests, and should not be a lengthy procedure. If a large amount of information is necessary in order to plan a programme, the assessment of the child should be spread over several short sessions. One is basically seeking answers to the following four key questions.

- What can the child already do without help? What skills and strategies has the child developed?
- What can the child do if given a little prompting and guidance?
- What gaps exist in the child's previous learning?
- What does the child need to be taught next, in order to make good progress?

Figure 2 summarizes the key steps involved in implementing a diagnostic approach to an individual learner. It begins with assessment and leads to programme planning and implementation. The procedure is applicable to all the main areas of the curriculum, and it will be referred to again in the chapters dealing with writing, spelling and arithmetic.

The various stages in Figure 2 may be interpreted thus:

Stage 1   This may involve the use of checklists, tests, inventories, as well as naturalistic observation of the learner. In the domain of reading the most useful procedure is to listen to the child read from an appropriate text and to note the strategies used and the errors made. Is the child confident and fluent? Does the child self-correct? Is the child very dependent upon adult assistance?

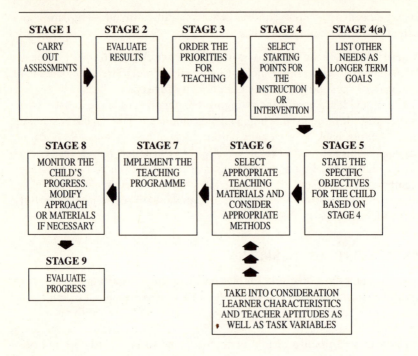

Figure 2 The diagnostic model

A running record of errors, self-corrections, requests for help, etc., can be noted on a photocopied version of the child's text.

Stage 2   This involves looking at what you have obtained from the assessment of the child performing in a particular skill area (e.g. reading) and applying the four diagnostic key questions referred to above.

Stage 3   This involves the identification of the most serious gaps in the child's previous learning which may need to be remedied.

Stages 4 and 5   These involve the selection of a starting point or teaching aim from the data analysed in Stage 3, and the writing of a specific student performance objective to make that aim: operational: e.g. teaching aim: 'to increase the child's basic sight vocabulary'; performance objective: 'given the twelve most commonly occurring words from the key words list presented on flashcards the child will read these aloud without hesitation or prompting.'

Stage 6   This involves the selection of appropriate resources (books, kits, apparatus, etc.) to assist in working toward the stated objective, and careful consideration of the most appropriate method of working with this child, based on a knowledge of his or her characteristics (e.g. learning strategies, interests, concentration span, etc.) and your own personal competencies in dealing with small group or individual tuition.

Stage 7   This involves implementing the teaching programme with the child for a period of sufficient duration and frequency to have some impact on progress. Ideally the programme may be operated within the whole-class setting, rather than in isolation. However, at times it will be necessary to provide such tuition in a withdrawal situation, particularly in the case of students with a learning disability.

Stage 8   This involves an overlap with Stage 7, in that you are required to determine whether your programme is working effectively by the use of an on-going (formative) evaluation of the child's performance.

Stage 9   This involves some definite procedure for assessing how much real change has occurred in the child as a result of the programme (summative evaluation). This is usually carried out at the end of the teaching block and is linked directly with the stated objectives at Stage 5.

Note that when working with and testing a child, it is important to observe the child's learning strategies and task-approach skills, as well as the actual responses being given. For example, has the child selected a particular answer after careful thought or was it an impulsive guess? Is the child hesitant and underachieving because he or she is wary of the adult and unwilling to take a risk?

Diagnosis must eventually involve a consideration of the total situation in which the learner operates. As well as learner characteristics it is important to evaluate also the learning task itself (e.g. level of difficulty, its relevance to the child's interests, etc.). It is also necessary to consider the teaching method being used, the physical environment in which the child is being taught, and the quality of the relationship between the child and the teacher and the child and the peer group. In other words, educational failure is rarely due only to factors within the child. Failure usually stems from a complex interaction among all the above variables, and intervention may require the teacher to adjust any or all of these variables.

Diagnostic approaches are referred to as either 'formal' or 'informal'. The term formal diagnosis usually implies that published tests (e.g. reading attainment tests or reading diagnostic tests) are used in order to obtain specific information about a learner's current status in certain selected areas such as comprehension, word recognition, phonic knowledge. Sometimes particular component skills are assessed, such as phonemic awareness, visual discrimination or short-term auditory memory. Formal assessment may be carried out for a whole class simultaneously, for example by the use of pencil-and-paper group testing. At other times formal assessment must involve the careful and detailed testing of one child alone, using standardized or criterion referenced tests. Formal assessment of this type is useful in indicating where current achievement stops and new learning needs to begin. It is usually supplemented by information from informal testing, and from observation and classroom records.

Informal diagnosis involves such procedures as direct observation of learners in action, and an examination of what they actually do or what they produce during a lesson. Informal assessment in reading includes, for example, listening to a child read aloud and detecting the presence or absence of particular strategies for word-attack, use of context, prediction, comprehension, general fluency and expression. The use of teacher-made informal reading inventories may be of value here. The inventories comprise sample paragraphs, graded from very easy to more complex, taken from books available in the classroom. A child's level of success on the inventory will provide a good indication of the readability level of books he or she can cope with independently and for instructional purposes. Performance on the inventory will also indicate the child's general approach to the task of reading (e.g. hasty and careless, hesitant and unwilling to risk a guess, etc.). Accuracy in reading the graded passages should be 95 per cent if the material is to be read independently by the child, and 90 per cent for material to be used for instructional purposes. Material with an error rate of 15 per cent or more is considered to be at frustration level (too difficult).

Over to you: Informal reading inventory

Prepare an informal reading inventory using photocopied passages from appropriate books in your classroom. The material should be carefully graded, beginning at the level of very simple vocabulary and short sentences in passages approximately fifty words in length. Extend this to more complex and demanding material in 150–200 word samples. Prepare six passages and use the inventory with a selected child. Evaluate the results in detail, indicating what the child can and cannot do in terms of word recognition, use of context, self-correction, etc.

The book *Watching Children Read and Write* (Kemp 1987) provides excellent advice and practical guidance for carrying out and analysing running records.

Level 1: Assessing the non-reader

If an individual, regardless of age, appears to be a non-reader it is worth obtaining the following information:

- Can the learner concentrate upon a learning task and attend to the teacher, or is he or she too preoccupied, distractible or hyperactive?
- Has the learner had adequate language experience (particularly listening to stories in the preschool years), and sufficient oral vocabulary development to begin reading?
- Is the learner capable of carrying out visual discrimination and matching of pictures, and letters and words?
- Has the learner developed adequate phonemic awareness to attend to the subtleties of speech sounds within words? (See also 'Auditory skills' in this chapter.)
- Does the learner understand what 'reading' involves? (Ask, 'What do we *do* when we read to someone? If you had to teach a friend to read what would you tell them to do? How do we read?').
- Does the learner understand 'word concept' – that words are separate units in print, and that the spaces between words have some significance?
- Does the learner have the concepts of a 'sound', and a 'letter'?
- Does the learner have an awareness of the left-to-right progression in a printed sentence?
- Does the learner recognize any words by sight? (e.g. own name; environmental signs such as 'CLOSED' or 'KEEP OUT').
- Can the learner complete picture-to-word matching activities correctly after a brief period of instruction?
- Can the learner carry out a simple learning task involving sight recognition of three words taught from flashcards without picture clues (e.g. 'MY', 'KEY' and 'BOOK')?
- Does the child know the names or sounds of any letters when these are presented in printed form?

Marie Clay's (1985) book, *The Early Detection of Reading Difficulties*, is very useful for appraising a child's concepts about print, and his or her understanding of the reading task. Her assessment procedures cover several of the factors listed above. Also of value is the *LARR Test of Emergent Literacy* (Downing, Schaefer and Ayers 1993).

Level 2: Assessment above beginner level

For the child who is not a complete non-reader and has at least some functional skills, the following areas are worthy of assessment:

Basic sight vocabulary   What can the child already do in terms of instant recognition of the most commonly occurring words in print? The Dolch Vocabulary List, the Key Words to Literacy List or the lists in the book *Reading Rescue* (Gillet and Bernard 1989) all provide appropriate material for this area of assessment.

Miscues and use of context When the child is reading aloud from age-appropriate material what types of error are made? Do the words conform to the meaning of the sentence or are they totally out of keeping with the message? Does the child tend to self-correct when errors are made in order to restore meaning? (See Kemp 1987.)

Word-attack skills When reading aloud does the child attempt to sound out and build an unfamiliar word, even without being instructed to do so? If not, can the child do this when he or she is encouraged to try? Has the child developed a fully functional set of phonic skills? In particular, does the child know all the common single letter sounds, digraphs, blends, prefixes and suffixes? Can the child divide a regular but lengthy word into its component syllables?

Auditory skills Can the child discriminate between similar but not identical speech sounds when these are presented orally in word-pairs (e.g. MOUSE–MOUTH, CAT–CAP, MONEY–MONKEY). Teachers can devise their own word lists for this purpose.

Can the child analyse and segment familiar words into their component sounds? This is a listening and oral test, not a reading test. If the child hears the work 'REMEMBER' can he or she break this into the units RE-MEM-BER? If testing this, you must first give some practice so that the child understands what is required.

Can the child blend or synthesize sounds in order to pronounce a given word (e.g. CR-I-SP). Again, this is a listening test and not a reading test; the child does not see the word in print. The following diagnostic test is useful for assessment of this skill.

Instructions

Say: 'I am going to say some words very slowly so that you can hear each sound. I want you to tell me what the word is. If I say "I-N" you say "IN". Sound the phonemes at rate of about one each second. Discontinue after five consecutive failures.

The words

i-f	g-o-t	sh-o-p	c-r-u-s-t
a-t	m-e-n	s-t-e-p	b-l-a-ck
u-p	b-e-d	l-o-s-t	f-l-a-sh
o-n	c-a-t	j-u-m-p	c-l-o-ck
a-m	d-i-g	t-r-u-ck	s-p-i-ll

Auditory discrimination, auditory analysis (segmentation), and phoneme blending are now regarded as parts of a more general metalinguistic ability termed 'phonological awareness' (Sawyer and Fox 1991). It is claimed that phonological knowledge is essential for beginning readers if they are to learn the orthographic code, and that specific training in such skills as rhyming, alliteration, segmentation, blending, and isolation of sounds within words results in improvement in early reading and spelling (Vandervelden and Siegel 1995; Ayers 1995; Frost and Emery 1996).

Comprehension

Reading can hardly be called true reading unless children are understanding the meaning behind the print, therefore evaluation of this key aspect of performance is crucial. Informal questions can be asked after a child has read a passage silently or aloud. The questions should not be solely at a factual-recall level (literal comprehension), e.g. 'How old is the girl in the story?'; 'What is the boy's name?'; but should probe for understanding at higher levels of inference and critical interpretation. (e.g. 'Why did the man act in that way? Was he angry or shocked?'; 'When the lady suggested they look for the goods in another shop was she being helpful or rude?'; 'What do *you* think of the suggestion the leader of the team makes?').

Exercises using 'cloze procedure' are sometimes useful in both testing and developing comprehension and contextual cueing. A passage of some 100 to 150 words is selected and every fifth or sixth word (approximately) is deleted leaving a gap. Can the child read the passage and provide a word in each case which conforms to the meaning of the passage and the grammatical structure of the sentence?

A particularly valuable instrument for the evaluation of reading rate, accuracy and comprehension is M.D. Neale's *Analysis of Reading Ability* (1988, 1989). The test also allows for appraisal of the student's auditory skills in discrimination, blending and simple spelling. An analysis sheet is provided to facilitate the recording and classification of errors.

Level 3: Assessing the child who has reached a reading plateau

Some children appear to reach a temporary plateau in their reading development at or about a reading age of 8 to 9 years. Many of the assessment techniques covered in the previous section may help to uncover the possible areas of difficulty in these children. The following procedures are also helpful at this level.

Error analysis

It is with children who have reached a reading plateau that error analysis can be extremely valuable in pinpointing specific gaps in the child's current reading skills. Possibly the child has not yet mastered certain letter clusters as phonic sight habits, and will either make random guesses or will refuse or mispronounce unfamiliar words containing these letter clusters.

To employ the error analysis procedure it is usual to listen to the child read aloud on several different occasions using material which is reasonably challenging but not at frustration level. The performance is recorded on tape for later analysis.

Kemp (1987) suggests that errors can be recorded on a running record sheet, and classified as: self-correction (SC); appeal for help (A); teacher intervention (TTA if the child is told to 'try that again'; or T for 'told' if the word is supplied by the teacher); substitutions (S – the substituted word is written above the text word); omissions (line drawn above the word omitted); repetition (underline word each time the child repeats it). Attempts at decoding a word should also be recorded in terms of phonemes and syllables. Kemp's procedure also allows for quantitative evaluations to be made leading to the calculation of error rate, self-correction rate and dependency rate. These measures can be used to compare a student's performance before and after an intervention programme.

Readability of the text

Consider the difficulty level of the material the child is attempting to read. Has he or she selected books which are at frustration level? Reading skills will not advance if the child is constantly faced with text which is too difficult.

The simplest check is to apply the 'Five finger test'. Take a passage of approximately 100 words and ask the child to read aloud. Each time an error is made you fold one finger into the palm of your hand. If you run out of fingers before the student reaches the end of the passage, the material is too difficult for independent reading (error rate more than 5 per cent).

There are several other more technical procedures which have been used over the years to calculate approximate readability level of texts. One system involves the following steps, using a sample of thirty sentences:

• count thirty sentences;
• count a number of words with 3 or more syllables in those sentences;
• calculate the nearest square root of that number;
• add a constant of 3 to your answer;
• the result obtained represents the school year level at which the material would usually be read successfully.

For example, if there are fifty-four words with three or more syllables, the nearest square root is seven. Add three, which gives ten. The material is typical of school Year 10 and could be read successfully by the average student of that age level.

However, readability level is determined by more than the number of multisyllabic words. The ease with which a text is read is also related to the reader's familiarity with the topic, the complexity of the syntax used and the sentence length. Even the size of the print and format of the pages can influence readability, especially for students with learning difficulties. The most useful index of readability is a student's actual performance on the text.

When selecting texts for students to read teachers should consider the following points:

- Is the topic within the experience of the students?
- Is it meaningful and relevant?
- Is the book itself attractive and appealing?
- Is the language used in the text natural and easy to predict? Are there many unfamiliar words? Are the sentences complex? Are the sentences stilted (as they often are in early reading books)?
- Are there many useful contextual and pictorial clues?
- Will this type of text expand the student's experience of different forms of writing for different purposes?

Affective factors

With a student who has ceased to make progress it is vitally important to consider affective as well as cognitive factors. For example, has the student developed a very negative, 'couldn't-care-less' attitude toward reading, avoiding the task whenever possible? Does the student experience any enjoyment from reading? Is the material in the book in keeping with the student's real interests? Is the working relationship between the student and the teacher (or tutor) a positive one? Is there any incentive to improve? Where difficulties are detected in these areas it is just as important to attempt to change matters, if possible, as it is to concentrate merely on the skills aspect of reading development.

The handbook prepared by Johns (1986) contains some useful question-naires, inventories and scales for the appraisal of affective and attitudinal factors. Also of value is the *Reader's Self-perception Scale* designed by Henk and Melnick (1995).

When setting performance objectives in the affective domain it is usually necessary to specify particular indicators which will signify changes in such areas as motivation, attitudes or values. For example: 'Jason will show improvement in his attitude toward reading by an increased willingness to (i) borrow books from the class library (ii) take books home to read (iii) discuss the books he has read (iv) stay on task for longer during periods of reading'; 'Lucy will demonstrate increased confidence in her oral reading performance by volunteering more frequently to read aloud in class.'

Over to you: *Informal assessment of reading skills*

Assemble appropriate materials for use in assessing a student's current abilities in the following areas:

• phonological awareness;
• sight recognition of commonly occurring words;
• phonic knowledge;
• word-attack skills;
• comprehension.

Use the materials with a student and seek answers to the four key questions presented earlier in the chapter.

SUMMARY

All the assessment procedures described in this chapter are applicable to students with very varied forms of physical, sensory or intellectual disability. A particular disability does not require a specific and unique form of diagnostic evaluation; one is simply attempting to find out with some degree of precision what the student can and cannot do at the present time in this skill area. It may well be that the student with the more severe form of disability, or with multiple disabilities, will be assessed in the readiness-type skills typical of a much younger child, but the actual procedure involved in assessment does not differ.

According to how the student performs on the initial diagnostic assessment a teacher would either focus on the early or prereading skills (e.g. sentence building, word-to-picture matching, letter knowledge, etc.), on intermediate skills such as word-attack, contextual cueing, etc., or higher-order reading skills such as prediction and literal, interpretive or critical levels of comprehension. Activities will then be programmed to assist the student to develop beyond the present stage. The next chapter provides a description of a number of methods which may be employed to assist students with reading difficulties, regardless of the cause of such difficulties. Most of these methods can be used within the regular classroom and do not require the students to be withdrawn for remedial assistance.

Discussion point

Imagine that you are appointed to a school where no systematic check is made of children's reading progress at any age level.

You are asked by the head teacher to devise some appropriate system for assessing the overall reading attainment in the school and for identifying those children in need of special assistance.

After considerable time and effort you plan what seems to be a viable set of procedures and you present your plans at a staff meeting.

Much to your surprise several of your colleagues object very strongly to your suggestions, stating that they do not believe in testing children in any formal way. They say that tests don't tell them anything they don't already know. They also imply that testing makes children anxious; and when parents get to know their children's results this can cause a great deal of unnecessary concern in some cases.

What are you going to do?

One obvious action would be to withdraw your plan and give in to your colleagues' arguments. However, you feel quite strongly that some monitoring of reading progress is necessary and you are prepared to argue your case.

Try to summarize the points you would make to support your suggested programme. Try also to answer the specific objections raised by your colleagues.

Further reading

Adams, M.J. (1990) *Beginning to Read: Thinking and Learning about Print*, Cambridge, Mass.: MIT Press.

Au, K.H., Mason, J.M. and Scheu, J.A. (1995) *Literacy Instruction Today*, New York: Harper Collins.

Campbell, R. (1995) *Reading in the Early Years Handbook*, Milton Keynes: Open University Press.

Clay, M.M. (1985) *The Early Detection of Reading Difficulties* (3rd edn), Auckland: Heinemann.

Froese, V. (ed.) (1995) *Whole Language: Practice and Theory* (2nd edn), Boston: Allyn and Bacon.

Holdaway, D. (1990) *Independence in Reading* (3rd edn), Portsmouth: Heinemann.

Kemp, M. (1987) *Watching Children Read and Write*, Melbourne: Nelson.

Miller, L. (1995) *Towards Reading: Literacy Development in the Preschool Years*, Buckingham: Open University Press.

Smith, B. (1994) *Through Writing to Reading*, London: Routledge.

Spafford, C. and Grosser, G. (1996) *Dyslexia: Research and Resource Guide*, Boston: Allyn and Bacon.

Tester, B. and Horoch, S. (1995) *Whole Language Phonics*, Melbourne: Longman.

Valencia, S.W., Hiebert, E.H. and Afflerbach, P. (eds) (1994) *Authentic Reading Assessment*, Newark: International Reading Association.

Chapter 8

Reading: making a start

[Teachers need to] guide student learning through a strategic sequence of teacher-directed and student-centered activities. Teacher-directed instruction is necessary if students are to catch up and advance with their able-reading peers. Children will not automaticaly bloom by being immersed in a literacy hothouse rich with literacy events and activities. While these activities enrich students' literacy development, they are not sufficient for children who are behind.

(Kameenui 1993: 381)

Following the careful assessment of a learner's abilities as suggested in the previous chapter, it should be possible to plan the appropriate starting points for intervention. Chapters 8 and 9 provide a compendium of ideas and methods from which to select, ranging from a beginning-reading level to post-secondary school level. These ideas may be used within or alongside the general language and reading curriculum in the regular classroom.

PREREADING AND EARLY READING EXPERIENCES

For most children a carefully structured prereading programme is un-necessary (McCoy 1995). Once the child has adjusted to the demands of school life, instruction in reading can and should begin. For a few, particul-arly those with significant intellectual impairment or perceptual difficulties, it may be valuable to provide prereading experiences which prepare these children for beginning-reading, to take them to the threshold of simple word recognition (Choate and Rakes 1993). Training in listening skills, en-couraging a liking for stories, ensuring familiarity with language patterns, all form important parts of the programme. Indeed, aural-oral language enrich-ment activities form the basis of beginning-reading programmes.

When the beginning-reading activities involve word-to-word matching, word-to-picture matching and letter and word copying, the child is ready to enter the next stage of development. The golden rule to remember is to make the work link as closely as possible with educational skills and media the child needs to use at this time. For instance, in prereading activities, if the child needs to improve in visual discrimination it is likely to be of maximum benefit if letter and word matching are utilized, rather than the matching of pictures and geometrical shapes.

Form perception and visual discrimination

For a very few children, particularly those with vision impairment or those with neurological problems, form perception may need to be improved. If oral language is adequate and if the child has realized that the marks on paper represent words which can be spoken, the next important skill to consider is that of form perception, which at its highest level is reflected in the fine discrimination of individual letters and sequences of letters.

If a young or disabled child is very poor at form perception the teaching will need to begin with the fitting of hardboard shapes into inset formboards, matching and sorting simple regular shapes and feeling these shapes hidden within a puzzle box where the child can handle but not see them. He or she then identifies the shape just handled from a set of line drawings outside the box. Later the activity can be reintroduced using small plastic letters of the alphabet in the puzzle box, these being handled and identified in the same way. This activity is useful for holding attention through active participation and enjoyment.

Other useful activities which will help to develop awareness of shape and form and encourage attention to detail include: copying regular shapes using drinking straws, drawing around templates, drawing within stencils, tracing figures, completing unfinished figures on worksheets. These activities are of particular importance to young children with impaired vision or with perceptual problems.

The sequence for training visual discrimination should follow the progression:

- picture matching;
- shape matching;
- letter-like shape matching;
- letter and word matching.

The point of entry for a particular child into this sequence will be determined from diagnostic assessment.

Word-to-picture matching is a useful activity in the beginning stages of word recognition. Colourful pictures can be cut from magazines and mail-order catalogues, or the child's own drawings and paintings can be used. Appropriate words or captions are provided on slips of card. The child places the card on or next to the picture and reads the word. The activity can be used with groups of children, particularly if a magnetboard is used to display the words and pictures.

If a child is able to sort and match word shapes and has adequate language development, he or she is ready to read through one of the various whole word and meaning-based approaches, even though phonics readiness may not be present. The child will benefit from a language-experience or shared-book approach (see later).

Visual retention and visual sequential memory

It is helpful for some children to be trained in the careful observation of material which they are then required to reproduce from memory in correct sequential order. This is sometimes done using picture cards (for example, cow, house, man, ball, cup), but it is more useful if the material provides letter cards which can be arranged to spell simple words. The training should then require the child to write the sequence after brief exposure on a flashcard. This aids early spelling skills as well as word recognition skills for reading.

Undoubtedly, one of the most valuable activities at this level is sentence building. At any age level, a learner who is beginning to read should be given the opportunity to construct and reconstruct meaningful sentences from word cards.

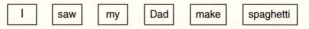

This procedure has been strongly advocated by Kemp (1987) as both an assessment and teaching technique. A child's ability to construct, reconstruct and transform sentences reveals much about his or her language competence and memory for words. Sentence building can be incorporated into the language-experience approach described later.

Hand–eye co-ordination and motor control

Building, cutting, sticking, threading, tracing, jigsaw-making and games activities which go on in all preschool and junior classrooms are already developing fine motor co-ordination for most children. A few will need much longer at such tasks and may benefit from specific training. Large chalkboard work using big movements is a very useful starting point. In cases of very poor control, it is helpful if the teacher guides the child's hand in order to make the movements smooth and rhythmical and to establish a correct motor pattern. Simple mazes and dot-to-dot patterns produced as worksheets are a useful extension from large-scale movements to finer control. Writing patterns can be used for both chalkboard work and practice sheets. It is vital that children who do have some degree of difficulty in co-ordination are taught correct letter formation. The acquisition of handwriting should not be left to incidental learning. This applies particularly to children with cerebral palsy, spina bifida, hydrocephalus or with neurological dysfunction resulting in clumsiness.

Problems of laterality (that is, choice of hand for manual tasks and dominant eye in visual tasks), and poor directional sense (orientation) are sometimes found to be present in students with learning difficulties. These factors are rarely the cause of a child's learning problems, but rather are another symptom of inefficient functioning. Some older American programmes stress the need to establish a strong lateral preference in a child before attempting remediation in academic skills, and suggest exercises for doing this. However, such programmes have not proved to be particularly successful and most teachers today would not deliberately set out to rectify crossed laterality or to alter hand preferences in their children with special needs.

If the child's balance and general co-ordination are very poor, teachers may need to plan specific activities for inclusion in a daily PE programme (e.g. hopping, beam-walking, small ball catching, etc.). In some schools these children may be receiving special physical education or therapy from a visiting teacher, and close liaison with this teacher will be essential if the activities are to be integrated and reinforced in the regular class programme.

Reversal problems

Crossed laterality, lack of firmly established lateral preference and poor directional sense frequently result in a marked tendency to *reverse* shapes (e.g. letters or words in reading, numerals in arithmetic). In extreme cases mirror-writing may be produced by the child. It is quite normal for children up to the age of 6½ years to confuse letters like p, b, d and q in their reading and writing, so undue attention to this problem would be out of place below that age. However, reversal problems which continue in some cases through to the secondary school level do require attention. A few ideas for remediation are provided here.

If a child above the age of 7 years is still confusing p, b, d, q or u, n, it is essential that he or she should be given a motor cue (kinaesthetic training) to establish the correct direction for these letters. Finger-tracing one of the letters until mastered is probably the most positive way to overcome the problem. First the child should close eyes or wear a blindfold while the teacher guides the index finger of his or her preferred hand over the shape of the letter 'b' on the blackboard. The letter is simultaneously sounded or named as tracing is repeated several times. The teacher now takes the child's finger over a series of other letters and the child must indicate quickly and clearly, but still with eyes closed, each time a letter 'b' is traced. The aim here is basically to give a child a physical image against which to discriminate d and b.

It is also useful to provide the child with a self-help card showing that the 'little b' is really only the bottom half of a capital B. This card can be left displayed in the classroom for some time after training. It is important to stress that if the child is given the correct motor cue for letter and numeral formation in the early stages of handwriting instruction many of the reversal problems would not persist.

Auditory training

It has been shown conclusively that auditory skills play a major role in the process of learning to read (Pressley and McCormick 1995; McGuiness, McGuiness and Donohue 1995). Progress beyond the stage of building up a basic sight vocabulary using whole word recognition is dependent upon the development of phonic decoding skills. As previously stated, the acquisition of phonic skills is in turn dependent upon 'phonemic awareness', including in particular adequate auditory discrimination, auditory analysis and phoneme blending. It is likely that these processes are also involved to a significant extent in spelling ability.

Auditory training need not always precede any introduction to reading, unless a child's auditory perception is markedly deficient (Frost and Emery 1996), or where a child has a known hearing loss and auditory training is recommended as part of a programme to increase the child's use of residual hearing. Usually auditory training can be provided alongside the child's early reading experiences while a basic sight vocabulary is being built up. Many of the activities which are being used to teach basic phonic knowledge are also simultaneously training listening skills.

The principal aim of auditory training is to increase awareness of sound patterns within words. Brief consideration will be given to three of the most important auditory processes, auditory discrimination, auditory analysis (the segmentation of words into sound units) and sound blending.

Auditory discrimination

A teacher will find it useful to collect pictures from mail-order catalogues and colour supplements to use in games requiring auditory discrimination. The pictures may be set out in pairs and the child must quickly touch one of a pair of pictures when the word is called: for example, 'pear' (pictures show 'bear' and 'pear'), 'three' (pictures show '3' and 'tree'). Worksheets can also be made with pictures of objects which the child must identify when the initial sound is given. When games like these have been played it is sometimes useful to get the child to say the name of each pictured object clearly and then to listen to his or her own voice played back on a tape recorder, thus dealing with articulation alongside auditory discrimination.

Classroom games which involve 'Finding the odd one out' (for example, boy, bag, hand, band) and which may involve rhyme (for example, sand, hand, feet, land, band) are popular. With young children 'I spy' games using initial letter sounds rather than letter names are useful.

Auditory analysis (segmentation)

Some of the activities listed above have included a simple level of auditory analysis, that of isolating the initial letter sound in a word. Games can be extended to listening for final sounds (for example, 'Put a line under the pictures that end like sn*ake*'. Pictures show *rake*, bucket, *cake*, ball).

Auditory analysis can be taught, or at least encouraged, by spending a little time in taking words apart into their component sounds, raising the actual process to the level of awareness in the child. For example, 'What's this picture, Jackie? Yes. Good. It's a frog. Let's listen to that word FROG. Let's say it very slowly. Let's stretch it out. FR-O-G. You try it.' This activity involves listening, not reading.

Phoneme blending

This is also referred to as auditory blending or sound blending, and is the complementary process to auditory analysis. Encourage the children to gain experience in putting speech sounds together to build a word. 'I spy with my little eye a picture of a FR-O-G.' Use the same technique while reading or telling a story to the children. 'The boy came to the wall. He couldn't get over. The door was st-u-ck . . .'. Children quickly supply the words as the story goes on. Sound blending is also used in the early stages of word-building from print with simple consonant-vowel-consonant words (l-o-t; m-a-n). Teachers should be on the look-out for children who find this process difficult, since it is a vital subskill for reading and can be actively developed.

PHONEMIC AWARENESS AND READING PROGRESS

Phonemic awareness appears to be important not only for development of phonic decoding skills but also as a direct aid to rapid word recognition. Studies have shown that children can be helped to increase their phonemic awareness through specific training, both separate from and embedded within their reading programmes (Hatcher, Hulme and Ellis 1994; Ayers 1995; Vandervelden and Siegel 1995).

Olson (1990) and North and Parker (1994) suggest that young children should be exposed to activities which raise their awareness of speech sounds, rhymes and alliteration through daily activities in preschool settings. They recommend as useful listening games and puzzles which, for example, require the children to clap out the number of syllables in their names, the number of words in a phrase and later the number of sounds within a familiar word. Activities can also be introduced which require children to blend sounds or syllables together to make words.

In most training programmes, six aspects of phonological awareness are specifically taught alongside the reading of texts for enjoyment and information. These six aspects are:

- rhyming: listening to and saying nursery rhymes; finding words which rhyme; generating a new word to rhyme with a given word;
- alliteration: 'the greedy green gremlins are grinning'; 'Hannah's house is high on the hill';
- blending: sounds into syllables and syllables into words;
- segmentation: sentences into words, words into syllables; syllables and words into separate sounds;
- isolation: identifying the initial, final and medial sounds in a target word;
- exchanging: substituting a new initial sound for another sound to produce a new word: 'met' becomes 'pet'; 'lost' becomes 'cost'.

Olson (1990) considers that one of the strengths of the whole language approach is the emphasis it places upon writing from the earliest stages. The use of invented spelling by the children almost certainly helps them develop phonemic awareness and an understanding of the alphabetic principle. It is helpful to inspect young children's invented spelling in their early attempts at writing as this can reveal the extent to which they have developed phonemic awareness. The same is true of older students with learning difficulties.

Children's use of word processors for story creation may also indirectly assist the development of phonic analysis and segmentation. Jackson (1987) suggests that word processing forces students back to a situation where they need to pay attention to the phonological and orthographic bases of language in order to key in correct sequences of letters to spell words correctly.

In general, research in recent years has confirmed that difficulties in learning to read are more likely to be related to problems with phonological awareness than to problems with visual perception. Students with hearing loss, and others with a specific learning disability which involves weakness in auditory processing, are obviously most at risk since their ability to access the phonemic aspects of the language around them is impaired. For them it will be helpful at first to focus more upon predominantly visual approaches to reading, such as flashcard work, sentence building and transformations using word cards, and written recordings for language-experience books. It is also essential to teach these students self-help strategies for word identification and comprehension, using explicit methods of instruction (Frost and Emery 1996).

Over to you: *Planning for a student with a significant disability*

Describe the methods and resources you might use to provide a useful introduction to the first stages of reading for a student with mild intellectual disability in the early years of primary school.

Indicate how you might incorporate some of these activities within the regular classroom programme.

SELECTING AN APPROACH

Assuming that the learner has the necessary entry skills of adequate visual discrimination, phonological awareness and at least some ability to converse in simple sentences, two complementary approaches might be used: shared-book experience and language-experience reading. The two approaches are entirely compatible with modern theories of language acquisition and reading skill development. In both cases, when used for remedial teaching purposes they require a much greater degree of structuring than is necessary when applied to children without learning problems. Neither method precludes the teaching of word-attack skills, as will be illustrated in the descriptions below.

Shared-book experience

This approach owes much to the influence of the New Zealand educator, Don Holdaway (1982, 1990).

In the shared-book approach children are brought to an enjoyment of reading through stories read by the teacher using a large-size, specially prepared book which can be seen easily by the group or class of children. Holdaway says that the book should have the same visual impact from 10 feet away as a normal book would have on the knee of the child. Stories, poems, jingles and songs which children love and which present an opportunity for them to join in, provide excellent material for the early stages. Familiarity with the language patterns involved in the stories is developed and reinforced in a natural way. Attention (on-task behaviour) is easily maintained by the teacher who can present the material with enthusiasm and whole-hearted enjoyment. The pages of the book become a giant teaching-aid on which the teacher can develop word recognition and decoding skills informally, as well as convey the story. The teacher may, for example, place a hand over a word (or mask it in some other way) so that the group of children must suggest what the word is likely to be, thus helping them to develop an awareness of contextual cues, language patterns and prediction. By covering only part of the word, the teacher helps children to utilize initial letter or final letter cues.

It should be noted that shared-book experience embodies all the basic principles of effective teaching, particularly the important elements of teacher demonstration and modelling, active participation and successful practice. The approach is also soundly based upon, and replicates, those aspects of 'the bedtime story at home' which Holdaway found to be important influences on early reading progress in school. As a beginning-reading method the approach has proved equal or superior to other methods, and produces very positive attitudes toward reading, even in the slower children. By its very nature, shared-book sessions are *inclusive* of all children.

Language-experience approach

The language-experience approach uses the child's own language to produce carefully controlled amounts of reading material. It could be described as a form of 'dictated story' approach. From the viewpoint of the slow learner or failing reader the approach combines two major advantages. There is the possibility of utilizing the child's own interests to generate material for reading and writing; and the teacher is able to work within the child's current level of language competence at all times. This is of tremendous value for children who are well below average in general language development. The work produced is usually relevant and motivating.

With the young child or the child of very limited ability the starting point for the language-experience approach can be the labelling by the teacher or aide of some of the child's artwork or drawings, no matter how primitive, with captions which the child suggests. 'This is my cat, Dotty'; 'I can ride my BMX bike fast'. The child and teacher together read these captions and revise them for a few minutes each day, without at this stage drawing attention to individual letters or words. The child can be encouraged to build these sentences using word-cards.

During this early stage of the programme the child can be helped to contribute a dictated sentence following some class excursion to the airport or a farm. 'I saw a Jumbo Jet'; 'The cow licked David on the face'. These sentences are added, along with others from the class, to the picture-map which the class has produced as part of the follow-up to the excursion. Again, they are not in any way analysed or drilled, and serve the purpose of establishing in the learner's mind the notion that 'What I say can be written down'.

After a few weeks of this introductory work the child is ready to make his or her first book. A topic is carefully selected: e.g. 'speedway'. The teacher produces some visual material which will provide the illustration for the first page, perhaps a picture of the child's favourite speedway rider from a magazine. Teacher and child talk about the rider and from the discussion they agree upon one brief statement which can be written under the picture: 'This is Chris Copley.' The teacher writes (prints) the agreed statement for the child who then copies it carefully under the teacher's version. If the child cannot copy due to perceptual-motor or co-ordination problems, he or she can trace over the words with a coloured pencil or wax crayon. Both teacher and child then read the statement together once or twice and the child is left to paste the picture carefully into the book. Even this activity must be closely supervised with some children in order that the page looks attractive rather than messy. With some older children they can be encouraged to type the same sentence on a sheet of paper and paste that into the book to help generalization from handwritten to typed form of the same words.

Next day the child is presented with the same statement written on a strip of card: 'This is Chris Copley.' Without reference to the book the child is encouraged to read the words. He or she may have forgotten the material so some brief revision is needed. The child then cuts the strip of card into separate word-cards. These are placed at random on the desk and the child has to arrange them in correct sequence. If the child fails he or she must spend time matching the word-cards against the original in the book until the sequencing task can be performed correctly. At this point the teacher picks up one of the cards, perhaps the word 'is', and using it as a small flashcard asks the child to pronounce the word. This is continued until the child can recognize each word out of context. The word-cards are then placed in an envelope stapled in the back cover of the book, ready to be revised the following day.

Over the next week the child continues to produce a page of his or her book with much guidance from an adult. Revision of the previous day's words ensures repetition and overlearning to the point of mastery. The teacher's control over what is written will ensure that not too much is added to the book each day which might otherwise result in failure to master the new words. If the child is allowed to dictate too much material this will result in failure to learn and loss of satisfaction.

Once important sight words are mastered these can be checked off or coloured in on a vocabulary list in the front cover of the child's book. McNally and Murray's *Key Words to Literacy* list or the Dolch sight vocabulary lists (see Preen and Barker 1987) are very appropriate for this purpose. Such charting of progress in the book gives the child visual evidence of improvement, and also indicates to the teacher what has been covered so far and what still needs to be taught. If certain words seem to present particular problems for the child games and activities can be introduced to repeat and overlearn these words until mastered (e.g. word bingo). Gradually the amount written can be increased and after some months a child will need less and less direct help in constructing his or her own sentences. The approach may sound slow and tedious but it does result in even the most resistant cases of reading failure making progress. It is highly structured and the growth in word recognition skills is cumulative.

At some stage in the programme the teacher must help the child to expand his or her word-attack skills. For example, perhaps the child has used the word 'crash' in writing about the speedway interest. In a separate booklet the teacher can help the child to learn the value of the blend 'cr' by collecting other 'cr' words (crab, crook, cross, cry, etc.). Similarly they can experiment with the unit 'ash' from the word 'crash' (b-ash, d-ash, c-ash, r-ash, etc.). This incidental word study linked with meaningful material from the child's own book is important, but it will still be inadequate for developing fully functional decoding skills. It will be necessary to teach word-attack and spelling skills quite explicitly for certain students.

Clearly the shared-book experience can operate in parallel with the individualized language-experience approach in both whole class and remedial group situations. Once a child has made a positive start using this language-experience approach he or she can be introduced to a carefully selected 'real' book. It is wise to prepare the way for this transition by including in the child's final language-experience book most of the words which will be met in this new book.

The basic principles of the language-experience approach can be used with non-literate adults and those learning English as a second language (Wales 1994).

The visuo-thematic approach

Jackson (1987) described a carefully structured variation of the language-experience approach which he had found useful in clinical settings. He called the approach 'visuo-thematic'. The learner (child or adult) is presented with a visual stimulus picture which has a number of ideas in it to generate discussion and to suggest a story, without too much imagination being required. Jackson found detailed cartoons from magazines or newspapers to be useful and he suggests that the learner be encouraged to seek out suitable material to bring to each session. Jackson outlines the procedure in the following steps.

The child obtains a picture which he or she pastes on a piece of cardboard, together with a pocket or envelope in the corner. This pocket is to house small cards containing all the words the child can think of to describe various aspects of the picture. The child is then required to have three columns ruled on a page headed *naming words, describing words, action words*. He or she is then asked to try to think of at least six words which can be placed in each of the above columns, thus giving a total of at least eighteen words for the picture. The words are written out at home or during the lesson in their appropriate columns and the child is then asked to put each word on a small card and place it in the pocket. In this way a 'library' of pictures and their associated vocabularies is built up by the child. When the child comes to the lesson the teacher or aide checks the words for accuracy and tests the child's ability to recall them. Some practice is then given in spelling one or two of the words.

The next step is for the child to construct his or her own series of questions about aspects of the picture. The child is then asked to write a story about the picture and to select a title. The story is read by the child and adult together and any corrections noted. After this the child is asked to rewrite the story or type it in its final form and to paste it in the book beside the vocabulary lists. This procedure is repeated at least once a week, using on each occasion a different story but the same format and structure. Each story is filed and kept available for rereading later.

Jackson (1991) has provided extremely useful suggestions for working individually with a student with severe reading problems in his book *Discipline: An Approach for Teachers and Parents*. His 'structured alphabet kit' is also clearly described in that text.

Over to you: *Selecting a beginning method*

Take one of the basic approaches presented in the section above and discuss how it might be accommodated in a classroom where the general language arts programme is based upon whole language philosophy.

READING RECOVERY

Reading Recovery is an early intervention programme first developed in New Zealand (Clay 1985) and now used in North America, Britain and Australia. Children who are identified as having reading difficulties after one year of school are placed in the programme and receive daily intensive tuition on a one-to-one basis. They remain in the programme for approximately fifteen weeks, or until they have reached the average level of their class (De Ford 1991). The aim of the programme is to reduce substantially the number of children who experience on-going and cumulative literacy problems. This is achieved by providing the opportunity for accelerated learning.

Evidence has accumulated to indicate that Reading Recovery as an early intervention programme is very effective in raising young children's reading achievement and confidence (Trethowan, Harvey and Fraser 1996). It is claimed that the programme can be so effective that only 1 per cent of children attending the individualized sessions require further, long-term assistance with reading and writing (Clay 1990). It should be noted, however, that this level of efficacy has been questioned by some observers who believe that gains made in the programme are not always maintained over time (Chapman and Tunmer 1991). It has also been observed that advantages gained in the Reading Recovey programme do not necessarily spill over into better classroom performance, partly because the reading resources provided in the regular setting are not carefully matched to the child's ability level (Wheldall, Centre and Freeman 1993).

A typical Reading Recovery lesson includes seven activities:

- rereading of familiar books;
- independent reading of the book introduced the previous day;
- letter identification activities with plastic letters;
- writing of a dictated or prepared story;
- sentence building and reconstruction from the story;
- introduction of a new book;
- guided reading of new book.

The texts selected are designed to give a high success rate; and confidence is boosted by frequent rereading of the familiar stories. Optimum use is made of the available time, and students are kept fully on-task. Some attention is given within the instructional time to listening for sounds within words and practising phonic skills. Iversen and Tunmer (1993) found that when increased attention was given to phonological training, together with explicit instruction in letter–sound correspondences, the students in Reading Recovery programmes made even more rapid progress.

The obvious stumbling block with Reading Recovery is the need to find time and appropriately trained personnel to provide daily tuition to the selected students. It is probable that volunteer helpers used within Learning Assistance Programmes (LAP) in schools would improve the quality and impact of their assistance if they utilized the teaching strategies from Reading Recovery under the teacher's direction.

Details of the Reading Recovery programme, including instructional strategies, practical ideas and use of time are given in Clay's (1985) book *The Early Detection of Reading Difficulties*.

DO LEARNING DISABLED STUDENTS NEED DIFFERENT METHODS?

Children with a specific reading disability do not, in general, need a totally different approach for instruction in reading. It was stated in Chapter 1 that their priority needs are for a carefully structured and effectively taught programme, which emphasizes the functional aspects of literacy and places a clear focus upon acquiring appropriate strategies for comprehending text. The methods advocated for learning disabled students are the same as those advocated for any students, but applied with greater precision. In particular, students with a specific reading disability require the following issues to be adequately addressed.

• Having a real reason for reading, writing and spelling is essential. There is a real danger that children with severe reading problems may receive, if tutored individually, a remedial programme which contains too many isolated skill-building drills. There is a need to apply these skills realistically as they develop.

• Many dyslexic children benefit from being taught more about the structure of language (for example, the meaning of the terms 'syllable' and 'prefix', etc.) as part of their programme. It is essential to help the student understand the close interrelationship between oral language, reading and writing.

• A structured use of the language-experience approach is widely advocated for learning disabled children.

• The use of strategy training and task-approach training, as described in Chapter 4, will help the student gain better control over his or her reading and writing. This is particularly important in higher-order reading skills, such as comprehension (Butler 1995; Dole, Brown and Trathen 1996).

• Emphasis usually needs to be placed upon the systematic teaching of phonic decoding skills (that is, the teaching of letter sounds and how to blend these into words). Phonemic awareness may need to be developed in some students.

• Multisensory approaches seem to help the learning disabled child assimilate and master particular units, such as letter–sound correspondences and sight words.

• Material must be selected very carefully to match the child's current ability and interest level. Some LD students profess to *like* the books in basal reading schemes (Reetz and Hoover 1992). This can be an advantage in terms of controlling the difficulty level of text in the early stages.

• Teachers should not present too much material at once. They should determine as rapidly as possible how much a particular student can handle successfully at one sitting, and avoid tiring or frustrating the student. However, regular and intensive practice sessions are essential, and the ultimate long-term aim is to *accelerate* rate of learning.

• There is a need to revise and review previously taught skills or concepts at frequent intervals. Practice and overlearning are vital for success.

SUMMARY

In this chapter attention has been given to appropriate prereading and early reading experiences, necessary for some students with learning difficulties or disabilities. It was pointed out that prereading activities are not routinely required by all students.

Particular attention was given to the important topic of auditory training, since phonemic awareness has been identified in a number of research studies as an essential prerequisite for early reading success. Where phonological skills are weak, they can be significantly improved through explicit teaching.

Several beginning-reading approaches were described in detail. In general, most remedial reading approaches do not differ greatly from mainstream approaches. Much useful help can be provided for many children with special needs simply by a more carefully structured use of the regular class programme and applying more direct teaching. Where this is possible it is to be preferred to offering a totally different programme requiring one-to-one tuition in a withdrawal room situation. However, some children's learning difficulties are so acute, or their attitude toward reading so negative, that their needs can only be met by a carefully designed programme which requires methods and materials that differ markedly from those in regular use. The following chapter contains some additional ideas to use in such cases.

Discussion points

• Review the teaching methods presented in this chapter. Which would you find most useful in your present teaching situation?

• How would you begin to teach reading to a student from a non-English-speaking background whose oral language is limited?

Further reading

Beimiller, A. (1994) 'Some observations on beginning reading instruction', *Educational Psychologist* 29, 4: 203–9.

Beveridge, M., Reed, M. and Webster, A. (1996) *Managing the Literacy Curriculum*, London: Routledge.

Blachman, B.A. (1991) 'Early intervention for children's reading problems', *Topics in Language Disorders* 12, 1: 51–65.

Cunningham, P.M. (1995) *Phonics They Use*, New York: Harper Collins.

Cunningham, P.M. and Allington, R.L. (1994) *Classrooms that Work: They Can All Read and Write*, New York: Harper Collins.

Funnell, E. and Stuart, M. (1995) *Learning to Read*, Oxford: Blackwell.

Glazer, S.M. and Burke, E.M. (1994) *An Integrated Approach to Early Literacy*, Boston: Allyn and Bacon.

Heilman, A. (1993) *Phonics in Proper Perspective* (7th edn), Columbus: Merrill.

Owens, P. and Pumfrey, P.D. (eds) (1995) *Children Learning to Read: International Concerns. Volume 1: Emergent and Developing Reading*, London: Falmer.

Reason, R. and Boote, R. (1994) *Helping Children with Reading and Spelling*, London: Routledge.

Stuart, M. (1995) 'Prediction and qualitative assessment of five and six-year-old children's reading: a longitudinal study', *British Journal of Educational Psychology* 65: 287–96.

Wagner, R.K., Torgesen, J.K. and Rashotte, C.A. (1994) 'Development of reading-related phonological processing abilities', *Developmental Psychology* 30, 1: 73–87.

Chapter 9

Reading: additional techniques and resources

> Good teachers are committed to balanced, eclectic approaches; they provide whatever a child needs to achieve optimal growth in language and reading development.
>
> (Mather 1992: 92)

The approaches described in the previous chapter, used selectively, are all useful for helping a student to make some initial progress in learning to read. This chapter provides some additional practical ideas which may be incorporated within the general programme to provide variety, enjoyment, motivation and additional practice for those students requiring extra assistance.

An important final section of the chapter looks at ways of improving comprehension skills in students who experience difficulty in extracting meaning from text.

EXPLICIT INSTRUCTION IN PHONICS

It is clear from the research evidence that helping young children develop better sensitivity to the phonological aspects of language is a necessary but insufficient condition to influence early reading and spelling progress (e.g. Torgesen, Wagner and Rashotte 1994; Ayers 1995; McGuiness, McGuiness and Donohue 1995). Phonological training appears to be of maximum value when the auditory experience with speech sounds and syllables is combined with explicit instruction in letter–sound correspondences. Training activities need to progress to the point where the connections between speech sounds and letters are thoroughly understood.

As a general principle, phonic knowledge and decoding skills should not be introduced and practised in isolation. Very important phonic principles can be established from children's daily reading and writing experiences. For example, a group of young children may wish to send a card to their friend Sam, who is in hospital. The teacher helps them to work out how to write the name by getting them to listen very carefully to each sound in the word. 'Let's say it slowly. Let's stretch it out. SSS-AA-MMM.' The teacher then helps the children to write the letter corresponding with each sound. She continues 'Now, let's write "We miss you". What letters do we need for "we"? Stretch it out: /W/ – /EEE/. We write "w-e". Now "MISS". Who can tell me how "miss" starts? Good! /MMM/. Then /I-I/ -/SSS/. Here is how we write "miss". Watch me.' Much valuable phonic knowledge is acquired in this informal way through writing. This is evident in young children's invented spelling, which reflects their current understanding of the alphabetic code. Basic ideas about phonics can also emerge naturally from shared-book experience and from rhymes, jingles and word-plays.

This informal approach to phonic skill acquisition is all that is required by many young children who are making good progress in early learning. However, it should not be assumed that this approach used alone provides sufficient coverage for students with learning problems. For some students, teaching phonic skills *only* from everyday reading and writing activities proves to be inadequate. In addition to these informal encounters with letter–sound correspondences, many students with learning difficulties need to have phonic skills taught much more directly. They also need regular and systematic practice in the application of these skills. Most studies suggest that at least 30 per cent of children require explicit instruction in phonic decoding and encoding principles in the early stages of learning to read and write. Beck and Juel (1992: 101) have stated: 'Failure to teach the code in a straightforward manner can leave many children without the ability to independently enter the world of quality literature.'

Teaching letter–sound associations

The common associations between letters and sounds may be introduced in any order, and in practice, the order is often dictated by the nature of the reading material the children are using and the writing they are doing. However, when working with students who have difficulties in mastering basic phonics, it is useful to consider how the task of learning the letter–sound correspondences may be organized into a logical sequence.

Holdaway (1990) recommends beginning by selecting highly contrastive sounds such as /m/, /k/, /v/, and avoiding confusable sounds such as /m/ and /n/, or /p/ and /b/. There is certainly some merit in applying this principle in the beginning stages. It is also helpful to teach first the most consistent letter–sound associations (Heilman 1993). The following consonants represent only one sound, regardless of the letter or letters coming after them in a word: j, k, l, m, n, p, b, h, r, v, w.

Identifying initial consonants can be made the focus within many of the general language activities in the classroom. For example, when children are consolidating their knowledge of single letter–sound links, they can begin to make picture dictionaries. Each letter is allocated a separate page and the children paste or draw pictures of objects beginning with that letter on the appropriate page. The 'T' page might have pictures of a Table, a Tree, a Tape recorder, and a Tricycle. Lists or charts can also be made with items grouped according to initial letter:

Children's names: **M**adelaine, **M**ichelle, **M**artin, **M**ark, **M**ary, **M**ichael
Animals and birds: **p**arrot, **p**enguin, **p**ig, **p**ython, **p**latypus

Vowel sounds are far less consistent than consonants in their letter-to-sound correspondences. After first establishing the most common vowel sound associations (/a/ as in apple, /e/ as in egg, /i/ as in ink, /o/ as in orange and /u/ as in up) variations are best learned later in combination with other letters when words containing these units are encountered (e.g. -ar-, -aw-, -ie-, -ee-, -ea-, -ai-, etc.).

With the least able children, it is likely that even more attention will need to be devoted to the mastery of letter sounds. This can be achieved through games, rhymes and songs rather than 'drills'. Stories can also be used to help establish links between letters and sounds. For example, the *Letterland* system developed by a very imaginative teacher in England, uses alliteration in the names of the key characters (e.g. Munching Mike, Ticking Tom, Golden Girl, Robber Red), to help the children associate and remember a sound with a symbol and to create a story link in the child's mind (Wendon 1992). This approach could easily be integrated into the shared-book programme. The pictograms used in *Letterland* are capital and lower-case letters with features superimposed. The h is presented as the Hairy Hatman who walks along in words whispering h, h, h, for hhairy hhat. The w is introduced as the Wicked Water Witch, with her two pools of water held within the shape of the letter. More complex combinations are also covered in the scheme. For example when /a/ (for apple) is next to /w/ (for Water Witch) the witch casts a spell which makes the apple taste awful, thus introducing the tricky /aw/ unit.

There are, of course, other programmes designed to teach phonic knowledge in a very systematic way. One example is *Alpha-Phonics* by Blumenfeld (1991), a step-by-step intensive introduction to phonics, beginning with the most basic letter knowledge and progressing to word-building and decoding. Another example of a very successful programme is 'Jolly phonics' (Jolly 1992). Also of value is Heilman's (1993) text, *Phonics in Proper Perspective*, which presents many practical ideas for classroom use.

Word-building experience

It is important that simple word-building and sound-blending activities are included as soon as the common vowel sounds and a few consonants have been taught. For example, adding the sound /a/ to the /m/ = am; adding /a/ to /t/ = at; adding /o/ to /n/ = on; adding /u/ to /p/ = up, etc. As well as reading these small units in print, the children should also learn to *write* them unaided when the teacher dictates the sounds. As simple as this basic work may sound, for many students with learning problems it is often the first real link they make between spoken and written language. It is vital that children who have not recognized the connection between letters and sounds be given this direction early. The only prerequisite skills required appear to be adequate visual discrimination of letter-shapes and adequate phonemic awareness (Mauer and Kamhi 1996).

An ability to deal with the concept of 'onset' and 'rime' appears to be important for early progress in reading and spelling (Adams 1990; Gunning 1995). The term 'onset and rime' refers to the way in which single-syllable words can be broken into a beginning sound (onset), and a unit comprising the vowel and all that follows it (rime). Examples: dog = onset /d/, rime /og/; shop = onset /sh/, rime /op/, etc. The rime units, in printed form, are often referred to as 'phonograms', although this term can also be applied to any other letter strings which represent a consistent sound unit within words, such as -ight, -ous, pre-, un-, *etc*.

Practice for onset and rime can include the following activities, making new words by combining a given initial sound with the rime. At this stage, plastic letters may be used for word-building and blending (see also 'alphabet kits' below). Example: 'Add the sound and say the word'.

t: -ag, -en, -ub, -op, -ip, -ap
s: -ad, -ix, -un, -it, -ob, -et
c: -up, -ot, -ap, -an, -ub etc.

Attention may also be given to final sounds:

d: da-, ha-, be-, fe-, ki-, ri-, ro-, po-
g: sa-, be-, le-, pi-, di-, ho-, lo-, ru-, tu-, etc.

Experience in attending to the middle vowel in consonant-vowel-consonant (CVC) words should also be provided:

a: r-g, b-t, t-p, b-d, c-n,
e: t-n, p-g, n-t, f-d, g-m
i: p-n, b-t, b-d, r-g, etc.

Weisberg and Savard (1993) have discovered that young children's blending ability is greatly improved if they are encouraged to sequence the sounds in quick succession, rather than pausing between each phoneme. They claim that pausing between the sounds makes it much more difficult to combine the phonemes and pronounce the word. Direct training in this skill improved the children's performance.

Later these simple word-building activities can extend to the teaching of digraphs (two letters representing only one speech sound, as in sh, ch, th, wh, ph, etc.) and blends (two or three consonants forming a functional sound unit: br, cl, sw, st, str, scr, etc.).

sw: -im, -ing, -ell, -eep
ch: -eer, -in, -op, -urch, etc.
ck: ba-, de-, ro-, du-, etc.

For the highest level of proficiency in recognizing and spelling unfamiliar words, children need experience in working with longer and more complex letter-strings, such as: -and, -age, -eed, -ide, -ight, -ound, -own, -tion, etc. Gunning (1995) provides a useful core list of 101 of these most common phonograms.

It must be remembered that all word-building activities are used as a *supplement* to reading and writing for real purposes, not as a replacement for authentic literacy experiences. For example, the words used to generate certain lists containing important phonograms for children to learn can be taken from words encountered in their shared-book experience or from their daily writing. The aim is to help students recognize important phonic units and to seek out these pronounceable parts of words (Gunning 1995). As Stahl (1992: 620) indicates, 'Good phonics instruction should help make sense of patterns noticed within words'.

Alphabet kits

An inexpensive but extremely useful resource to use with beginning readers of any age is a set of plastic letters. For many years their use with dyslexic students has been strongly advocated for word-building and spelling practice. Jackson (1991) includes them as an important component in his approach for students with severe reading disability, and he devised a 'structured alphabet kit' to be used in individual tutorial sessions. The use of plastic letters also forms an essential part of Bryant and Bradley's (1985) programme to assist children to categorize and identify sounds. These writers suggest that the use of groups of letters, arranged to spell simple words in front of the child, allows for the removal of a particular letter while still leaving the rest of the word visually intact. The child can then substitute other letters to make new words, and in doing so develop valuable insight into word structure and sound–symbol relationships. Plastic letters are used for precisely this purpose in the 'Reading success' programme (Reynolds and Dallas 1991).

It can be argued that the use of plastic letters adds a 'concrete' level of representation which some students may cope with more successfully than the purely auditory or purely graphic. Cashdan and Wright (1990) strongly support the use of such aids in not only helping the development of an awareness of the written language system, but also adding to the interest and enjoyment of the teaching session.

BUILDING SIGHT VOCABULARY

It is essential that children acquire, as rapidly as possible, a bank of words they know instantly by sight. Much of a child's learning in this area arises naturally from daily reading and writing experiences. The more frequently a child encounters and uses a word, the more likely it is that the word will be retained in the long-term memory.

Some students, particularly those with reading difficulties, may need to have sight words presented and practised more systematically. The use of flashcards can be of great value here. Playing games, or participating in other activities involving the reading of important words on flashcards, can help to provide the repetition necessary for children to learn to read the words with a high degree of automaticity. Immediate recognition of these words contributes significantly to swift and fluent reading of text.

Teachers often remark on the child who can recognize words on one day, but appears to have forgotten them by the next day. In part, this can explained by what learning theory tells us about the acquisition of new knowledge (e.g. Gagne, Briggs and Wager 1992). New information is not necessarily fully assimilated on first exposure. Acquisition of a correct association, say, between the oral form of a word in speech and the printed word-pattern on the page, involves two distinct stages. The first stage is that of recognizing the word and distinguishing it from other words when the teacher says it aloud. For example, given an activity where word-cards are spread out on the table, the teacher may ask: 'Kathryn, point to the word London. Dennis, pick up the card saying caravan. Show me the word castle', etc. The second stage involves recall of the word from long-term memory without prompting. The teacher shows the child a particular word on the card and asks, 'What is this word, Mary? Read this word to me, Dermot.' Children with learning problems usually need much more practice at stage one (aural/oral matching to print) than teachers realize. Often the children are expected to recall the words from memory before they have had sufficient practice at matching the spoken word to the printed equivalent. A learner cannot retrieve from long-term memory material that has not been effectively stored through adequate exposure and practice.

So important is basic sight vocabulary acquisition to early reading progress that many writers have produced lists of words, arranged in frequency of usage, beginning with the most commonly used words (e.g. McNally and Murray 1968; Preen and Barker 1987; Gillet and Bernard 1989). The list below contains the first fifty most commonly occurring words derived from those lists:

a I in is it of the to on and he she was are had him his her am but we not yes no all said my they with you for big if so did get boy as at an come do got girl go us from little when look

Other high-frequency sight words, often confused by beginning readers include:

were where when went with want which will
here there their they them then

For a comprehensive list of important sight words refer to Preen and Barker (1987).

ADDITIONAL TECHNIQUES AND RESOURCES

Games and apparatus

In almost all texts dealing with remedial or corrective reading teachers will find abundant encouragement to use games and word-building equipment as adjuncts to their programmes. Games, it is argued, provide an opportunity for the learners to practise and overlearn essential material which might otherwise become boring and dull. Such repetition is essential for children who learn at a slow rate or who are poorly motivated. The use of games and equipment may also be seen as 'non-threatening', serving a therapeutic purpose within a group or individual teaching situation.

There can be little doubt that well-structured games and apparatus can perform a very important teaching function. However, it is essential that a specific game or piece of equipment has a clearly defined purpose and that it is matched with a genuine learning need in the children who are to use it. The material should contribute to the objectives for the lesson, not detract from them. Too often games are used in a very random way, almost to amuse the children or to keep them occupied. While this may be justified on therapeutic grounds it cannot be defended pedagogically. A study carried out by Baker, Herman and Yeh (1981) with second and third-grade children found that the unstructured use of games, puzzles and supplementary material was *negatively* related to achievement in reading and mathematics.

It is also important that the use of games or apparatus be closely monitored by an adult, if time is not to be wasted by the children and if the material is to be used correctly.

Multisensory or multimodal approaches

The names Fernald, Gillingham, Stillman and Orton usually come to mind when multisensory approaches are mentioned. All of these educators advocated methods which use as many channels of input to the learner as possible. The methods usually involve the learner finger-tracing over the letter-shape or word-shape to be mastered, or tracing it in the air, while at the same time saying and hearing the auditory component and seeing the visual component.

The Fernald approach involves four stages:

- First the learner selects a particular word which he or she wants to learn. The teacher writes the word in blackboard-size writing (cursive) on a card. The child then finger-traces the word, saying each syllable as it is traced. This is repeated until the learner feels capable of writing the word from memory. As new words are mastered they are filed away in a card index for later revision. As soon as the learner knows a few words these are used for constructing simple sentences.

- The second stage involves the elimination of direct finger-tracing and the child is encouraged to learn the words through studying their visual appearance and then writing them from memory. This stage improves visual imagery and may thus be used also for remedial instruction in the correct spelling of irregular words. The words are still stored on card and used for frequent revision. The material is usually consolidated by the child producing his or her own small books.

- The third stage continues to develop visual word-study techniques and encourages a more rapid memorization of the words, followed by swift writing. The word-card drill is usually retained only for particular words which give difficulty. At this stage the child also begins to attempt to read new material prepared by the teacher.

- The final stage involves the child becoming almost entirely independent in his or her reading skill, having generalized an understanding of word structure and having been helped to make use of contextual cues.

The Gillingham and Stillman approach and the Orton approach are basically the same as the Fernald approach, employing a visual-auditory-kinaesthetic-tactile (VAKT) method. The only significant difference is the emphasis given to sounding-out rather than slowly pronouncing the word during the finger-tracing stages. More attention is given to learning the letter sounds and applying these in word-attack.

It can be argued that multisensory approaches using several channels of input simultaneously help a child to integrate, at a neurological level, what is seen with what is heard, whether it be a letter or a word. On the other hand VAKT approaches may well succeed where other methods have failed because they cause the learner to focus more intently on the learning task. Whatever the reason, this teaching approach, which brings vision, hearing, articulation and movement into play, does appear to result in improved assimilation and retention. It is obviously easier to apply this approach with younger children; but in a one-to-one remedial situation it is still a viable proposition with older students.

Carbo (1996) suggests that, where possible, choice of teaching approach should capitalize on students' preferred learning modalities. For some students, emphasis on phonemic awareness and phonic skills may not produce the best results; for them a predominantly visual memory approach may be indicated. For others, the use of multisensory resources and techniques bring about improved learning. Again, this is easier to accomplish in an individual tutorial session, rather than in a large class.

The overhead projector

The overhead projector can be a useful aid for presenting aspects of both reading and spelling in a predominantly visual way. Many teachers make their own transparencies and use colour to good advantage in developing word study skills. The overhead projector is also useful in presenting cloze exercises and preparing word webs, both of which are described below.

The tape recorder

The cassette tape recorder is also a useful resource in the remedial reading situation. Teachers can make their own instructional programmes for use with this equipment. The programme may be nothing more ambitious than the prerecording of popular stories which the children can listen to through headsets while following the text in the book. In this way more difficult material can be presented which would otherwise be at frustration level for the child. Other uses of tape may be to programme aspects of phonic work or spelling assignments, or to set comprehension activities involving questions at literal, interpretive, critical and creative levels.

The use of popular songs on audio-tape provides repetition with enjoyment and has proved to be useful in remedial or special class situations. A zig-zag book containing the words from a current song can be prepared for the child or for a small group. The children follow the words in the book as the song is played from a cassette. Later the words are read without the music and some key words may be put on flashcards to be recognized out of context.

The use of comic strips

The use of picture material from children's comics and cartoons can provide an enjoyable and motivating beginning-reading approach for primary or very slow-learning secondary students.

The children select a comic strip. They number each individual picture in logical sequence and cut and paste each picture in the top half of a blank sheet of A4 paper. They can dictate their own interpretation of the 'story' to the teacher or other tutor (e.g. parent, peer, aide). The teacher prints the words for each story below the appropriate pictures, reading these back to the child and then asking the child to read them unaided. Finally the pages are secured together and a cover is made. The children can then share their small booklets with others in the class. The story dictated by a child does not have to be identical with the one intended by the artist. The teacher should accept the children's own versions.

During the process of writing down the child's dictated story the teacher can draw attention to certain single letters and letter groups in order to begin to develop some basic word-attack skills. Words which are particularly difficult but important are put on flashcards for revision and practice. At a later stage the child copies the story into his own book. Gradually the child will be able to construct more of the story without adult help.

Another possible use of comic strips and cartoons for remedial reading and writing involves the removal of the captions or the speech balloons using some form of correcting fluid or white ink. The child then discusses with the teacher what the characters might be saying and is helped to write the words into the speech balloons. These are then read to the teacher and other children.

Rebus reading approaches

Any approach which uses a picture or symbol in place of a particular word may be described as a 'rebus' approach. The method allows a child to feel that he or she is reading at a functional level by replacing difficult nouns or concepts with a picture or symbol. A simple illustration of this principle is presented below from a series called *Truckin' with Kenny* (Rogers 1982).

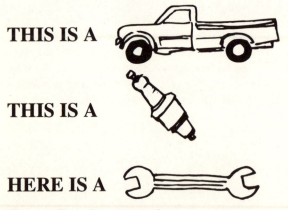

Figure 3 The rebus approach

It is an approach which can serve to boost confidence in the early stages and can allow a story-line to be developed without tight constraints of vocabulary control.

The rebus approach can also be adapted as a group activity, where children work together to construct the story which is then read aloud to others. This provides opportunities for children at all levels of ability to contribute and is

Figure 4 Example of a group rebus approach

a useful example of inclusive practice. The example in Figure 4 was collected from a group of primary students.

The Impress Method

The Impress Reading Method is a unison reading procedure in which the student and the teacher read aloud together at a natural rate. The student is permitted to use the index finger to keep the place on the page, and may even be physically guided to do so by the teacher.

The Impress Method is particularly useful when a child has developed some word recognition skill but is lacking in fluency and expression. It is recommended that sessions should last roughly fifteen minutes and be provided on a very regular basis for several months. It may be necessary to repeat the same sentences or paragraphs several times until the student becomes fluent at reading the material alone.

The Impress Method is very appropriate for use in peer tutoring, where one child who is a better reader provides assistance for a less able friend. In such cases the 'tutor' usually needs to be shown how to act effectively as a helper.

Eldredge (1990) has had good success using a variation of read-along with a group of poor readers. He uses the term 'group-assisted reading' to describe an approach which uses reading in unison to emphasize correct phrasing, intonation and pitch. The decoding burden is removed, allowing students to concentrate upon meaning. Eldredge's system involves reading a challenging text several times with the students while each student follows or tracks the print in the book. Students then practise the reading in pairs without teacher assistance. Significant achievement gains in reading comprehension and vocabulary were reported.

Repeated readings

A very similar approach to the Impress Method, which simply requires non-fluent readers to practise reading a short passage aloud until fluent, has also been found useful in building confidence and increasing skills (Bowd 1990). The teacher first models the reading, while the student follows in the text. The student then practises by reading the material aloud, with corrective feedback from the teacher. The student then continues to practise until perfect, and finally records the reading on tape. When the recording is played back, the student hears a high-quality performance which is equal in standard to the reading of even the most competent student in class. This is an important boost to this student's confidence and self-esteem.

Word processors

Word processors can be used most effectively to help students acquire confidence in creating their own reading material (Montague and Fonseca 1993). It has been suggested that the use of word processors for desk-top publishing adds a valuable new dimension to the language programme in any classroom (Wray and Medwell 1989). Creating and printing one's own stories can enhance a child's interest in books, and at the same time develop skills in composing, editing, proof-reading, spelling and design.

At a more basic level computer programs exist which will help students to improve their word recognition, decoding, sentence completion and spelling skills. For example, a target word may be displayed on the screen and the student required to copy it using the keyboard. The word is then embedded in a sentence for the student to read and copy. The word is presented again with the initial letter missing and the student is required to complete it. Gradually the cues are removed until the student is reading and writing the word correctly with a high degree of automaticity.

Computer programs can also be used to improve comprehension skills (Anderson 1990), and programs can be devised to provide additional study material related to texts and novels being used by the class (Wepner 1991).

In general, word processors are valuable because they integrate reading with writing and require the student to interact with the text which is being presented. Computers are infinitely patient, allow for self-pacing by the student, present material in carefully sequenced steps and provide immediate feedback. Students are required to be active throughout the learning session and are found to have higher levels of motivation when working at the keyboard (Loughrey 1991). Whether used by one student alone, or by students working together, the computer is an excellent tool within the regular classroom.

In the home situation the computer can aid literacy development. Children can work with a parent on early reading skills, such as word recognition, simple spelling and following instructions (Rickleman and Henk 1991).

LISTENING TO CHILDREN READ

Regardless of which approach or blend of approaches a teacher decides to use in working with individual children, listening to the child read aloud should be an essential part of the programme. It permits the teacher to monitor such features as self-correcting behaviour, use of context, word-attack skill, fluency and phrasing. This writer has found it valuable to use such time as a 'reading together' experience, rather than merely listening to the child read. Having selected an appropriate book the session may take the following form.

• You (the teacher) volunteer to read the first page or two while the child follows in his or her copy of the book. The teacher's fluent reading of the text serves not only to model appropriate expression and rate but allows the child to get the flavour of the story. Names of characters will have cropped up and topic-specific terms will have been encountered by the time the child's turn comes to read. Allow the child to finger-point to keep the place in the text if necessary, rather than become lost and left behind in the story.

• Now invite the child to read the next page or half-page. As you listen to the performance anticipate any difficult words and simply provide them to maintain continuity and meaning.

• Praise the child briefly for the reading, then continue yourself with the next page.

• Again invite the child to read the next page, providing help only when necessary. Don't destroy continuity by suggesting that the child sound out a word. You might, however, suggest that the child read the rest of the sentence if he or she can't recognize a word. This will usually enable the reader to self-correct or make a contextual guess.

• After reading at least four or five pages together in this way, the child will feel that a significant part of the story has been read. Indeed the story content (plot) will be emerging and a few minutes may be spent in talking about the key points to aid recall and comprehension. (This approach might be contrasted with the typical classroom ritual of hearing a child read one page, then marking his or her card and putting the book away until the next day or later in the week. So little of the actual story is covered each day that it is almost impossible for the child to understand what it is really about. The least able readers suffer most in this system.)

- In later sessions the amount that you read is gradually reduced, allowing the child more time to perform independently. It is at this stage that you can gain insights into the child's skills by attending to the nature of miscues which may occur from time to time.

- It is important that a child be helped to read a significant amount at each session. By breaking into the vicious circle of 'I can't read well – so I avoid reading – so I don't get much practice – so I don't improve', you are able to prove to the child that he or she is, indeed, making progress. Some form of daily charting of pages read can be very useful here.

It is important to aim to make the child an *independent* reader. The amount of correction and feedback given to a low-ability reader may tend to maintain that child's dependence on adult support and guidance. Frequently the feedback tends to be drawing the child's attention to the phonic properties of a word, or simply supplying the word, rather than helping the reader to pick up cues from context and thus become more independent in performance. Less frequent and less direct support seems to provide more opportunity for the child to self-correct and maintain attention to meaning. In particular, teachers should pause longer before prompting a student.

Pause, prompt, praise (PPP)

A procedure known as 'pause, prompt, praise' was developed by Professor Glynn and his associates at the University of Auckland. It has been applied very successfully in many remedial intervention programmes, and can be taught to parents, aides, peer-tutors and volunteer helpers in schools as a strategy to use with the children they are assisting (Pumfrey 1991; Wheldall 1995).
The procedure involves the following simple steps:

- the child encounters an unfamiliar word;
- instead of stepping in immediately and giving the word, the teacher/tutor waits a few seconds for the child to work it out;
- if the child is not successful, the teacher/tutor prompts the child by suggesting he or she perhaps guess from the meaning of the passage, or attend to the initial letter, or read on to the end of the sentence, etc.;
- when the child succeeds in identifying the word he or she is praised;
- if the child cannot get the word after brief prompting, the teacher/tutor quickly supplies the word;
- the child is also praised for self-correcting while reading.

Wheldall (1995) reports that low-progress readers make significantly more progress when tutored by volunteers trained in PPP than when tutored by untrained personnel. When combined with specific instruction in phonics and decoding, PPP resulted in an average increase in reading age of nearly fourteen months from seven weeks of daily tutoring in Wheldall's study.

SILENT SUSTAINED READING (SSR)

Silent Sustained Reading describes a specific period of time set aside each day in the classroom for students and the teacher to read material of their own personal choice. Often ten or fifteen minutes of the afternoon session are devoted to SSR across the whole school.

Fenwick (1988) reported that SSR, if well implemented, can result in students engaging in much more reading activity than previously. He states that in doing so, the students gradually develop their ability to concentrate on reading for longer periods. In some cases, the students are seen to become more discriminating readers and the range and quality of what they read improves. Fenwick also reports the development of a more positive attitude toward reading.

If SSR is implemented inefficiently it can result in students wasting time. A problem emerges if students with reading difficulties select books which are too difficult for them to read independently. Teachers need to guide book choice to ensure that all students can successfully read the material during these silent reading periods. Biemiller (1994: 206) warns that poor readers often spend substantial periods of SSR time 'covertly avoiding reading'. If true, this situation needs to be rectified.

COMPREHENSION

Reading comprehension is not something which comes *after* learning the 'mechanics' of reading. Reading for meaning must be the focus of any literacy programme from the very beginning. Even in the earliest stages of reading acquisition, children should discuss and answer questions about what they read. When teachers read stories to children they should discuss the material and encourage children to think about and criticize the ideas in the story.

As long ago as 1969 Nila Banton Smith identified four levels of comprehension, each level containing a cluster of component skills and each being dependent upon competence at the previous levels. The most basic level is referred to as 'literal comprehension' (understanding, at least superficially, the basic information which is being presented). This level is dependent upon such subskills as: understanding word meanings; recognition of main idea; grasp of sequence and order of detail; and recognition of cause-and-effect relationships when these are stated in the text. To a large extent even this level depends upon the learner's own previous knowledge and experience. If the concepts being presented are very new, even literal comprehension and recall will be difficult. This raises the question 'Is reading a text the best way of introducing a new and unfamiliar topic?' For some learners the answer is certainly 'No'.

The second level of comprehension is 'interpretation'. This involves going beyond what is actually presented in the text, inferring and reading between the lines and drawing conclusions. Subskills at this level include making generalizations, predicting outcomes, reasoning cause–effect when these are not stated and discovering relationships.

The third level of comprehension is 'critical reading'. This involves judgement of the quality, value, accuracy and truthfulness of what is read, detecting bias or overstatement.

The final level is referred to as 'creative reading'. At this level the reader goes beyond the writer's material and generates new ideas or develops new insights which were not explicit in the text.

It is argued that in many classrooms comprehension exercises rarely demand responses other than at the literal (factual recall) level. While this level *is* important, since it is basic to the other three levels, a programme which sets out to develop comprehension skills in children should include questions (oral and written) which demand some thinking at the interpretive, critical and creative levels. For example, following a short story about the crash of a passenger aircraft these questions might be posed:

• How many passengers escaped the crash? (literal)
• Why did the failure of cabin pressure lead to the crash? (interpretive)
• From the way he behaved before the crash what kind of man do you think the pilot was, and could his judgement be trusted? (critical)
• Many air crashes involving loss of life occur each year. How might flight be made a safer method of transport? (creative)

If a child has difficulties in comprehending what is read, particularly at the first two levels, it is worth considering whether there is a serious mismatch between his or her own vocabulary knowledge and the words being used to convey the information in the text. A child may be able to read a word correctly but not know (or may misunderstand) its meaning. In such cases there is a need to devote more time to word study and vocabulary building when comprehension activities are used in classroom.

Children who read very slowly or much too fast often comprehend poorly. Attention to rate of reading is thus indicated as a specific intervention in some cases.

For some children, the actual recall of information is poor. Recall is dependent upon attention, vividness of content, intention to remember, rehearsal and any connections with the reader's previous experience. These factors may help to identify why a particular child is having problems.

Improving comprehension

According to Dole *et al.* (1991) there are five key components to successful comprehension of text: locating the main idea; drawing inferences; generating questions; monitoring one's own understanding; and making a summary. Research has indicated that these aspects of comprehension can be improved if given due attention, and if taught explicitly as components of an integrated study-skills strategy (Pressley *et al.* 1995). In particular, students with reading difficulties appear to benefit from specific training in self-monitoring and in summarizing (Malone and Mastropieri 1992). However, it must be noted that this type of strategy training is time-consuming and effort-intensive, with effects often taking months to occur (Dole, Brown and Trathen 1996).

Cole and Chan (1990) have reviewed the classroom-based research on what is known as 'reciprocal teaching'. In this approach to the improvement of study skills, teachers and students work together in the initial stages, sharing ideas, generating questions which may be answered by a specific text, predicting answers, checking for meaning and finally collaborating on a summary. The teacher's role is one of demonstrating effective ways of gaining meaning from text; but the long-term aim is to have the students internalize these strategies for themselves.

The reading comprehension skills of all children can be increased when teachers spend more time modelling and demonstrating strategies such as:

- previewing material before it is read to gain an overview;
- locating the main idea in a paragraph;
- generating questions about the material by 'thinking aloud';
- predicting what will happen;
- summarizing or paraphrasing the content.

Fielding and Pearson (1994) suggest that a successful programme for the development of comprehension should include four components:

- large amounts of time devoted to text reading;
- teacher-directed instruction in comprehension strategies;
- opportunities for peer and collaborative learning using texts;
- occasions provided for students to talk with the teacher and with one another about their responses to a particular text.

Hints for developing comprehension skills

The following specific suggestions may help to improve the comprehension of all students, but are particularly applicable to with learning difficulties.

- Ensure that the material presented is interesting to the child and at an appropriate readability level.

- Always apply comprehension strategy training to real texts and read the texts for some genuine purpose. Don't rely upon contrived comprehension exercises used in isolation.
- Prepare for entry into the printed material. Ask, 'What might we find in this chapter? What do the illustrations tell us? What does this word mean? Let's read the subheadings before we begin', etc. Refer also to the PQRS strategy described in Chapter 4.
- Encourage students to set comprehension questions for each other; then use these questions to discuss what is meant by critical reading, inferring, predicting, etc.
- Read through any comprehension questions *before* the story or passage is read so that the student enters the material knowing what to look for.
- Use daily newspapers and magazine articles as the basis for some class-room discussion and comprehension activity. Highlighter pens can be used to focus upon key ideas, important terms, facts to remember, etc.
- For the more limited readers make frequent use of instruction sheets which the student must read, interpret and act upon. For example, instructions for a simple science experiment; following a recipe; making a model.
- Making a summary is an excellent way of ensuring that students have identified main ideas.
- In general, make sure that students are aware of the goal in reading a particular text. Teach them how to make use of strategies which will help them to extract meaning from what is read. Don't simply test comprehension, teach it!

The cloze procedure

Cloze procedure is a simple approach designed to make a reader more aware of context cues and meaning as aids to guessing unfamiliar words. The procedure merely requires that certain words in a sentence or paragraph be deleted and the reader asked to read the paragraph and supply the possible words which might fill the gaps:

> It was Monday morning and Leanne should have been going to sch. . . . . .
> She was still in . . . . . . She was hot and her throat was. . . . . .
> 'I think I had better send for the d. . . . . .,' said her . . . . . . 'No school for you . . . . . .'

Variations on the cloze technique involve leaving the initial letter of the deleted word to provide a clue; or at the other extreme, deleting several consecutive words, thus requiring the student to provide a phrase which might be appropriate. The use of the cloze procedure can be integrated as part of the shared-book experiences already described.

These cloze activities can involve group work. The prepared paragraphs are duplicated on sheets for the children or displayed on the overhead projector. As a group the children discuss the best alternative and then present these to the teacher. Reading, vocabulary and comprehension are all being developed by a closer attention to logical sentence structure and meaning.

Graphic organizers and word webs

Another useful activity which aids comprehension and study skills is that of 'word webbing'. The process of word webbing is also known as 'thought mapping' or 'concept mapping'. The 'web', or diagram, produced is often referred to as a 'graphic organizer'.

Word webbing is advocated as a way of preparing the student for entry into a text and for recording information while reading (Hickerson 1992). It is also useful for organizing ideas prior to writing on a new theme. Charts containing key words to be encountered in the text are prepared in advance by the teacher, or the teacher and students together brainstorm ideas and write key words on the blackboard. Tentative connections are made between some of the words, and these connections are discussed. As the reading of the text proceeds, new connections are made and additional important words added to the web.

Figure 5 illustrates a word web relating to a magazine article which has an illustration of a woman changing the tyre on her car on a country road.

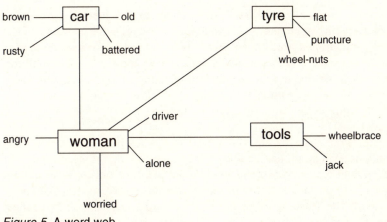

Figure 5 A word web

Word webs help students to organize their thoughts and link new ideas with what they already know. The final chart serves as a useful aid for students when they begin to write a summary for the topic studied.

When students have become proficient at word webbing they may use the technique as individuals, or apply it collaboratively in groups.

Over to you: Developing a comprehension strategy

- Read through the sections in this chapter dealing with comprehension, and also again read the appropriate sections of Chapter 4.

- Select a novel, a magazine article or a subject textbook which is suitable for the students you teach. Devise a procedure which you could use with the students to study and extract meaning from the material you have selected.

- Don't forget the importance of your own modelling of important strategies.

- How might you extend the activity into independent practice for the students?

- How will you attempt to provide for generalization of the new strategies to other reading materials?

SUMMARY

This chapter provided some additional ideas for teachers to use when adapting a reading approach for an individual student's needs. Many of the techniques mentioned are not, in themselves, total approaches to reading; they can be used to complement and extend existing approaches. The majority of students will not require major adaptations to their programme, but where appropriate, these suggestions may help to maintain a student's interest and enjoyment while at the same time providing successful practice of essential skills.

When programming for special assistance in reading the teacher must constantly keep in mind that the long-term goal is to help the student become an independent reader, capable of reading for pleasure and for information; and in the case of the student with intellectual disability, reading for social competence. The teaching of phonic skills, word-attack and so forth must never become an end in itself, but must be recognized as a step on the ladder to fully functional reading ability.

All teachers, and all helpers in learning assistance programmes, should develop skills in listening to children read and providing appropriate support and feedback. Advice on this issue was provided in this chapter.

The suggestions for improving comprehension skills presented above have wide application and should readily find a place in the whole class programme.

Discussion points

• Which of the techniques or approaches described in this chapter could be used with adults who have literacy problems?

• 'If you gave me a pencil and paper, or a blackboard and chalk, I could teach a child to read.' Give your views on this statement.

• Discuss some of the difficulties a teacher might encounter in trying to apply in a mixed-ability classroom some of the strategies and techniques described in this chapter. How might these problems be minimized?

• What are your views on using Sustained Silent Reading periods in school?

Further reading

Armbruster, B., Anderson, T. and Meyer, J. (1991) 'Improving content-area reading using instructional graphics', *Reading Research Quarterly* 26, 4: 394–416.

Campbell, R. (1995) *Reading in the Early Years Handbook*, Milton Keynes: Open University Press.

Gunning, T.G. (1995) 'Word building: a strategic approach to the teaching of phonics', *The Reading Teacher* 48, 6: 484–8.

Miller, L. (1995) *Towards Reading*, Milton Keynes: Open University Press.

Morris, D., Ervin, C. and Conrad, K. (1996) 'A case study of middle school reading disability', *The Reading Teacher* 49, 5: 368–77.

Palinscar, A.S. and Klenk, L. (1992) 'Fostering literacy learning in supportive contexts', *Journal of Learning Disabilities* 25, 4: 211–25.

Samuels, S.J. and Farstrup, A.E. (eds) (1993) *What Research Has to Say About Reading Instruction* (2nd edn), Newark: International Reading Association.

Schunk, D.H. and Rice, J.M. (1992) 'Influence of reading comprehension strategy information on children's achievement outcomes', *Learning Disability Quarterly* 15, 1: 51–64.

Vacca, R.T. and Vacca, J. (1993) *Content Area Reading*, New York: Harper Collins.

Van Daal, V.H. and Van der Leij, A. (1992) 'Computer-based reading and spelling practice for children with learning disabilities', *Journal of Learning Disabilities* 25, 3: 186–95.

Chapter 10

Fostering development in writing

The ability to communicate well in writing is a prerequisite for success in school. Students with learning disabilities typically have a hard time meeting the writing demands of school because they have problems related to mastery of the more mechanical aspects of written expression such as spelling, handwriting and punctuation, as well as the higher level skills of composing.

(Vallecorsa, Ledford and Parnell 1991: 52)

Perhaps more than any other area of the curriculum, writing presents major problems for the student with learning difficulties. According to Zipprich (1995) and Wong *et al.* (1996), these students exhibit difficulties with the composing skills of planning, sequencing ideas, editing and revising. They also have problems with the more mechanical aspects, such as handwriting, spelling and punctuation. In Isaacson's (1987) review, where unskilled writers were compared with skilled writers, the following problems were identified in the unskilled writers:

- they spent very little time in planning before they started to write;
- no rough draft notes were prepared before writing;
- ideas were not composed in a logical order;
- either very simple sentence structures were used, or long and rambling sentences were constructed with repetitive use of conjunctions;
- simple words were favoured over more interesting and expressive words;
- certain words were used repetitiously (e.g. 'and then', 'nice', 'really big', 'really small', 'really fast', etc.);
- not much material was produced in the available time;
- the writers were reluctant to review and revise their work;
- many spelling errors were made;
- punctuation was often omitted, or was added idiosyncratically.

Writing is certainly the most demanding of the language arts. It is fortunate that contemporary approaches to the teaching of writing have done much to alleviate the anxiety and frustration which, in years gone by, many of the lower-ability students experienced whenever 'writing' or 'composition' appeared on the timetable. To them it meant a silent period of sustained writing, with little or no opportunity to discuss work or ask for assistance. Great importance was placed on accuracy and neatness at the first attempt and many children must have felt extremely inhibited. Even when the teacher wasn't a severe judge of the product, the children themselves sometimes carried out self-assessment and decided that they couldn't write because their product was not perfect. An attitude quickly developed in the child, 'I can't write', and a failure cycle was established.

The change that has occurred in recent years has been a shift of emphasis from finished product to the actual processes of composing and revising. The method is represented best in the 'process-conference approach' of Donald Graves (1983).

THE PROCESS-CONFERENCE APPROACH

Briefly, the process-conference approach embodies the following principles.

- Writing, as a process, usually involves a number of separate stages, from the initial hazy formulation of ideas to the first written draft, though subsequent revision and editing to a final product (although not *all* writing should be forced to pass through all stages). Students need to have these stages made explicit.

- Teachers themselves should write in the classroom and thus demonstrate the composing, editing and publishing stages in action.

- When writing, the choice of topic should usually be made by the writer, as personal narrative is likely to result in the most lively and relevant communications.

- The teacher should confer with each and every student about the writing being produced. This involves far more than the automatic dispensation of praise and encouragement: and it will involve quite different amounts of time and advice according to individual needs and abilities.

- A student writing in a classroom has a potential audience not only in the teacher but also the peer group. A friend or partner can be used as a sounding board for ideas and can read, discuss and make suggestions for written drafts.

- When possible and appropriate students' work should be 'published' for a wider audience (class book, display board, school library, etc.).

- The results appear to be particularly encouraging when the process approach is combined with use of a word processor.

It should be noted that the process-conference approach to writing can certainly be regarded as an inclusive practice as it involves collaboration between students, and between teachers and students. Each and every student can be helped to produce and share something of personal worth in the form of a written recording.

According to Milem and Garcia (1996) the three important guidelines to apply when first introducing process writing are:

- allow students to ease into the writing process as a group before asking them to write as individuals;
- initially, help the students choose topics about which they have strong opinions and ideas;
- model frequent writing and sharing yourself; and also model mature acceptance of constructive criticism.

Milem and Garcia (1996) have strongly supported the use of 'process writing' with learning disabled students, including those in high-school settings.

PROVIDING SPECIAL ASSISTANCE

General principles

The first important step in improving writing skills is to allocate sufficient time for writing within the school day. It seems that writing is often seen as an adjunct to other subjects, rather than something which needs to have specific time devoted to it. If writing occurs daily there is much greater likelihood that motivation, confidence and writing skills will improve (Vallecorsa, Ledford and Parnell 1991).

It is also essential to give students an adequate stimulus for writing. The topic must be interesting and relevant, and students must see a purpose in transferring ideas to paper. Regardless of whether the activity involves writing a letter to a friend or composing a science-fiction fantasy story, the students should perceive the task as enjoyable and worthwhile.

In general, students need help most in two basic stages of the writing process, namely planning to write and revising or polishing the final product. The teaching of each of these stages of writing should embody the basic principles of effective instruction, namely, modelling by the teacher, guided practice with feedback (mainly via the conference process between teacher and student) and independent practice.

Students with writing difficulties need to be given a clear structure which they can use whenever they write. In particular, novice writers appear to benefit most if they are taught specific strategies for generating ideas, composing and editing (Graves and Hauge 1993; Martin and Manno 1995; Wong *et al.* 1996). They need to be given guidance in how to begin, how to continue and how to complete the writing task. In this context, students could be taught a set of questions to ask themselves which will facilitate the generation of ideas for writing, and will assist with the organization and presentation of the material across different writing genres.

Unskilled and reluctant writers

Students who exhibit difficulties in written expression fall into one of two groups. The groups are not mutually exclusive and there is some overlap in terms of instructional needs. The first group comprises those students of any age level who have learning difficulties or who have a genuine learning disability. For these students, the teacher needs to make any writing task very clear and structured enough to ensure their successful participation. The second group comprises those students of any age who can write but don't, the reluctant and unmotivated students. These students appear not to see the relevance of writing, or have not experienced the excitement of written communication and get no satisfaction from it. Some of these students may have encountered negative or unrewarding experiences during the early stages of becoming writers. They may have acquired what has been termed 'writing apprehension', which now causes them to avoid the task whenever possible. Their problem is one of poor motivation leading to habitually low levels of productivity. Here the teacher must try to regain lost interest and build confidence.

The classroom atmosphere which encourages all children to experiment and take risks in their writing without fear of criticism or ridicule is a very necessary condition for the least able students. However, in many cases, particularly with the upper primary or secondary student with a history of bad experiences in writing, simply creating the atmosphere is not enough; more than the ordinary amount of guidance and encouragement from the teacher will also be needed. Indeed, Graves (1983) describes some such children in his chapters titled 'How to help children catch up' and 'How to help children with special problems of potential'. His studies of the ways in which very young children begin to write and compose throw some light on the performance and needs of older children with difficulties in writing. In particular these studies indicate how important it is to view a child's writing attempts *diagnostically*, to determine how much a child can achieve unaided, and to observe the strategies he or she brings to the planning, composing, spelling and revising stages.

With some students with learning difficulties, the initial stimulus for writing may have to come from the teacher rather than from free choice. On the other hand, many students will have interests and experiences about which they can talk freely and can then be helped to write. The link here with the language-experience approach to reading for such children should be obvious: 'What I know about I can talk about. What I can talk about someone can help me to write. What I have written I can read.'

Graves (1983) suggested the following possible sequence in assisting young children with difficulties to produce something satisfying. In addition he says that such students need to be helped *daily* and usually during the first ten minutes of the lesson:

- initial 'warm up' – perhaps a few minutes spent with handwriting patterns or letter formation, or copying of something previously written;
- discussion of new topic for writing;
- a drawing for the topic;
- further discussion with teacher;
- composing one or two sentences;
- feedback from the teacher.

With low-achieving students, or those lacking in confidence, the teacher may have to structure the discussion very tightly at various stages, even to the extent of writing down key vocabulary and possible sentence beginnings for the student to use. Graves advises teachers not to be afraid of saying, at times, 'Try doing it this way'. Teachers are still permitted to teach! However, during the discussion and feedback stages (the 'conferring') the teacher should not overcorrect, but rather encourage the student to talk and to think. The main aim is to help the student generate ideas and then to sort these into an optimum sequence.

In the early stages it is important not to place undue stress upon accuracy of spelling since this can stifle the student's attempts at communicating ideas freely. Invented spelling gives students the freedom to write with attention to content and sequence. Charles Cripps (1983: 22) makes an excellent point when he says, 'it is essential that a misspelling is never referred to as something "wrong" but instead as something nearly right'. As the student becomes more confident and productive, the teacher, while still remaining supportive, will make the conferring stage rather less structured. Enabling-type questions are still used to extend the student's thinking and to build upon the writing so far produced. The term 'scaffolding' has been used to suggest this surreptitious support which can be reduced gradually.

In the case of the least able students, particularly in upper primary and secondary classes, it will be mainly the teacher who monitors the work in progress and who has most to offer when they confer. Extreme care must be exercised in using peers to read and comment upon the writing of other children with difficulties. In many classrooms the more able students will have a sufficiently positive attitude toward students who are less able, and can offer very useful assistance in a peer tutoring role. In other classrooms, or in some individual cases, the able writer may be inclined to ridicule any naive contributions and thus rapidly undermine the confidence and motivation of the student with difficulties. Peer critiquing is often written about and talked about as if it is a simple strategy to employ in the classroom, but actually it needs to be done with great sensitivity. Teachers must spend time in modelling the critiquing process before expecting students to implement it skilfully: e.g. how to highlight the good points, how to detect what is not clear, how to help with the generation of new ideas, how to assist with adding or deleting material and polishing the work.

Many of the lower-achieving students have, in the past, written very little during times set aside for writing. This is part of the vicious circle which might be described thus: 'I don't like writing so I don't write much, so I don't get much practice, so I don't improve . . . etc.'

Humes (1983) has advocated frequent writing practice (daily) and even to the extent of using 'speed writing' against a time limit (e.g. for five minutes), with students copying existing material as rapidly as possible to convince themselvers that they can indeed 'write a lot' when style and accuracy are not to be judged. A modified form of precision teaching can be used to increase output of some students. The number of words or sentences written in a set time during writing lessons can be counted and charted each day (Lindsley 1992).

Small booklets are usually better than exercise books for students who are unskilled and reluctant writers. The opportunity to make a fresh start almost every week is far better than being faced with the accumulation of evidence of past failures which can accrue in an exercise book. For students of all ages a loose-leaf folder may be very useful as a replacement for the traditional exercise book. There is a place for the daily diary, journal or news book; but teachers should avoid such writing becoming merely habitual, trite and boring. There is a danger of this being the case, even with students who can write well.

Leading from the points above it is obvious that our notion of 'free writing' for the least able students should be interpreted as 'freely-guided writing' in the early stages. Quite original ideas may be there, but the process of organizing them before getting them down on paper needs to be teacher-supported. As confidence and proficiency increase with the passage of time, the amount of direct help can be greatly reduced for most students.

Since the process-conference approach depends so much upon the student-writer having someone with whom to confer, it is important to consider other possible sources of assistance in the classroom. In addition to the teacher and the peer group, help may also be provided by teacher aides, older students (cross-age tutoring), college and university students on field placements, and parent volunteers. In all cases these helpers must know what their role is and will require some informal training by the teacher if they are to adopt an approach which is supportive rather than too demanding of perfection.

Over to you: Advice to helpers in a writing programme

- Assume that you need to provide some in-service training for a group of parents who have offered to help children write within a school-based learning assistance programme.

- List the basic principles you would wish them to apply when they work with the children.

- Add to your list as you move through the remaining sections of this chapter.

SOME SPECIFIC STRATEGIES

Providing a framework

The skeleton story

Getting started is the first obstacle faced by many students who find writing difficult. One simple way of helping them complete a story is by giving them the framework for a story, with sentence beginnings to be completed using their own ideas. Example:

Something woke me in the middle of the night.
I heard . . . .
I climbed out of bed quietly and . . . .
To my surprise I saw . . . .
At first I . . . .
I was lucky because . . . .
In the end . . . .

With groups of low-achieving students it is useful, through collaborative effort, to complete one version of the skeleton story on the blackboard. This completed story is read to the group. Each student is then given a sheet with the same sentence beginnings, but he or she must write a different story from the one on the blackboard. The stories are later shared in the group.

Cues and prompts

In helping students generate ideas and compose in writing Graham, Harris and Sawyer (1987) and Martin and Manno (1995) suggest that they be taught a framework of questions which they can ask themselves if necessary during the initial stages of planning – e.g. 'What happened first?' 'Where did it happen?' 'To whom did it happen?' 'What happened next?'

Questions such as 'What does it look like (size, colour, shape, etc.)'; 'What does it feel like?', will help students become more descriptive in their writing. These temporary props are very useful for students who have difficulty in the planning stage of writing, but the students must not become too dependent upon such starting points.

Story webs

Story webs are very similar to the word webs referred to in the previous chapter. They can provide students with learning difficulties with a useful starting point from which to generate ideas for writing (Zipprich 1995).

A web is created by writing the main idea in the centre of a sheet of paper, then branching off from the main idea into different categories of information. These ideas and categories might include: the title in the centre, the setting for the story, the type of action to take place, the characters involved, the outcome, etc. Prompts and cues, as above, may need to be used to stimulate the students' thinking as the web is constructed. The brief notes in the web can then be elaborated into sentences and the sentences gradually extended into paragraphs.

Story planner

Gross (1993) uses a variation of the story web idea. In her approach, the title for a story is placed in the centre of the blackboard. Radiating lines, like the spokes of a wheel, are drawn out from the title. The students then brainstorm for ideas that might go into the story. In random order, each idea is briefly noted against a spoke in the wheel.

The class then reviews the ideas and decides upon an appropriate starting point for the story. A number '1' is written against that idea. How will the story develop? The children determine the order in which the other ideas will be used, and the appropriate numbers are written against each spoke. Some of the ideas may not be used and can be erased. Other ideas may need to be added at this stage, and numbered accordingly. The students now use the bank of ideas recorded on the story planner to start writing their own stories.

By preparing the draft ideas and then discussing the best order in which to write them, the students have tackled two of the most difficult problems they face when composing, namely planning and sequencing.

Step-by-step planning

A task-approach strategy with a 'prompt word' can help some students to organize their thoughts for writing. An example is LESSER ('LESSER helps me write more!').

L = List your ideas.
E = Examine your list.
S = Select your starting point.
S = Sentence one tells us about this first idea.
E = Expand on this first idea with another sentence.
R = Read what you have written. Revise if necessary. Repeat for the next paragraph.

Expanding an idea

Begin by writing a short, declarative sentence that makes one statement.

We have too many cars coming into our school parking area.

Next, write two or three sentences which add information to, or are connected with, the first sentence. Leave two lines below each new sentence.

We have too many cars coming into our school parking area.
The noise they make often disturbs our lessons.

The cars travel fast and could knock someone down.

What can we do about this problem?

Now write two more sentences in each space.

We have too many cars coming into our school parking area.
The noise they make often disturbs our lessons. The drivers sound their horns and rev the engines. Sometimes I can't even hear the teacher speak.
The cars travel fast and could knock someone down. I saw a girl step out behind one yesterday. She screamed when it reversed suddenly.
What can we do about this problem? Perhaps there should be a sign saying 'NO CARS ALLOWED'. They might build some speed humps or set a speed limit.

Edit the sentences into appropriate paragraphs. Combine some short statements into longer, complex sentences. Edit for style. Use of a word processor makes each of these steps much faster and makes the process of editing and checking spelling easier.

The teacher demonstrates this procedure, incorporating ideas from the class. Students are then given guided practice and further modelling over a series of lessons, each time using a different theme.

Shuffling ideas

A strategy that helps to establish the value of planning and sequencing points before writing is that of 'shuffling ideas'. As ideas for writing are generated, each is written on a separate card. Finally, the cards are reordered until the most suitable and appealing sequence is obtained. The sequence can become the focal point for discussion between teacher and student or between two students. The procedure avoids the problem of reluctance which sometimes occurs when a student is asked to revise and rewrite a draft.

Group editing

To assist further with the development of revising and editing skills the whole class (or a small group of students) might look at a duplicated essay, or one displayed by an overhead projector, and make suitable alterations and improvements to it after discussion. The focus might be on adding more descriptive words, or on making ideas clearer by including more detail.

Sentence combining

Another useful editing activity is that of 'sentence combining'. Often the lower-achieving students will tend to write very short sentences, lacking fluency and variety. Suitable exercises can be devised to help students develop skills in combining sentences.

I went to watch netball.
I went with my friend Hannah.
We had a good time.
Our team got beaten.

These sentences can be combined in various ways, e.g.:

When I went to watch netball with my friend Hannah we had a good time, but our team got beaten.

To avoid the common problem of failure to generalize this type of learning to new contexts, students' attention will need to be directed back to this experience when they are editing and improving their own written work.

Writing a summary

The complementary skills of reading and writing come together in the task of writing a summary or precis of a passage, a chapter or a book. Casazza (1992) suggests that summarizing text helps students to focus on key points and to sequence these in writing in a coherent way. She presents three basic rules for preparing a summary, and states that students should be taught these rules explicitly and trained to use them independently. First they must identify the main idea and generate a statement which embodies the main idea. Then they identify minor or irrelevant detail and redundant information. Finally, they must combine statements or ideas which have similar information, and link these to the main idea statement.

By using an overhead projector the teacher can model the application of the three rules to several different pieces of text. Students are then given guided practice and feedback. Casazza (1992) also advocates having students evaluate the summaries of their peers and of the teacher. A checklist can be used with a rating scale to allow for appraisal using such descriptions as:

- identifies topic clearly;
- identifies main idea correctly;
- paraphrases accurately;
- omits irrelevant detail;
- combines similar ideas coherently;
- stays within required word-length.

The use of such a checklist is also recommended by Zipprich (1995) and Martin and Manno (1995).

Even this degree of direct guidance in summary writing is insufficient for some students. They need to have the task broken down into much more manageable steps. One or more of the following procedures can be helpful to such students.

- The teacher provides a set of true and false statements based on the text just read. The statements are presented on the sheet in random order. The student must read each statement and place a tick against those which are true. The student then decides the most logical sequence in which to arrange the true statements. When written out these statements provide a good summary of the text.

- The teacher provides some sentence beginnings, in a sequence which will provide a framework for the summary. The student completes the unfinished sentences and writes the summary.

- The teacher provides a summary with key words or phrases omitted. The words may be presented below the passage in random order, or clues may be given in terms of initial letters of word required, or dashes to represent each letter of the word. The student completes the passage by supplying the missing words.

- Simple multiple-choice questions can be presented. The questions may deal with the main ideas from the text and with supporting detail. In selecting the appropriate responses and writing these down the student creates a summary.

Word processors

Undoubtedly, the arrival of word processors in the classroom heralded a new opportunity for students of all levels of ability to enter the realm of writing and composing with enthusiasm and enjoyment. In particular, students with learning difficulties can gain confidence in creating, editing, erasing and publishing their own unique material through a medium which holds attention and is infinitely patient (Kerin 1990; Montague and Fonseca 1993).

In the previous chapter the use of word processors for developing lower-order reading skills such as word recognition and phonic decoding was discussed. Their use is not, however, confined to such drill and practice procedures, and higher-order reading comprehension and writing skills can be enhanced through word processing (Au and Bruce 1990; Lewis and Doorlag 1991).

The present writer found that students with learning difficulties need first to develop at least some basic keyboard skills if the word processing is to be achieved without frustration. It is usually necessary to teach only the most essential skills to enable the student to access the program, type the work and save the material at regular intervals. Even this simple level of operation can give some students a tremendous boost to confidence and can encourage risk-taking in writing and composing. Printing can be left to the teacher or classroom aide in the beginning stages.

By combining the conference approach to writing with the use of a word processor, the student's story in draft form can be printed, first without using the in-built spelling check. Student and partner, or student and teacher can then check the print-out and discuss good features of the story, and identify sentences or phrases or particular words that might be improved. It is useful for the teacher to note which words the student can self-correct in terms of spelling, and which misspelt words are not detected without assistance. A second draft of the story can then be made after the student does the necessary revisions and uses the spell-check.

Lewis and Doorlag (1991) reviewed research evidence on the benefits of using word processors with learning disabled students. Among their conclusions were that word processing seems to be of great benefit to students who don't usually write very much, and to those with the most severe spelling problems.

MOTIVATING THE RELUCTANT WRITER

Book production

Extending the earlier suggestion of using small booklets, it is useful to have the students prepare somewhat more ambitious products. The following topics have proved to be particularly motivating for reluctant writers.

'A book about myself'   My family. Where I live. What I do. Things I like. Things I hate. My friends. The book can also include factual material: e.g. height, weight, pulse rate, etc.

'A book about this school'   Descriptions. Photos. Plans. Interviews with teachers.

'A book about my class'   Descriptions. Photos. Interviews.

'Our book of jokes'   Don't forget to censor these before parents' evening!

'Our neighbourhood'   Location. Personalities. Shops. Industries. Entertainment.

'Our visit to . . .'   Impressions and summaries following field trips and excursions. (Don't make this a regular feature of *every* trip or you will find yourself in the position of the old joke where a class was on an excursion and two children saw a UFO land in a field. 'Look! Look!', one child began. 'Shut up you fool!' said the other. 'We'll only have to write about it.')

'A visitor's guide to Planet Zargok'   Sections describing the people, the cities, the food, the transport, the animals and plants. A dictionary section to translate the planet's vocabulary into English.

'My book of monsters'   An opportunity for creepy creatures to become the focus of both artwork and story-writing.

Video or film scripts

Much use is made of improvised drama, without a set script, in both primary and secondary classrooms. A useful variation is to get the students, particularly the reluctant writers, to prepare a script in detail and then film or record the action after rehearsal. The combination of practical work, writing and production of something which can then be seen and discussed is usually adequate stimulus for even the most reluctant student.

'You write the rest' stories: an anecdote

One technique which this writer used when teaching in special classes was to prepare a story about a popular character currently appearing on children's television. The story is told or read to the class for enjoyment; but just when it gets to a cliff-hanger climax, the story stops. What happens next? Individuals can write their own episode or you can brainstorm ideas from the group.

It was particularly useful to type a simplified version of the story, spreading this over several half-pages of a small booklet and providing a frame for an illustration above each passage of print. The children, who were not proficient readers, could cope with the simplified material since it dealt with a story just read to them; the plot was familiar. The second half of the booklet was blank to allow the children to write their own endings and provide illustrations.

This example is from a *Doctor Who* story. Teacher's story ends with this paragraph:

He was in for a shock when he switched on the televiewer. The giant spiders were spinning a web over the Tardis. The strands looked as strong as rope. Suddenly the lights went out. He dashed to the controls and frantically flicked the switches. Nothing happened. The Tardis refused to move. They were trapped!!!

Patricia's story continues:

Dr. Who was cross. The spiders sat on the Tardis and sang a jungle song. Dr. Who took the plants he had collected and did an experiment on them. The plants turned into little people. The doctor put the little people outside and they began to chew through the web. Soon the wind came and the web blew away. The Tardis was free again.

Letter writing and project exchange between schools

It is very useful indeed to set up an exchange system between schools, particularly if one school is in the city and one in the country. It can start out as a 'pen pal' scheme but extend to exchange of class books, project materials, etc., and even result in visits between schools.

Choose a story

Prepare eight sets of small cards (four cards in each set), to correspond with the following categories:

Hero
Heroine
Action
Setting
Time
Feeling
Thing
Weather

In each category provide four different words. For example:

Hero: Batman, yourself, Spiderman, the Prime Minister
Heroine: Spiderwoman, Helga the Horrible, yourself, Cinderella
Action: fighting, escaping, flying, chasing
Setting: the jungle, under your bed, the moon, on a train
Time: 100 years ago, 100 years from now, midnight, school holiday
Feeling: anger, love, excitement, fear
Thing: monster, ghost, wild pig, meat pie
Weather: stormy, windy, cold, heatwave

Students take turns to choose, read and replace one card from each set until each student has the eight ingredients for a story they are to write. They can introduce the elements in any order in the story. The results can be shared with the group at the end of the session.

Over to you: *Using the frameworks*

- Apply any of the suggestions from this chapter to a student with learning problems.

- Evaluate the effectiveness of the strategy, and note any modifications you may have to make.

- List some stimulating opening lines, or introductory paragraphs, for stories which students can complete.

- Devise a set of notes and prompts which could be used by a student to help him or her write a brief summary from a passage of text.

SUMMARY

This chapter has provided practical suggestions for helping poorly motivated and lower-ability students to write. Most of the techniques can be used within the normal classroom setting and require only minor modifications to the mainstream language arts programme.

The reader will have noted in this and earlier chapters the importance placed upon the teacher modelling effective ways of approaching a task, whether it be generating and composing ideas for a story, or revising the final draft. Students should be helped to develop and use effective task-approach skills for themselves, and in doing so, to feel good about the work they produce and the improvements they make.

Discussion point

- Discuss with your colleagues their ideas for writing which have proved to be very successful with mixed-ability classes.

- Devise a set of notes and prompts which could be used by a student to help him or her write a brief summary from a passage of text.

- 'Students with learning difficulties find writing very difficult and frustrating. It is best to avoid setting them too many writing tasks.' Discuss this statement.

Further reading

Australian Council for Educational Research (1995) *The Best of Set: Writing*, Camberwell: ACER.

Danielson, K. and LaBonty, J. (1994) *Integrating Reading and Writing Through Children's Literature*, Boston: Allyn and Bacon.

Dowis, C.L. and Schloss, O. (1992) 'The impact of mini-lessons on writing skills', *Remedial and Special Education* 13, 5: 34–42.

Englert, C.S. and Mariage, T.V. (1991) 'Shared understandings: structuring the writing experience through dialogue', *Journal of Learning Disabilities* 24, 6: 330–42.

Graham, S. and Harris, K. (1989) 'Improving learning disabled students' skills at composing essays', *Exceptional Children* 56, 3: 201–14.

O'Brien, D. (1992) *Writing in the Primary School*, Melbourne: Longman Cheshire.

Pumfrey, P. and Elliott, C. (1990) *Children's Difficulties in Reading, Writing and Spelling*, London: Falmer.

Smith, B. (1994) *Through Writing to Reading*, London: Routledge.

Smith, D.G. (1996) 'Choose your own writing', *The Reading Teacher* 49, 5: 420–4.

Sperling, M. (1996) 'Revisiting the writing-speaking connection: challenges for research on writing and writing instruction', *Review of Educational Research* 66, 1: 53–86.

Temple, C.A. (1993) *The Beginnings of Writing* (3rd edn), Boston: Allyn and Bacon.

Chapter 11

Developing spelling skills

The contention that learning to spell should primarily take place through incidental learning from reading and writing is highly questionable for students with special needs, as well as for many normally achieving students. In our opinion, advocates of incidental learning in spelling are overly optimistic.

(Graham and Harris 1994: 283)

For many low-achieving students, spelling continues to present a problem long after reading skills have improved. This is sometimes due to the fact that too little attention is given to the explicit teaching of spelling skills and strategies. Instruction in spelling no longer features as prominently now in the primary school curriculum as it did some years ago.

WHOLE LANGUAGE PERSPECTIVES ON SPELLING

The advent of the whole language philosophy has seen the teaching of spelling become fully integrated into children's daily writing activities, rather than being treated as a subject in its own right. It is argued that spelling instruction is kept within a meaningful context at all times when students are helped individually to spell the words they need to use as they write. This integrated approach is deemed to be the 'natural' way of acquiring spelling skill, and is therefore regarded as preferable to any form of direct teaching based upon the content of a predetermined spelling programme or word list. Children are taught the precise information they need at the exact moment that they need it. For example, a student may want to write the word 'please' but is unsure of the /ea/ sound within it. The teacher spells the word, and takes a moment to explain that often the letters 'ea' together make the long /e/ sound, as in sea, feast, deal, leap, seat, read, etc.

Used alone, the integrated approach to spelling seems to be inadequate for students with learning difficulties (Graham, Harris and Loynachan 1996). In classrooms containing twenty-eight or more students it is virtually impossible to find the necessary time to devote to such a personalized system. Even if a few moments can be devoted to each student within the writing lesson, helping the student with a spelling difficulty for a very brief period of time inevitably results in very superficial coverage of the specific spelling principle. Simply because the teacher has explained a particular rule on one day, there is no reason to suppose that the student will remember this information the next day unless it is reviewed and practised.

Dealing with words and spelling principles only as they are needed can also result in undesirable fragmentation of experience. For example, a child taught to spell the word 'fight' may not recognize that it belongs to the word family comprising right, sight, might, tight, light, bright, flight, etc. An essential part of understanding how words are constructed involves students in recognizing that many words share predictable letter patterns. It does not make sense to leave students to pick up this important knowledge through incidental learning. As Templeton (1992: 455) has observed, 'Spelling knowledge grows out of, and supports reading, writing and vocabulary study. *It also grows out of examining words in and of themselves*' (emphasis added).

DEVELOPMENTAL STAGES IN SPELLING ACQUISITION

It is important for teachers to be aware of the normal stages of development through which children pass on their way to becoming proficient spellers (Bentley 1990). Students pass through these stages at different rates, and it is unrealistic to expect a student to achieve a level of independence or accuracy in spelling which is beyond his or her current developmental level. The stages have been described in the following way:

Stage 1: Prephonetic   At this stage the child 'plays' at writing (often using capital letters) in imitation of the writing of others. There is no connection between these scribbles and speech sounds or real words.

Stage 2: Phonetic   At this stage the child relies mainly upon auditory perception and phonemic awareness. In the child's spelling there is evidence of an emerging knowledge of letter-sound correspondences, picked up through incidental learning. The invented words are quite recognizable as children begin to apply basic phonic principles as they write. Sometimes the phoneme they identify is equated with the letter name rather than the sound, as for example in 'rsk' (ask), 'yl' (while), 'lefnt' (elephant).

Toward the end of the phonetic stage, approximations move much nearer to regular letter-sound correspondences, as in 'sed' (said) or 'becos' (because). Even at this stage, some children have difficulty in identifying the second or third consonant in a letter-string and may write 'srong' (strong) or 'bow' (blow). Or they may fail to identify correctly the actual sound in the word and may write the incorrect letter, as in 'druck' (truck), 'jriv' (drive), 'sboon' (spoon).

It should be noted that the majority of individuals with poor spelling have reached this phonetic stage in their development but have not progressed beyond it. They now need to be taught to use strategies such as visual checking of words and spelling by analogy, in order to move to the next stage.

Stage 3: Transitional At this stage there is clear evidence of a more sophisticated understanding of word structure. The child has become aware of within-word letter strings and syllable junctures. Common letter sequences, such as -ough, -ious, -ea-, -ai-, -aw-, -ing, etc., are used much more reliably. The children who are gaining real mastery over spelling at this stage also begin to spell by analogy, using words they know already in order to spell words they have never written before.

Stage 4: Independence At this stage the child has mastery of quite complex grapho-phonic principles, and also uses visual imagery more effectively when writing and checking familiar words. Flexible use is made of a wide range of spelling, proof-reading and self-correcting strategies.

DO WE SPELL BY EYE, BY EAR OR BY HAND?

The answer to the question do we spell by eye, by ear or by hand is almost certainly that we use all three modalities on the way to becoming proficient spellers. However, for many years teachers have regarded the encoding of words as predominantly a *visual* processing skill. For this reason, if students were fortunate enough to receive some guidance in spelling, the strategies they were taught to use have been mainly concerned with improving visual memory for word forms, for example the 'look-cover-write-check' strategy. Much less importance has been attached by teachers to *auditory* processing strategies as they relate to spelling. Indeed, some authorities actively dissuade students from attending closely to the sound values heard within spoken words since the individual letters used to represent these sounds may not be entirely predictable. It is argued that because up to three words in every ten are not written precisely as they sound, with perfect letter-to-sound translations, it is not beneficial to teach children to utilize phonic information when spelling. Counter to this argument is evidence to suggest that learning to read and learning to spell, particularly in the beginning stages, are far more closely related to auditory processing abilities than we previously believed (Goswami 1992).

Let us consider the general contributions made to spelling acquisition by visual perception, auditory perception and kinaesthesia.

Visual perception: spelling by eye

Very proficient spellers appear to make great use of visual information when writing words. It is obvious that visual clues are, indeed, extremely important for accurate spelling. The most common way of checking one's own spelling and detecting errors is to look carefully at the written word and ask oneself 'Does this word look right?' Strategies which involve the deliberate use of visual imagery, such as look-cover-write-check, are very effective for the learning of what are termed 'irregular' words, those with unpredictable letter-to-sound correspondences. To this extent we certainly do learn to spell by eye. The effective use of visual perception in learning to spell results in the student building up a memory-store of visual images of word patterns and of commonly occurring letter strings. The knowledge in this store can be called upon when the student attempts to write an unfamiliar word.

Learning to spell 'by eye' does not mean, however, that learners simply acquire incidentally the ability to spell by 'seeing' words as they read. Just 'looking' at words does not seem to be enough for most learners. It is necessary for them to examine a word very carefully, with every intention of trying to commit its internal structure and configuration to memory. As this behaviour does not come naturally to every learner, it is important that any student who lacks this experience be given the necessary instruction and practice. By implication, this may mean devoting specific time and attention to word study, over and above any help given to individual students as they write. It is most unlikely that such an important skill as word analysis could be adequately developed through incidental learning alone.

It must be noted that there is some indication that even good spellers may not really spell by visual imagery alone to the extent we once imagined. They may use visual memory effectively only to check the final appearance of a word written mainly by using other cues (Adams 1990). The current viewpoint is that spelling actually involves the co-ordinated use of several different complementary process and strategies, including listening carefully to the component sounds and syllables within the word and by developing kinaesthetic images of the most commonly written words (Weckert 1989; O'Brien 1992).

Auditory perception: spelling by ear

Research has indicated that in the early stages of learning to read and spell it is important that a child can identify the different sound units within spoken words (phonemic awareness). The basic knowledge upon which successful reading and spelling develop seems to depend upon the child's awareness that spoken words can be broken down into smaller units and that these units can be represented by letters. In order to spell, young children in the first years of schooling may have to use auditory perception to a much greater extent than older children, simply because they have not yet had as much exposure to letter patterns within words through daily reading and writing experiences. Building up a bank of visual images of words and letter strings takes time and experience. The extent to which early attempts at spelling do rely upon attention to sounds in words and to letter–sound correspondences is evident in children's early attempts at inventing spelling.

Those who doubt the importance of auditory perception for spelling might ponder the fact that the spelling of many dyslexic individuals is frequently described as 'bizarre' in the sense that the letters written down often have no logical connection with the speech sounds they represent in the word (Perfetti 1992). It is also clear that one of the most common problems exhibited by many dyslexic students is an inability to analyse words they hear in terms of syllable units and separate phonemes (Clark 1992). It is likely that the bizzare spelling is a reflection of this auditory processing problem.

When spelling a word there is actually a complementary association between auditory perception and visual perception. The process of writing an unfamiliar word requires the child first to identify the common sound units within the word, and to match these sound units with the appropriate letter clusters stored as visual images in what is termed 'orthographic memory' (Jorm 1983). Having identified the sound values in the word to be attempted, and having associated these sound units with specific letters, visual perception is then used to check that what the student writes on paper also has the correct appearance.

Kinaesthesia: spelling 'by hand'

Kinaesthesia can be defined as the sensation which produces an awareness of the position and movement of parts of the body by means of sensory nerves within the muscles and joints. Since the spelling of a word is typically produced by the physical action of writing, it is fair to assume that kinaesthetic memory may also be involved in learning to spell. Indeed, the extremely rapid speed and high degree of automaticity with which a competent speller translates a very familiar word, such as 'they', directly from its meaning to its graphic representation, supports the view that motor memory is involved. Nichols (1985: 3) has written, 'Spelling is remembered best in your hand. It is the memory of your fingers moving the pencil to make a word that makes for accurate spelling.' The frequent action of writing may be one of the ways of establishing the stock of images of commonly occurring words and letter strings in orthographic memory. The process of building up orthographic images in memory is also facilitated by the study of word families with common letter sequences, for example, 'gate, date, late, fate, mate, etc. (Varnhagen and Das 1992; Templeton 1992; Gunning 1995).

It is often recommended that we should not think of spelling words letter-by-letter, but rather by concentrating upon the functional letter strings which form common units in many words. This has some implications for the way in which we teach handwriting in the early years of schooling. Some evidence exists to support the notion that it is beneficial to teach young children to join letters together almost from the beginning of their instruction in handwriting, rather than teaching print script first and linked script much later. It is believed that joining the letters together in one smooth action helps children to develop an awareness of common letter strings (Cripps 1990).

The relative contributions of vision, audition and kinaesthesia

The extent to which visual perception, auditory perception and kinaesthesia contribute to the act of spelling a particular word seems to depend upon how familiar the word is to the writer. Unfamiliar words appear to require an analysis into their component sounds before an attempt can be made to write them. What has been written can then be checked for accuracy in terms of visual appearance. For example, when trying to spell the word 'WORK', the /W/ and the /RK/ can probably be encoded from their sound values, but the writer's orthographic visual memory has to be checked for the information that the vowel is O and not E in WORK (Jorm 1983). Very familiar, high-frequency words, such as 'and', 'the' and 'are', etc., are probably written mainly from kinaesthetic memory and checked simultaneously for visual appearance.

INDIVIDUAL DIFFERENCES AMONG SPELLERS

As we have seen, three types of imagery appear to be used in spelling a word:

- visual – the way the word looks;
- auditory – the way the word sounds;
- kinaesthetic – the way the word feels when written.

To this list some experts would add:

- Speech-motor – the way the word 'feels' when spoken.

It seems that some students rely much more heavily on one type of imagery than on another and may need to be taught to use as many types of imagery as possible. For example, as indicated previously, dyslexic students are often found to be particularly weak in phonological skills and they rely too heavily on visual memory for recall of letter patterns. Training them in phonemic awareness and the application of basic phonic knowledge appears to have a positive effect on spelling ability (Ball and Blachman 1991).

Examination of the written work produced by students with learning difficulties can reveal a great deal about their current skills and specific needs in spelling. One of the most common problems is the tendency of the student to be overdependent on phonic knowledge and therefore to write irregular words as if they are regular. They appear to have remained at the phonetic stage of development for too long. Close examination of a student's exercise books, or the use of dictated word lists, will quickly reveal the extent to which the individual has this problem. The students producing these errors seem to lack the necessary strategies for carefully checking the visual appearance of a word, and even when encouraged to proof-read their material will fail to identify the errors.

TEACHING APPROACHES

The whole word approach

This approach requires the student to memorize the overall letter patterns of individual words. Rather than attending to the sounds and syllables within the word, the student attempts to store the image of the word in long-term memory. Research has suggested that children can be trained to focus more attentively on a word and to improve their visual imagery for letter sequences (Sears and Johnson 1986).

To improve visual processing of whole words, one of the simplest aids to make and use is the flashcard. These cards are particularly useful for teaching irregular words and for the student who needs to be weaned away from a predominantly phonetic approach to spelling. The words are introduced to the student on cards about 30cm × 10cm. The word is pronounced clearly, and attention is drawn to any particular features in the printed word which may be difficult to recall later. The child is encouraged to make a 'mental picture' of the word, and examine it. With the eyes closed the child is then told to trace the word in the air. After a few seconds the student writes the word from memory, articulating it clearly as he or she writes. The word is then checked against the flashcard. The writing of the whole word avoids the inefficient letter-by-letter copying habit which some students have developed.

The general look-cover-write-check approach advocated by Peters (1985; Peters and Smith 1993) is based on these principles. To accommodate the possible importance of clear articulation to accurate spelling, some teachers add the word 'say', making the strategy look-say-cover-write-check. The strategy involves the following steps.

• Look very carefully at the word in the list. Say the word clearly. Try to remember every detail. For some students, finger-tracing over the word may help with assimilation and retention of the letter sequence.
• Cover the word so that it cannot be seen.
• Write the word from memory, pronouncing it quietly as you write.
• Check your version of the word with the original. If it is not correct go back through the four steps again until you can produce the word accurately.
• Teachers should check for recall several days and weeks later.

The look-cover-write-check approach is far better than any verbal rote learning and recitation procedure for learning to spell. It gives the student an independent system which can be applied to the study of any irregular words set for homework or to corrections or omissions from free writing. Students can work in pairs where appropriate, to check that the procedure is being followed correctly by the partner. It is claimed that children as young as five years old can be taught this visual strategy for spelling (Peters and Smith 1993).

Several computer programs designed to develop spelling skills have come on to the market (e.g. *Spell It Plus*, Davidson and associates 1991). Teachers should ensure that the way in which the words are presented on the screen causes the students to attend carefully to the sequence of letters, to identify these letter strings within words and to type out the words from memory. Programs which focus too much attention on spelling letter by letter are far less effective.

The phonemic approach

It is inappropriate to use the look-cover-write-check strategy if the target word could be written as it sounds. The phonemic approach encourages students to attend carefully to sounds and syllables within words, and to write down the letters or letter strings most likely to represent these sounds. While it is true that some 30 per cent of English words are not phonemically regular, some 70 per cent of words do correspond reasonably well with their letter-to-sound translations.

The phonic knowledge necessary for this approach goes well beyond knowing the common sounds associated with each single letter. It is necessary to draw on a knowledge of letter strings which represent larger units within words. When students have acquired this level of proficiency the percentage of words which can be spelled as they sound increases very significantly (Jongsma 1990).

The morphemic approach

This approach to spelling teaches the students to use a knowledge of the smallest unit of meaning within a word, the morpheme, to work out its probable spelling. For example, the word 'recovered' comprises three morphemes (re-cover-ed), as does 'unhappiness' (un-happ[y]-ness). The latter example also illustrates the use of a rule (y to i) when combining certain morphemes. When using a morphemic approach, teachers also need to teach these rules.

Spelling rules

Some experts advocate teaching spelling rules to students. The present writer found it difficult to teach spelling rules to students with learning difficulties.

Cripps has said that because rules are often more complex than the word itself they are not recommended (Cripps 1978). In many cases, it is easier to help the students spell the words they genuinely need for their writing, and also teach them the strategies to use when attempting to learn any new word, rather than to drill complex rules. However, rules may be of some value for some students, particularly those of at least average intelligence who have a specific learning disability. The rules which are simple and have few exceptions are obviously of value and should be explicitly taught (e.g. 'i' before 'e' except after 'c').

Dictation

Dictation has traditionally been used for testing students. However, unless the results are to be used for diagnostic purposes, e.g. the analysis of errors, there is little to support the continued use of dictation exercises.

It is sometimes suggested that dictation develops listening skills and concentration, and at the same time gives students experience of words in context. It is recommended under this system that the material be presented in written form for the children to study *before* it is dictated. In this way there is an opportunity to point out any particularly difficult words.

Another approach encourages proof-reading and self-correction. An unseen passage at an appropriate level of difficulty is dictated for students to write. They are then given a period of time to check and alter any words which they think are incorrect, perhaps using a different coloured pen. The teacher then checks the work and can observe two aspects of the student's performance. First, it is useful to look at the words the child has been able to correct (or at least knows to be wrong). Second, the teacher can record words which were in fact wrong but were not noticed by the student. If, based on their level of difficulty, these words should be known by the student, the teacher must make every effort to teach their correct spelling since they have become firmly set as incorrect responses.

Finally the use of phonic dictation, where the teacher deliberately stresses the sequence of sounds in a tricky word or breaks words into syllables, can be helpful in developing a student's sensitivity to the phonemic components of words.

Should spelling lists be used?

The notion that lists can be compiled which contain words which *all* students should know and use at a particular year or grade level has, to some extent, been abandoned. However, spelling lists continue to form the core of many classroom spelling programmes. The question most often asked by teachers is, 'Do students learn to spell best from lists?' If the question refers to lists of words which individual students actually use and need in their writing, the answer is certainly 'yes'. If the lists are based on other criteria, e.g. words grouped according to visual or phonemic similarity, the decision to use such a list with a particular student or group of students must be made in the light of their specific learning needs.

The value of lists or word groups is that they may help the student to establish an awareness of common letter sequences, e.g. -ight, -ought. This awareness may help a student take a more rational approach to tackling an unfamiliar word. The limitation of formal lists is that they always fail to supply a particular word a student needs at the appropriate time. The most useful list from the point of view of the weakest spellers will be one compiled according to personal needs and common errors. The list might be given the unofficial title 'Words I find difficult'. A copy of this list can be kept in the back of the student's exercise book and used when he or she is writing a rough draft or proof-reading a final draft of a piece of work.

DEVELOPING STRATEGIC SPELLERS

Students have become truly independent in their spelling skills when they can look at a list of words and select the most appropriate strategy to use for learning each word. For example, they need to be able to look at a word and decide for themselves whether it is phonemically irregular or regular. For an irregular word, they may need to apply the look-cover-write-check strategy, coupled perhaps with repeated writing of the word for practice. For some irregular words they may also need to call upon prior knowledge of simple rules about doubling letters, or dropping or changing a letter. If the word is regular they need to recognize that they can spell it easily from its component sounds. When students can operate at this level the shift is from rote learning to an emphasis on studying words rationally.

This level of independence does not come easily to all students. Many individuals need to be taught how to learn material. Some students, left to their own devices, fail to develop any systematic approach. They may just look at the word. They may recite the spelling alphabetically. They may copy letter-by-letter rather than writing the whole word. They may use no particular strategy at all, believing that learning to spell is beyond them. Any serious attempt at helping children with spelling difficulties will involve determining *how* they set about learning a word or group of words. Where a student has no systematic approach it is essential that he or she be taught one.

In cognitive and metacognitive approaches to spelling instruction, students are taught specific self-regulatory strategies to use when learning new words or checking the accuracy of spelling at the proof-reading stage of writing. For example, they are taught to ask themselves, 'How many syllables do I hear in this word?; Do I have the right number of syllables in what I have written?; I'll try it again. Does this word look correct?', etc. According to Wong (1986: 172), 'Effective spelling instruction appears to contain two components: knowledge of phonics and knowledge of spelling strategies'. In particular, spelling strategies must include steps that cause the students to check for accuracy without being constantly reminded to do so.

As with all other examples of strategy training described in this book, the teacher's key role is to model effective strategies, to 'think aloud' and demonstrate ways of going about the task of spelling, checking and self-correcting.

REMEDIAL APPROACHES

Simultaneous oral spelling

This approach was first developed by Gillingham and Stillman in 1960. It has been applied very successfully by Bryant and Bradley (1985) for remediation of spelling problems in individual tutorial settings, and is appropriate for any age level. The approach involves five steps:

- select the word you wish to learn, and have the teacher pronounce it clearly;
- pronounce the word clearly yourself while looking carefully at the word;
- say each syllable in the word (or break a single syllable word into onset and rime);
- name the letters in the word twice;
- write the word, naming each letter as you write it.

Repeated writing

The practice of having a student correct an error, by writing the correct version of the word several times is believed by some teachers to serve no useful purpose. They consider that it is a form of rote learning that can be carried out without conscious effort on the part of the learner, and that words practised in this way are not remembered later. It is true that if the student carrying out the repeated writing is thinking of other things, or is distracted by noise or activity, the procedure is of little value. However, repeated writing of a target word can be very helpful if the learner has every intention of trying to remedy an error and is attending fully to the task. It is one way in which kinaesthetic images of words can be more firmly established.

Old Way: New Way method

Lyndon (1989) has identified the psychological construct of 'proactive inhibition' as a possible reason for the failure of many conventional remedial methods to actually help a student 'unlearn' incorrect responses, such as habitual errors in spelling. Proactive inhibition (or proactive interference) is the term used to describe the situation where previously learned information interferes with one's ability to remember new information or to acquire a new response. What the individual already knows is protected from change.

Lyndon's approach, called 'Old Way: New Way' uses the student's error as the starting point for change. A memory of the old way of spelling of the word is used to activate later an awareness of the new (correct) way of spelling the word. The following steps and procedures are used in Old Way: New Way:

- Student writes the word in the usual (incorrect) form.
- Teacher and student agree to call this the 'old way' of spelling that word.
- Teacher shows student a 'new way' (correct way) of spelling the word.
- Attention is drawn to the similarities and differences between the old and the new.
- Student writes word again in the old way.
- Student writes word in the new way, and discusses the differences.
- Repeat five such writings of old way, new way and articulation of differences.
- Write the word the new way six times, using different colour pens or in different styles. Older students may be asked to write six different sentences using the word in its 'new' form.
- Revise the word or words taught after a two-week interval.
- If necessary, repeat this procedure every two weeks until the new response is firmly established.

The Directed Spelling Thinking Activity (DSTA)

This approach is advocated by Graham, Harris and Loynachan (1996) for use with learning disabled students. It is basically a word-study activity in which a group of students are helped to compare, contrast and categorize two or more words based on discovery of points of similarity and difference. The goal is to raise the students' awarenesss of spelling patterns and the more complex grapho-phonic principles. For example, students may explore words with the long /a/ sound, as in 'pay', 'pail', 'male', etc. They discover that the long /a/ is represented not only by 'ay', but also by 'ai' (nail) and by the letter 'a' in several words with the final 'silent e' (as in lake, mate, made, late, etc.). The students then classify other similar words into these groups, or decide that a particular word is an exception to the principle. Follow-up activities might include looking for words conforming to the rule in reading material, scanning their own writing for such words, adding similar words to a class list over a period of time.

SOME FINAL POINTS

When planning an individualized programme in spelling the following points should be kept in mind.

- For the least able spellers daily attention will be needed, with weekly revision and testing for mastery.

- Over a period of time, collect a list of words frequently needed by students to whom you are giving special help. Use this list for regular review and assessment.

- Once a special programme is established, students should always work on specific words misspelled in free writing lessons, as well as on more general word lists or word families in order to develop insight into word structure.

- Since repetition and overlearning are important, it is useful to have a range of games and word puzzles available to reinforce the spelling of important words. The games must be closely matched to the objectives of the programme, or they may simply keep students amused without leading to improvement.

- Teachers in high schools should try to give students help in learning to spell words from specific subject areas: e.g. ingredients, temperature, chisel, theory, etc.

- Use some form of visual record of improvement, an individual progress chart or simple graph to indicate the number of new words mastered each week.

- When making a correction to a word, a student should rewrite the whole word not merely erase the incorrect letters.

- The value of having students spell words aloud is very questionable, as spelling is essentially a writing activity. The visual appearance, and the flow of the letters in sequence, provide important clues to the speller which are absent when the word is spelled aloud.

- A neat, careful style of handwriting which can be executed swiftly and easily by the student is an important factor associated with spelling ability. It cannot be inferred that good handwriting *per se* causes good spelling; but laboured handwriting and uncertain letter formation almost certainly inhibit the easy development of spelling habits at an automatic response level.

Over to you: Putting it all together

Write a brief article for a parents' magazine indicating ways in which spelling can be taught in a mixed-ability class of children in the age range 7 years to 9 years. Also suggest strategies parents might use at home to assist their children to improve their spelling skills.

SUMMARY

Most of the techniques for teaching and improving spelling described above can be used within the normal classroom setting and require only minor modifications to the mainstream language arts programme. It is implied in this chapter that teachers need to set aside time each week for word study, otherwise this important topic may never receive the systematic attention it deserves. However, it is equally important that spelling skills are also tackled within the context of the children's daily reading and writing experiences. Too much attention to word-study in isolation will develop skills that do not generalize to real writing situations.

Discussion points

- 'Spelling ability is caught, not taught.' Discuss this statement.

- How might a classroom teacher develop a core list of words most commonly needed by students in their daily writing? How might such a list be used within the language arts curriculum in that class?

- Examine and evaluate some computer programs designed to increase spelling ability.

Further reading

Andrews, M. (1994) *Reading and Spelling Made Simple*, Camberwell: Australian Council for Educational Research.

Bentley, D. (1990) *Teaching Spelling: Some Questions Answered*, Earley: University of Reading.

Cheetham, J.S. (1990) *Teach your Child to Spell*, Melbourne: Hyland House.

Dykes, B. and Thomas, C. (1989) *Spelling Made Easy*, Sydney: Hale and Iremonger.

Fehring, H. and Thomas, V. (1989) *Spelling Companion for Writers*, Sydney: Horwitz Grahame.

Graham, S., Harris, K.R. and Loynachan, C. (1994) 'The spelling for writing list', *Journal of Learning Disabilities* 27: 210–14.

MacArthur, C.A., Graham, S., Haynes, J.B. and DeLaPaz, S. (1996) 'Spelling checkers and students with learning disabilities: performance comparisons and impact on spelling', *Journal of Special Education* 30, 1: 35–57.

Peters, M.L. (1985) *Spelling: Caught or Taught? A New Look* (2nd edn), London: Routledge.

Peters, M.L. and Smith, B. (1993) *Spelling in Context*, Windsor: NFER-Nelson.

Pumfrey, P. and Elliott, C. (1990) *Children's Difficulties in Reading, Writing and Spelling*, London: Falmer.

Watkins, G. and Hunter-Carsch, M. (1995) 'Prompt spelling: a practical approach to paired spelling', *Support for Learning* 10, 3: 133–8.

Wirtz, C.L., Gardner, R., Weber, K. and Bullara, D. (1996) 'Using self-correction to improve the spelling performance of low-achieving third graders', *Remedial and Special Education* 17, 1: 48–58.

Chapter 12

Developing numeracy and problem-solving skills

> In striving for educational excellence and higher standards we must
> provide students with disabilities with instruction to help them become
> problem-solvers and move beyond rote application of basic skills.
>
> (Parmar, Cawley and Frazita 1996: 427)

Many children with disabilities and learning problems experience difficulty
in acquiring number concepts and coping with the demands of calculation
and problem-solving. In this chapter some of the reasons for this situation
will be discussed. Teaching methods will be examined, and suggestions will
be made for assessing students' abilities in basic mathematics. Practical ideas
for programming for students' individual needs will be presented.

CONTEMPORARY APPROACHES TO MATHEMATICS TEACHING

Constructivism

In most primary schools today, mathematics teaching utilizes a 'constructivist' approach, often referred to as 'process maths' or 'activity-based'
mathematics. Rather than using explicit teaching methods based on the
transmission of information and the direct teaching of skills, the teacher's
role now is to create learning situations which provide opportunities for
children to discover mathematical relationships, solve real problems and
construct meaning for themselves (Green 1993; Elliott and Garnett 1994;
DeVries and Zan 1995). It is believed that constructivist methods have most
to offer in the development of higher-order cognitive skills and strategies.

Constructivist approaches are not without their critics (e.g. Ernest 1996;
Harris and Graham 1996). The notion that mathematics can be taught
successfully by the same type of student-centred, immersion approach as is
advocated for language arts learning has been challenged by Hunting (1996).
He suggests that there is so much for students to learn in the domain of
mathematics that skilled teaching and the efficient use of time are essential

prerequisite ingredients for the effective classroom. It is also remarked that process and discovery methods appear to be unsuccessful with some children, and may even be a primary cause of their learning difficulties. Some students appear to make better progress when directly taught (Pressley and McCormick 1995).

The conclusion to be reached is that a balanced approach to the teaching of mathematics must include a significant measure of explicit teaching, as well as the valuable 'hands-on' activities and situations which typify constructivistic programmes. The amount of explicit instruction required will vary from student to student, with the direct teaching being of most benefit for students with learning difficulties and disabilities. The perspective presented in this chapter reflects this conclusion.

Group work

The use of an explicit teaching approach does not mean that the teacher makes no use of group work and collaborative learning in the mathematics classroom. Studies have shown that lessons which include well-planned group work do facilitate student achievement and can increase motivation (Good, Mulryan and McCaslin 1992). Group activities which involve students in discussion and the sharing of ideas appear to help individuals negotiate a better understanding of key concepts and processes. It should be noted, however, that certain students don't seem to gain as much from small group processes, particularly those who remain passive and allow other students to make decisions and do most of the work. Teachers need to recognize this problem and attempt to structure group work in such a way that all students can usefully participate.

Another problem associated with group work in mathematics is the paucity of curriculum materials specifically designed for collaborative learning. It is usually left to the teacher to develop appropriate resources, and the additional work involved may result in some teachers opting out of this pattern of organization. It is not uncommon to find classes physically arranged for group work, with four or five students seated together, but actually working on *individual* mathematics assignments (Hastings and Schwieso 1995). This arrangement results in poorer achievement, probably due to difficulties in attending to task.

QUALITY OF INSTRUCTION

Sometimes the instruction given for students with learning difficulties in mathematics does not match their current aptitudes or learning rates (Elliott and Garnett 1994). The following features are characteristic of poor-quality instruction for students with a limited aptitude for mathematics.

- At some stage in the students' schooling the teacher's pacing of the work has outstripped the students' ability to assimilate the concepts and skills, and they have fallen behind and become discouraged.

- There was too little structuring of 'discovery learning' or 'process maths' situations, so they failed to abstract or remember anything from them. For many students the value of experiential learning will be lost unless the follow-up is carefully structured and consolidated.

- The teacher's use of language in explaining mathematical relationships or posing questions may not have matched the students' level of comprehension.

- Abstract symbols may have been introduced too early in the absence of concrete materials or real-life examples. Concrete aids may have been removed too soon for some students, or may have been used inappropriately and created confusion rather than clarity (Kouba and Franklin 1993; Schwartz and Curcio 1995; Threlfall 1996).

- Students with reading difficulties may have been condemned to a diet of 'pure arithmetic' because they couldn't read the problems in the textbook. Teaching only a set of computational tricks does not amount to efficient teaching (Thornton and Jones 1994). Such tricks are usually rapidly forgotten since they do not constitute meaningful learning.

- The students' grasp of simple relationships in numbers to ten or twenty may not have been fully developed before larger numbers involving complications of place-value were introduced.

- The curriculum may have been presented in a linear sequence, with only a few lessons devoted to one topic before moving on to the next topic. The mathematics programme should be planned as spiral, with key concepts and processes revisited at regular intervals in order to revise them and apply them to new situations. Regular revision is crucial for long-term retention and mastery of knowledge and skills (Dempster 1991). Less effective teaching of mathematics is characterized by infrequent review and revision, demonstrations which are too brief or unclear, insufficient guided practice, and too little corrective feedback (Rosenshine 1986).

Contrary to the beliefs of the more extreme constructivists, effective teachers of mathematics are good at constructing series of lessons that successfully transmit the curriculum content to the learner (Lloyd and Keller 1989; Secada 1992; Rosenshine 1995). Their lessons are typically clear, accurate and rich in examples and demonstrations of a particular concept, process or strategy. The teacher takes an active role in imparting information and skills, while still providing abundant opportunities for active participation by students.

In general, research on teacher effectiveness in the area of mathematics supports the use of a structured approach within a carefully sequenced programme. Evidence seems to prove that effective teachers can provide systematic instruction in mathematics in such a way that understanding can accompany the mastery of number skills and problem-solving strategies with a minimum of confusion. Within such an approach the use of practical work, collaborative group activities and open discussion will always have a vital role in developing understanding and positive attitudes in the learners (Sutton 1992).

In recent years the value of integrating mathematics with other subjects, and particularly using reading and writing skills in mathematics, has been recognized (LeGere1991; Whitin 1995). An integrated approach appears to enhance student motivation and involvement, and reduce the maths anxiety which is said to be present in certain students (Bosch and Bowers 1992). However, an integrated approach does not imply that basic skills of numeracy are devalued or left to incidental learning. It is clear that mastery of basic number skills must be given high priority in any programme (Agudelo-Valderrama 1996).

Manipulatives

The use of equipment, such as Dienes MAB, Cuisenaire Rods, Unifix and Mortensen Materials, is strongly advocated in the early stages of any student's mathematics programme (Schwartz and Curcio 1995). The material is particularly important for students with learning difficulties and learning disabilities as it helps them to retain visual representations of number relationships. The use of apparatus is also helpful for making word problems more visual and concrete (Marsh and Cooke 1996). However, it must be recognized that manipulatives have to be used effectively if students are to form the necessary connections between the materials and the underlying concepts and processes they are designed to illustrate. Problems arise if students come to rely too much on apparatus and do not progress to the pencil-and-paper processing of number relationships (Dougherty and Scott 1993; Therlfall 1996).

A DIAGNOSTIC APPROACH

There exists a variety of reasons to account for some students experiencing difficulty in mastering the facts, concepts and operations in arithmetic and applying these successfully to problem-solving. As with reading, writing and spelling, the most practical first step toward intervention is to ascertain what the student can already do in this area of the curriculum, to locate any specific gaps which may exist and to determine what he or she needs to be taught next. In other words, the diagnostic model presented in an earlier chapter can be applied to the assessment of skills in arithmetic, and can guide programme planning in mathematics.

With any approach to the teaching of mathematics there is an on-going need for regular assessment of individual progress. Periodic checks on the student's understanding of new work are essential; and such checks must usually involve working directly with the student to detect strengths and weaknesses in performance (Robinson and Bartlett 1995). Without this the teacher has little idea whether the student carries out an activity in rote fashion, through the help of other students or with partial or complete understanding.

The first step in the diagnostic evaluation of mathematical skills might involve formal testing of the student, using standardized tests to determine the level at which he or she is functioning. However, standardized tests are of rather limited value for programming purposes since they do not yield a comprehensive picture of a student's broad range of knowledge and skills. Far more useful information can be obtained from teacher-made tests which reflect the true content of the curriculum being taught in that classroom. Curriculum-based assessment is now widely acknowledged as the most helpful method for teachers to link assessment to instructional design. Teacher-made tests can be supplemented with information gleaned from an examination of the student's exercise books and worksheets. The nature of a student's errors can be appraised, and follow-up diagnostic tests which assess proficiency in particular processes can be used. Clarke (1992) and Olssen *et al*. (1994) advocate combining information from anecdotal records, examination of workbooks, practical tests and student self-assessment to obtain a valid picture of a student's current ability.

A task-analytic approach may be taken when attempting to find the point of failure or misunderstanding in basic arithmetical processes. By carefully grading the various steps involved in, say, long division, and providing test items to sample the child's competence at each stage, the teacher can detect the precise point of breakdown in computational skills or understanding. When preparing teacher-made tests in mathematics, it is helpful to include three items at each level of difficulty in order to discriminate between careless errors and persistent errors. An analysis of the actual errors made by the child can then further pinpoint the teaching which needs to be done (Enright and Choate 1993; Howell, Fox and Morehead 1993).

Reisman (1982) strongly advocated that teachers construct their own 'informal mathematical skills inventory' containing test items covering key concepts, knowledge and skills presented in earlier years together with essential material from the current year. Such an inventory can very conveniently indicate precisely what the student can and cannot do, and will assist with the ordering of priorities for teaching.

There are various levels of abstraction involved in diagnostic work in mathematics. Identification of these levels will help a teacher to answer the question 'What can the student do in mathematics if given a little help and guidance?' The levels are concrete, semi-concrete and abstract. At the concrete level the student may be able to solve a problem or complete a process correctly if permitted to manipulate real objects. At the semi-concrete level pictorial representations of the objects, together with the symbols, are sufficient visual information to ensure success. At the abstract level the student must work with the symbols only, either in printed form or as orally dictated by the teacher. During the diagnostic work with the student, the teacher may move up or down within this hierarchy from abstract to concrete, in an attempt to discover the level at which the child can succeed.

It may be helpful to keep the following thoughts in mind when attempting to discover the student's present functional level. Referring to any items which a student fails to solve in a test or during deskwork following a period of instruction, ask yourself these questions:

- *Why* did the student get this item wrong?
- Can he or she carry out the process if allowed to use concrete aids or count on fingers or use a number line, etc.?
- Can he or she explain to me what to do? Ask the student to work through the example step by step. At what point does the student obviously misunderstand?

The value of this last procedure cannot be over-stressed. If a student explains to you how he or she tackles the problem, you are likely to pick up at once the exact point of confusion, and can teach from there. Too often we jump in and reteach the whole process, but still fail to help the student recognize and overcome the precise difficulty.

Howell, Fox and Morehead (1993) advocate close investigation of the actual strategies used by a student in carrying out a computation or solving a problem. A discussion between teacher and student can reveal much about the student's level of confidence, flexibility of thinking and underlying knowledge. According to Salvia and Hughes (1990), teachers should probe for understanding in the following areas when appraising a student's problem-solving abilities: detecting what is called for in a problem; identifying relevant information; selecting correct procedure; estimating an approximate answer; computing the answer; and checking the answer. In many ways, assessing problem-solving skills in mathematics has much in common with assessing comprehension in reading. Additional information on teaching problem-solving strategies is provided later in this chapter.

Teachers must recognize that the main goal in teaching mathematics to *all* students is the development of everyday problem-solving skills (Cawley, Baker-Kroczynski and Urban 1992; Enright and Choate 1993); and diagnosis of a student's current ability in this domain should have high priority.

Three levels of assessment

The following three levels of assessment may help the teacher to design appropriate assessment materials. It is likely that the first two levels will be the most applicable for students with learning difficulties.

Level 1

If the student's performance in basic number is very poor, consider the following points. At this stage almost all the assessments will need to be made at an individual level, using appropriate concrete materials such as toys, blocks, pictures, number cards, etc.

- Check the student's grasp of vocabulary associated with number relationships (e.g. 'bigger than', 'altogether', 'less', 'share', etc.).
- Check the student's conservation of number.

Then check the following knowledge and skills in the following order. Can the student:

- sort objects given one attribute (colour, size, shape, etc.)?
- sort objects given two attributes?
- produce equal sets of objects by one-to-one matching?
- count correctly objects to ten? To twenty?
- recognize numerals to ten? To twenty?
- place number symbols in correct sequence to ten? To twenty?
- write numerals correctly from dictation to ten? To twenty?
- understand ordinal values (fifth, tenth, second, etc.)?
- perform simple addition with numbers below ten in written form (e.g. 3 + 5 =   )? With or without apparatus?
- perform subtraction with numbers below ten, in written form?
- count-on in a simple addition problem?
- answer simple oral problems involving addition or subtraction with numbers below ten?
- recognize coins and paper money (1p 2p 5p 10p 50p £1 or 5¢ 10¢ 20¢ 50¢ $1.00 $2.00)?

Level 2

If the student's performance in mathematics is slightly better than Level 1 consider the following areas. Can the student:

- carry out simple mental addition with numbers below twenty?
- carry out simple mental problem-solving without use of finger-counting or tally marks?
- carry out simple subtraction mentally as above? Is there a marked difference between performance in addition and subtraction?

- perform both vertical and horizontal forms of simple addition?

    3   and $3 + 5 =$
    +5
    —

- understand the commutative law in addition (i.e. that the order of items to be totalled does not matter)? Does the child see for example that $5 + 3$ and $3 + 5$ are bound to give the same total? When counting-on to obtain a total in such problems does the child always count the smaller number on to the larger; or are these problems always solved from left to right regardless? $(2 + 8 =$ $12 + 5 =$).
- understand additive composition (i.e. all the possible ways of producing a given set or total)? For example, 5 is $4 + 1, 3 + 2, 2 + 3, 1 + 4, 5 + 0$.
- understand the complementary or reversible character of addition and subtraction? $(7 + 3 = 10, 10 - 7 = 3, 10 - 3 = 7)$.
- watch an operation demonstrated using concrete material and then record this in written form?
- translate a written equation into a practical demonstration (e.g. using Unifix cubes to demonstrate $12 - 4 = 8$)?
- listen to a simple real-life situation described in words and then work the problem in written form? (Seven people were waiting at the bus stop. When the bus came only three could get on. How many were left to wait for the next bus?) Use numbers below twenty. Can the child work problems at this level mentally?
- recognize and write numerals to fifty?
- tell the time: read a digital clock correctly? An analogue clock to the nearest hour and half-hour?
- recite the days of the week?
- recite the months of the year?

Level 3

If the student is able to succeed with most of the items in the previous levels, or if he/she seems reasonably competent in many areas of basic math, consider these questions. Can the student:

- read and write numbers to 100? To 1000? Can he or she read and write sums of money correctly?
- halve or double numbers mentally?
- add money mentally? Give change by the counting-on method?
- recite the multiplication tables correctly and answer random facts from these tables?
- perform the correct procedures for addition of H T U and Th H T U. Without carrying? With carrying in any column?

- understand place value with T U? With H T U? With Th H T U?
- perform the subtraction algorithm, without exchanging in any column? With exchanging? It is important to note the actual method used by the child to carry out subtraction. Is it 'decomposition' using only the top line of figures; or the 'equal addition' method using top and bottom lines?
- perform the correct steps in the multiplication algorithm? To what level of difficulty?
- perform the correct steps in the division algorithm? To what level of difficulty?
- recognize fractions: ½, ¼, 3½, 7¼, ¹⁄₁₀, 5³⁄₁₀, 0.8, 5.9, etc.
- read and interpret correctly simple word-problems?

Over to you: *Curriculum-based assessment*

Prepare the materials and questions needed in order to carry out assessments at one of the three levels described above.

Devise a simple checklist to enable you to record an individual student's responses to your assessment items. For Level 3 you may be able to locate published arithmetic tests to include in your assessment; but failing this, teacher-designed questions and items are perfectly acceptable. Don't forget to grade your items in each area carefully and where possible include several items at each level of difficulty.

SOME BASIC TEACHING POINTS

Clearly it is impossible within a single chapter to summarize teaching procedures across the complete field of mathematics. One must be selective and is helped in this by Bowd's (1990) statement that in teaching mathematics to students with learning difficulties the two biggest hurdles to overcome will be number fluency and problem-solving. These two areas will be developed in the following pages.

Basic number concepts and skills

Conservation

Basic to all number work is the concept of conservation of number; that is, a group or set composed of N separate items remains a set of that number regardless of how it is arranged or distributed. Up to the age of 5 or even 6 years (and later with disabled learners) the number of items in a set may appear to alter if the members are rearranged spatially. Experience has to be given to children to help them understand conservation of number and not be misled by what their eyes seem to tell them. Much of the preschool and early school experience of sorting, counting, giving out materials, one-to-one matching of objects, etc., should be helping the basic concept of conservation to develop. For some children the process needs to be made more explicit.

The following activities and apparatus may help a student to develop the concept of conservation of number:

- teacher-made cards with pictures, dot patterns, and shapes in different groupings can be sorted into sets of equal size (numbers in sets should be below ten and no numerals will be introduced);
- matching or joining up various patterns with equal numbers of shapes presented on worksheets;
- counting activities to ten (or less) to establish one-to-one correspondence between the number rhyme 'one, two, three . . .' and the actual objects in given sets, and to establish 'equivalence' or 'difference' between sets;
- matching of objects (toys, unit blocks, etc.) with pictures or dot patterns containing different size groups;
- comparing and contrasting groups of different size.

The vocabulary of early number relationships needs to be introduced carefully and systematically alongside such experiences. For the least able students this vocabulary needs to be repeated and overlearned until completely mastered (for example, same, different, more than, less than, few, many, all, none, altogether, as many as). If a student's understanding of the vocabulary associated with number and mathematics is very restricted greater attention must be given to teaching the appropriate terms in a meaningful context. It is not just the vocabulary itself which is important, but the syntactical structures that accompany the verbalizations. For example, 'Are there more dogs than cats in the picture?'; 'How many more cars than buses can you see?'; 'Using a radius of 5cm, draw a circle', etc.

For students with learning difficulties, it is important that teachers analyse the actual vocabulary which is to be used in teaching a new concept, and simplify this where possible. Essential terms which cannot be simplified should be taught thoroughly and not left to incidental learning (Orton 1992). Students should also be taught to identify mathematical terms printed in their texts.

Counting

Counting is perhaps the most fundamental of all early number skills (Maclellan 1993). As indicated in the previous section it can assist with the development of conservation of number. If this skill of accurate counting of objects is not established it must be taught by direct instruction. The problem is often that the student fails to make a correct one-to-one correspondence between the word spoken in the 'number rhyme' and the objects touched in order. If the physical act of counting a set of objects appears to be difficult for the student, manual guidance of his or her hands may be needed. For young children the use of 'finger plays' and 'number rhymes and songs' may assist with the mastery of counting.

Counting of actual objects will eventually be extended to encompass 'counting-on' strategy for addition, and the 'counting-back' strategy for subtraction, in the absence of real objects. These strategies may have to be taught directly to certain students (Fuson and Fuson 1992).

Recognition of numerals

The cardinal value of number symbols should, of course, be related to a variety of sets of different objects. Teachers can make numeral-to-group matching games (the numeral 11 on a card to be matched with eleven birds, eleven kites, eleven cars, eleven dots, eleven tally marks, etc.). Also useful are teacher-made lotto cards containing a selection of the number symbols being taught or overlearned (one to ten, or one to twenty, or twenty-five to fifty, etc.). When the teacher holds up a flashcard and says the number the student covers the numeral on the lotto card. At the end of the game the student must say each number aloud as it is uncovered on the card. Later these same lotto cards can be used for basic addition and subtraction facts, the numerals on the cards now representing correct answers to some simple question from the teacher (5 add 4 makes . . .? The number 1 less than 8 is . . . ?).

Activities with number cards can also be devised to help students sort and arrange the numerals in correct sequence from one to ten, one to twenty, etc. The early items in the Unifix mathematics apparatus can be useful at this stage (e.g. the inset pattern boards, number indicators, number line to twenty).

The writing of numerals should be taught in parallel to the above activities. Correct numeral formation should be established as thoroughly as correct letter formation in handwriting: this will reduce the incidence of reversals of figures in written recording.

Recording

There is a danger that some students will be expected to deal with symbolic number recording too early. Pictorial recording, tally marks, and dot patterns are very acceptable forms of representation for the young child. Gradually, the writing of number symbols will accompany such picture-type recording and then finally replace it, by which time the cardinal values of the numerals are really understood (Stoessiger and Wilkinson 1991).

Number facts

Ashcraft (1985) suggests that functional knowledge in arithmetic involves two major components: mastery of number facts which can easily be retrieved from memory (to 9 + 9 and 9 × 9), and a body of knowledge about computational procedures. Both components are needed in typical arithmetic problem-solving situations. Number facts are involved in all steps of the subroutines carried out later in more complex computations.

It is essential that students be helped to develop automatic recall of the basic number bonds rather than having, for example, to calculate with fingers each time they need 7 + 3 = 10. Being able to recall number facts easily is important for two main reasons: it makes calculation easier and it allows time for the deepening of understanding (Ginsburg and Baroody 1983; Agudelo-Valderrama 1996). Knowing number facts is partly a matter of learning through repetition (remembered through constant exposure) and partly a matter of grasping a rule (e.g. that zero added to any number doesn't change it: 3 + 0 = 3, 13 + 0 = 13, etc; or if that 7 + 3 = 10 then 7 + 4 must be 'one more than ten', etc.).

Many students with learning disabilities have problems in learning and recalling number facts and tables and require extra attention devoted to this key area. The following suggestions may help.

Daily speed and accuracy sheets   One must not underestimate the value of something as simple as a daily worksheet to practise recall of number facts and tables for those students still needing such experience. Students should aim to increase their own scores each day in, say, a three-minute session, thus competing against themselves, not the class average. They are likely to get responses correct because they are working at their own rate (and can use counters, tally marks, etc., if necessary). This procedure is preferable to the daily session using 'ten mental problems', which can become nothing more than a morning ritual and only teaches some students how poor they are at rapid mental arithmetic.

Although they are important, daily speed and accuracy sheets must not be allowed to become an end in themselves. It is vital that a student has the opportunity to *apply* number facts and arithmetic skills to problem-solving.

Number games   Almost any simple game involving a scoring system can be used to practise recall of number facts or simple addition or subtraction. For example, a skittle game can be played using empty bleach or cordial containers with a value (score) painted on each. The student has to add the value for any knocked down with each roll of the ball. Card games can be designed which involve adding and subtracting scores at each turn.

Salmon (1990) has recommended that teachers devise or select games carefully in order to complement the objectives of the lesson rather than provide amusement. Students must be taught the appropriate way to play a game and they should be made aware of what the game is teaching them.

Computer programs have proved to be particularly useful in providing the necessary amount of drill and practice without boredom. Hasselbring, Goin and Brandsford (1988) combined drill sessions on a computer with training in recall of basic number facts from memory for students with learning difficulties. Their results suggest that such a procedure is effective in developing automaticity in recall of number facts.

Computation and algorithms   Once young students have evolved their own meaningful forms of recording in the early stages one must move on carefully to the introduction of conventional forms of both vertical and horizontal computation. A student should be able to watch as a bundle of, say, ten rods and two extra ones are added to a set already containing a bundle of ten rods and three extra ones and then write the operation as

$$12 + 13 = 25 \text{ or} \quad \begin{array}{r} 12 \\ +13 \\ \hline 25 \end{array}$$

The reverse of this procedure is to show the student a 'number sentence' $(20 - 13 = 7)$ and ask him or her to demonstrate what this means using some form of concrete material. Dienes' MAB blocks are particularly useful for this purpose. Stern's equipment and Unifix blocks, being larger in size, are more appropriate for children with poor manipulative skills.

This stage of development is likely to require careful structuring over a long period of time if the student with learning difficulties is not to become confused. The careful grading of the examples, and the amount of practice provided at each stage, are crucial for long-term mastery. Once the students reach this stage of applying the basic algorithms for addition (with and without carrying), subtraction (with and without borrowing), multiplication and division, the demands on their thinking and reasoning increase rapidly.

Skemp (1976) suggested that ideally students should achieve two levels of understanding in their application of arithmetical processes to problem-solving. The most basic level is termed 'instrumental understanding' (knowing what to do and when to do it, in order to select an appropriate process to solve a problem and complete the calculation correctly). At this level the learner knows *what* to do but does not necessarily have an in-depth understanding of why or how the procedure works. An example would be the application of the rule to invert and multiply when dividing a fraction by a fraction. The higher level of understanding is termed 'relational understanding'. At this level the learner understands fully how and why a particular process works, as well as when to use it. Ideally one would hope to assist all students to achieve both levels of understanding; but realistically the relational level may be beyond the grasp of lower-ability children. However, it is possible to teach many of these students who have mastered the basic number system to select and carry out the correct arithmetical procedure to solve a problem. For everyday purposes that ability is all that is required.

Indirectly, the issues above raise the question of the place of the pocket calculator as a means of bypassing the computational difficulties of some students. There is a valid argument that time spent on mechanical arithmetic is largely wasted on a student who cannot seem to retain the steps involved in carrying out a particular procedure when working through a calculation with pencil and paper. The use of the calculator as a permanent alternative is totally defensible in such cases (Drosdeck 1995). The use of the calculator removes a major obstacle for students with poor computational skills, and they can all compute with speed and accuracy. The instructional time saved can then be devoted to helping the students learn to select the correct type of operation needed to solve particular problems. The result is more time on problem-solving, not less! However, it is interesting to note that a few students prefer *not* to use a calculator, appearing to gain more enjoyment and satisfaction from mathematics lessons when they can obtain a solution to a problem through their own efforts (Ruthven 1995).

It is likely that in the foreseeable future many teachers will still wish to teach computational procedures in traditional written forms before a student is permitted to use a calculator. It is to these teachers that the following paragraphs in this section are directed.

It is, of course, valuable to teach students verbal self-instructions when carrying out the steps in a particular calculation. For example, using the decomposition method for this subtraction problem the student would be taught to verbalize the steps in some way similar to the wording below.

$$\begin{array}{r} 5 \ {}_7 8 \ {}^1 1 \\ - \ 1 \ \ 3 \ \ 9 \\ \hline 4 \ \ 4 \ \ 2 \end{array}$$

The child says: 'Start with the units. I can't take 9 from 1 so I must borrow a ten and write it next to the 1. Cross out the 8 tens and write 7. Now I can take 9 from 11 and write 2 in the answer box. 7 take 3 leaves 4 in the tens column. 5 take 1 leave 4. Write 4 in the answer space. My answer is 442.'

A support teacher or parent who attempts to help a student in this area of school work *must* liaise closely with the class teacher in order to find out the precise verbal cues which are used in subtraction, multiplication, etc., so that the same words and directions are used in the remedial programme to avoid confusion.

Rote learning of these verbal routines has fallen somewhat into disrepute in recent years. It is felt that these methods inhibit the more able students' thinking, and may prevent them from devising insightful and more rapid methods of completing a calculation. Slavishly following an algorithm may represent purely mechanical performance even below the instrumental level. Nevertheless, for students with poor aptitude for arithmetic, it is essential that the teacher does cover these paper-and-pencil skills thoroughly to the point of mastery. Without the verbal and mechanical procedures for working through a calculation the lower-ability students are likely to be totally confused and utterly frustrated. It is often the absence of these basic skills that causes students with learning difficulties to become frustrated and disheartened in 'process-type' mathematical activities.

Computational procedures can be elevated above the rote learning level if they are accompanied by some degree of 'self-monitoring' in the student (Frank and Brown 1992). Self-monitoring helps the student to remember how to complete the steps in a sequential task and how to self-correct where necessary.

It is important that students also be taught other strategies for solving addition and subtraction problems, preferably those which will help to develop insight into the structure and composition of the numbers involved. For example, if the student is faced with $47 + 17 =?$, he or she is encouraged to think of this regrouped as a set of $(40 + 7)$ added to a set of $(10 + 7)$. The tens are quickly combined to make 50, and the two 7's make 14. Finally 14 combined with 50 is obviously 64. Fewer errors seem to occur with this method than with the 'carry ten under the line' type of vertical addition. This is almost certainly because the approach is meaningful and does help to develop insight into the structure of number. It can also be easily demonstrated using MAB blocks or similar concrete materials.

With subtraction the procedure may be illustrated thus:

$(53 - 27 =)$ 53 can be regrouped as $40 + 13$
27 can be regrouped as $20 + 7$
Deal with the tens first: $40 - 20 = 20$
Now the second step: $13 - 7 = 6$
We are left with 26.

Once the method is established with relational understanding, it appears to result in few errors than either 'decomposition' or 'equal addition' methods. Equal addition, once considered to be the best method for tackling more difficult subtraction problems involving zeros in the top line, has fallen out of favour.

In the surveys which have been carried out to determine adult needs in arithmetic, multiplication and division do not appear to be of great value in everyday life. Certainly it is useful to be able to multiply, say, twenty-three lengths of wallpaper by 3m to find out how much to order to paper a room; but the adult who has difficulty with multiplication will usually solve the problem correctly as an addition process (setting down twenty-three three times and adding). It seems that if teachers are to identify the priorities for curriculum content in mathematics, addition and subtraction should be given high ranking, multiplication moderate ranking, and division low ranking. For students of limited ability, a pocket calculator may well be the most obvious answer for multiplication and division.

Over to you: *Calculators vs. pencil and paper*

The place of the pocket calculator in the mathematics course remains a vexed issue for many teachers. Set down your own views on the matter and address yourself particularly to its possible value for lower-ability children.

What are your views on the teaching of computational skills in fairly traditional ways involving set algorithms and verbal cueing?

One final word on the paper-and-pencil performance of students with perceptual difficulties or co-ordination problems. It is often necessary to rule up the pages of their exercise books in ways which will make it easier for them to set down the digits in correct spatial positions. Heavy vertical lines will assist with the correct placement of H, T and U, and thus maintain place values. Squared paper will usually assist with the general arrangement of figures on the page. Teachers must also anticipate the difficulties which some students will have in reversing not only single digits but tens and units (e.g. 61 written as 16). Much specific teaching, with cues and prompts such as small arrows or dots on the page, will be needed to overcome this tendency.

MENTAL ARITHMETIC: DOES IT STILL HAVE A PLACE?

Mental arithmetic – the 'daily ten' – has an almost sacred position in the primary mathematics lesson. If the activity is used to review and practise important skills or facts and if there is corrective feedback provided for the students who make errors, then the time is well spent. However, in many classrooms the session really is nothing more than a ritual if the questions are posed, the answers given and a mark given out of ten with no follow-up whatsoever for students with poor scores. The teacher must identify which questions caused difficulty and spend a few moments reteaching the necessary procedure to solve the problems.

One simple teaching strategy which is extremely helpful for students who are poor at processing purely auditory information is to write the numerals on the blackboard as the problem is posed orally. For example, the teacher says, 'Red team scored nine goals. Blue team scored seven goals. Green team scored twelve goals. How many goals were scored altogether?' The numerals 9, 7 and 12 are quickly written randomly on the blackboard. Having this key information available in a visual form will enable many more students to add the numbers mentally.

It is worth commenting that children with impaired hearing may have particular difficulties with mental arithmetic when the questions are dictated by the teacher. If the student relies heavily on speech reading, a number such as 'sixty' may *look* exactly like 'sixteen' on the teacher's lips. Again the use of the blackboard will help to minimize this confusion.

DEVELOPING PROBLEM-SOLVING STRATEGIES

According to Enright and Choate (1993: 280):

> Problem solving is the primary function of mathematics education. Students must learn how and when to use the computational and fact skills they develop, or these skills will be of no use at all. Solving problems involves the application of reading, computation, and a host of other skills specific to the process.

Students with learning difficulties frequently exhibit confusion when faced with a problem to solve (Parmar and Cawley 1994). They may have difficulty in reading the words in the problem, or with comprehending the meaning of specific terms. They may also be uncertain of which process or processes to use. They may fail to generalize from one form of successful problem solution to another. Most students with these difficulties need to be explicitly taught a range of effective strategies to use. The aim is to teach students how to approach a problem without a feeling of panic or hopelessness. They need to be able to sift the relevant from the irrelevant information and impose some degree of structure on the problem (Carpenter 1985).

Useful strategies for problem-solving have been devised by Darch, Carnine and Gersten (1984), Howell and Barnhart (1992), Wilson and Sindelar (1991), Enright and Choate (1993) and McIntosh and Draper (1995). Some of their ideas have been incorporated in the suggestions below.

Four steps to problem-solving

Example: A store sold 485 bottles of cold drink on one day in the summer. The drink bottles are packaged in cartons which hold six bottles each. How many cartons of drink were sold that day?

Step 1: Understanding the problem   The teacher focuses the student's attention on the relevant information in the problem through the use of questions.

'How many bottles were sold?'
'What does packaged mean?'
'What is a carton?'

Visual aid or blackboard sketch may be helpful even at this stage.

'How were the bottles packed?'
'If one carton holds six bottles how many bottles in two cartons?'
'What does the problem ask us to find out?'

Advice such as 'think!' or 'read it again!' will be of no help to the student.

Step 2: Planning to solve the problem   The teacher encourages the student or students to consider possible ways of solving the problem. If necessary the teacher may need to offer some suggestions.

Well could we do it like this? Could we get 485 bottles and put them into groups of six? Do we need to do that? How else could we do it? Could we make up some form of chart or table? Will a sketch help us to visualize what to do?

Most of the experts stress the immense value of having students draw sketches which help them to 'picture' the actual problem. Some students do not automatically apply the strategy of visualizing the problem.

Step 3: Attempting a solution   The student might now attempt, perhaps through trial and error, to come up with a plausible answer.

Step 4: Reviewing the problem and its solution   In this final stage the students are encouraged to consider the problem again and to check to see if their solution is what was asked for. 'John, you've got 2910 cartons. Does that make sense?'

Linda, you have written 80 and a bit cartons; tell us how you got that.

The final review stage in teaching problem-solving is very important indeed. It benefits the student who is having to think carefully *how* he or she solved the problem; and it is helping the other students who hear (in language they can readily understand) how someone else tackled the problem. 'Verbal mediation' of this type is also an essential part of the teacher's role when demonstrating how to break a problem down into its component steps. The teacher should describe the process aloud and then, during the guided practice, have the students talk themselves through the process, making the required procedural decisions (Howell, Fox and Morehead 1993).

Salend's (1994) approach to solving word problems involves seven steps:

• Read the problem. Look for clue words which suggest the procedure to use (e.g. altogether, lost, remain, spent, more than, etc.).

- Reread the problem. Identify key information. Ignore extraneous detail. What units will the solution be in (dollars? centimetres? eggs?).
- Visualize the problem. Draw a picture or imagine the picture.
- Write the problem. Set down the computational steps on paper.
- Estimate the answer. What will a reasonable answer be like?
- Solve the problem. Carry out the necessary calculations.
- Check the answer. Compare answer to estimate. Check calculation. Check units against original question.

A problem-solving strategy involving similar steps might use a particular 'cue word' to aid recall of the procedure. For example, in 'RAVE CCC' the word RAVE can be used to identify the first four possible steps to take:

- R = Read the problem carefully.
- A = Attend to key words which may suggest the process to use (for example, 'share', 'altogether', 'less than').
- V = Visualize the problem, and perhaps make a sketch or diagram.
- E = Estimate the possible answer.

Then the letters CCC suggest what to do next:

- C = Choose the numbers to use.
- C = Calculate the answer.
- C = Check against your estimate.

Hallahan and Kauffman (1994) provide a very simple example of a cue word 'DRAW' to represent a task-approach strategy for problem-solving:

- D = Discover the sign (add, subtract, multiply or divide?).
- R = Reread the problem and draw a representation using pictures, tally marks, etc.
- A = Answer the question.
- W = Write the solution in the correct terms.

The most important thing to teach students is how to sift out the key information from the facts that are presented. The students must be helped to perceive the relationships between the statements in the problem, and to detect the relevant facts. This is basically a reading comprehension problem.

Since there is evidence that students can be helped to become more proficient at solving problems, teachers of students with learning difficulties should devote more time to this area of work. As mentioned in an earlier section, perhaps the students' use of pocket calculators will enable teachers to spend more time on this, rather than restricting the students to a diet of mechanical arithmetic. Calculators do not inhibit the development of students' computational skills; and children who are permitted to use calculators often develop a better attitude toward mathematics (Campbell and Stewart 1993).

Over to you: Problem-solving

Briefly outline some strategies you would use to help a student with learning difficulties solve the following problem.

At the beginning of the new term Class 7, with twenty-five children in it, has been given a collection of ninety-eight new books to increase the size of their classroom library. Before the holiday they had one hundred and two books in the library. The teacher says, 'I want labels pasted in all the books, new and old. You can share the work out equally so that you all have a turn at pasting.' If the work is divided up fairly, in how many books will each child have to paste labels?

CURRICULUM CONTENT

Students with learning difficulties sometimes need a modified mathematics programme. Some traditional topics in mainstream mathematics courses are unnecessarily complex and too abstract for these students.

In trying to decide upon core content for a mathematics curriculum for students with learning difficulties one is helped by the results of surveys of community expectations of basic numeracy (Bourke 1981; Knight *et al.* 1995). Parents and employers agree that the key areas for functional numeracy are: counting, tables, use of the four basic processes, money management, time and measurement. Some grasp of common and decimal fractions and the ability to understand simple graphs are also useful in everyday life.

The following content was considered by a group of primary and secondary teachers to comprise a core of essential material basic to the needs of low-achieving school-leavers. Items marked with an asterisk could be omitted with children of very low ability.

Suggested core content

Basic number

- Digit (numeral) recognition. Ability to count actual objects correctly.
- Understanding of cardinal and serial aspects of number. Appreciation of place value. Emphasis on establishing a high degree of automaticity in recall of basic number facts.
- Standard processes (algorithms) of arithmetic. Emphasis on addition, subtraction. Emphasis on 'estimating' reasonable results for calculations. Greatest emphasis on problem-solving using basic processes.
- Multiplication and division to be taught later using realistic numbers.

Grouping. (No objection to table charts or desk calculators.) Counting in intervals (2s, 5s, 10s, 100s).

Money

- Coin and note recognition.
- Ability to handle money (count up totals using coins and notes; give change by 'counting-on' method).
- Ability to perform basic processes with $ and ¢, £ and p (especially addition and subtraction).
- Experiences with simple budgeting and banking.

Problem-solving

- Emphasis to be placed on applying all the above skills and processes to solving problems.
- Emphasis also on practical mathematics.
- Use of measurement scale in simple mapwork and interpretation.*
- Ability to interpret simple graphs and charts.*

Fractions, decimals, percentages

- Understanding and recognition of simple common fractions (½, ¾, ¼, ¹⁄₁₀).
- No rote learning of operations with fractions.
- Equivalence of simple fractions.
- Understanding and recognition of decimal notation: tenths and hundredths, particularly in connection with measurement (linear, temperature, etc.) and money.*
- Awareness of meaning of 100 per cent, 50 per cent, 25 per cent, 10 per cent, and particular reference to discount and '10 per cent off', etc.*

Measurement

- Ability to measure and construct using mm, cm and metres.
- Awareness of distance (km). Speed (km/hr) (and associated road signs).*
- Ability to weigh in g and kg.
- Awareness of common weights of goods (e.g. packet of sugar, potatoes, etc.).
- Basic understanding of tonne.*
- Ability to tell the time; digital clock and analogue clock.
- Awareness of the passage of time (e.g. 30 seconds; 1 minute; 5 minutes; 1 hour; 24 hours). Estimate how long will it take to do a certain task, or to travel a certain journey, or to get to the bus stop, etc.).
- Know days of the week, months of the year and seasons.

- Liquid measures (litre). Relate to petrol, cans of paint, carton of milk or juice, etc.*
- Temperature. Read thermometer.*

SUMMARY

In this chapter brief attention has been given to factors which may cause students to experience difficulty in learning basic mathematics, particularly those related to quality of instruction. A case was argued for a classroom approach which combines the best features of activity-based mathematics learning with explicit teaching of basic skills.

Practical suggestions were made for carrying out an appraisal of a student's mathematical knowledge and skills. Three levels of diagnostic assessment were described. A teacher using the items listed at each level should obtain a fairly accurate picture of what a student can and cannot do in number work and simple problem-solving.

Attention was given to practical ways of helping students develop number fluency, since this is basic to all problem-solving work. Students who have mastered the basic processes with numbers have more mental energy to devote to problem-solving. It was suggested that for some students a pocket calculator might be provided as a permanent alternative to pencil-and-paper computation. Suggestions were also provided for the teaching of problem-solving strategies.

Finally, a suggested 'core curriculum in mathematics' was presented. This may be helpful for teachers who need to plan priorities within individualized programmes.

Discussion points

- 'Mathematics is the most texbook-driven subject in the school curriculum.' Discuss this comment.

- Describe the key features you would expect to find in a maths textbook designed for lower-ability students.

- 'All students should be exposed to the mainstream mathematics curriculum. To water down the content for students with learning difficulties is not in their best interests.' Argue the points for and against this viewpoint.

- Mathematics learning is an area where it is only too easy for a student to enter a 'failure cycle'. How might teachers prevent this situation?

Further reading

Burns, M. (1993) 'The 12 most important things you can do to be a better math teacher', *Instructor* 102, 8: 28–31.

Burton, G.M. (1985) *Towards a Good Beginning: Teaching Early Childhood Mathematics*, Menlo Park: Addison-Wesley.

Chinn, S.J. and Ashcroft, J.R. (1993) *Mathematics for Dyslexics*, London: Whurr.

Heddens, J. and Speer, W. (1995) *Today's Mathematics* (8th edn), New York: Prentice Hall.

House, P.A. and Coxford, A.F. (1995) *Connecting Mathematics Across the Curriculum*, Reston: National Council of Teachers of Mathematics.

Lloyd, J. W. and Keller, C.E. (1989) 'Effective mathematics instruction', *Focus on Exceptional Children* 21, 7: 1–10.

Mannigel, D. (1992) *Young Children as Mathematicians*, Sydney: Social Science Press.

Perry, B. and Conroy, J. (1994) *Early Childhood and Primary Mathematics*, Sydney: Harcourt Brace Jovanovich.

Polloway, E., Patton, J., Payne, J. and Payne, R. (1992) *Strategies for Teaching Learners with Special Needs* (5th edn), Columbus: Merrill.

Reys, R., Suydam, M. and Lindquist, M. (1995) *Helping Children Learn Mathematics* (4th edn), Boston: Allyn and Bacon.

Sovchik, R. (1995) *Teaching Mathematics to Children* (2nd edn), New York: Harper Collins.

Thornton, C.A. and Bleys, N.S. (1994) *Windows on Opportunity: Mathematics for Students with Special Needs*, Reston: National Council of Teachers of Mathematics.

Chapter 13

Issues in inclusion and differentiation

In inclusive schools, the roles and responsibilities of general and special educators must change in fundamental ways. In addition, a shift has to occur in how educators collaborate, – from conferring only about individual student problems to making curriculum accessible to a diverse group of students.

(Warger and Pugach 1996: 62)

In the last few chapters attention has been given to what are commonly called 'the basic academic skills' – reading, writing, spelling and arithmetic. Strategies have been presented for adapting methods and curriculum content in these areas to meet the special requirements of some students. The basic academic skills are not the only curriculum domains which may need adaptation for groups of students with increasingly diverse needs. In this chapter some general principles for developing inclusive practices will be discussed, together with specific suggestions for adapting curriculum content and modifying the teaching approach for students with special needs.

INCLUSION AND DIFFERENTIATION

Inclusion defined

Staub and Peck (1995: 36) have defined inclusion as 'the full-time placement of children with mild, moderate, and severe disabilities in regular classrooms'. This definition assumes that regular class placement is a relevant option for all children, regardless of the degree of severity of their disabilities. However, the writers state that their definition does not preclude the use of withdrawal services or instruction in a self-contained setting when necessary. There are many other definitions of inclusion, but all focus on the rights of students with disabilities to be educated in regular schools.

According to Booth (1996), there is a basic difference between the integration movement of the 1970s and 1980s and the inclusive schooling movement of the 1990s. In the case of integration, extra support was provided to help the student with special needs participate in the mainstream pro-gramme without the content or delivery of that programme being changed in any significant way. Inclusive practice, on the other hand, requires significant changes to be made to the mainstream programme in terms of organization, content and delivery, in order to accommodate a much wider range of ability and disability than ever before. Much of the literature on inclusion talks of totally 'restructuring schools' to make them more responsive to the diversity of learning needs and characteristics in their student populations.

Contemporary views on social justice and equality of opportunity for all have led to the belief that *all* students have the right to be exposed to the mainstream curriculum in a reasonably unadulterated form (Ainscow and Muncey 1990). The move toward national and state-prescribed curricula and competency testing in several countries (e.g. Britain, North America, Aus-tralia), has reinforced this concern for the rights of every individual student to receive a broad and enriching school programme. However, actually implementing a common curriculum for a very wide ability range can be problematic. It is argued that some students require very significant modi-fications to the curriculum and teaching approach if their educational needs are to be met (O'Neil 1995). Some may even require separate programmes, with a focus on self-help and daily living skills. Yet the practice of 'watering down' the curriculum for students with disabilities and learning difficulties by reducing and simplifying the content (for example, as was suggested in the case of mathematics in the previous chapter), has come in for criticism over the years (Haigh 1977; Dyer 1991). It is sometimes argued that to reduce the curriculum is to reduce a student's opportunities in life.

While inclusion of all students in regular schools is seen by many teachers, parents and administrators as a very positive opportunity for students with special educational needs to benefit from the mainstream curriculum, the move has also been regarded by some as a 'highly ideo-logical crusade' which fails to take account of the realities of learning difficulties in this population of students (Emblem and Conti-Ramsden 1990). It is certainly true that in the first half of the 1990s much of the debate on inclusive schooling was conducted predominantly at the philosophical, sociological and political levels, without due consideration being given to the practicalities of implementation at classroom level (Sebba and Ainscow 1996). However, more practical guidelines are now beginning to emerge to suggest how students with severe learning problems can be effectively served in regular school settings (Roach 1995; Giangreco 1996; LeRoy and Simpson 1996; Farlow 1996).

One area which remains contentious is the feasibility of providing special services such as speech therapy, physiotherapy, orientation and mobility training, self-care training and the teaching of alternative methods of communication, in the regular school. Until now, these services were provided in reasonably cost-effective ways in special schools and centres. It is much more difficult to address these special needs in regular schools. James Kauffman, the highly respected special educator in the United States, has commented in an interview,

> Although it sounds very engaging and intriguing, I doubt that it is possible to provide all needed services in one place at the same time for all types of children one might have. People are eager to say that they don't exclude anybody from a particular classroom, but there is no credible research evidence showing that the regular classroom can actually provide superior services for all kids with disabilities.
>
> (O'Neil 1995: 10)

These are important issues which will need to be addressed in the coming decade.

Facilitating inclusion

Several writers have suggested key factors which are evident in settings where inclusion is working most successfully. The following list represents a compilation of ideas from Dyson (1994), Barry (1995), O'Neil (1995), Roach (1995), Jorgensen (1995), Vaughn and Schumm (1995), Farlow (1996), Sebba and Ainscow (1996) and LeRoy and Simpson (1996):

- Teachers and school administrators need to have a positive attitude toward the notion of inclusive schooling. A willingness to accept the challenge of adapting classroom practices and reviewing school structures is essential.

- Each school needs to develop a policy statement which includes the set of beliefs that guide that school's inclusive practices, together with a commitment to implement such practices. Administrators cannot hand down such policies to schools. It is essential that all teachers and support staff are involved in development of the policy if they are to feel genuine ownership and commitment. In Britain, the Code of Practice (Department for Education 1994) requires schools to establish policies which address the education of students with special needs. Beliefs about inclusive practice are likely to be embedded within that policy.

- Planning for inclusion needs to be proactive, not reactive. It is necessary to anticipate problems which may occur, both at classroom level and at school system level, when students with very significant learning needs are included in regular classes. It is essential to have in place some strategies for dealing with problems if they arise.

- All interested parties need to be involved in preparing for inclusion, and in the on-going monitoring of its effectiveness. The active support of teachers, parents, paraprofessionals and service personnel needs to be established and maintained.

- Support networks need to be identified for the student with special needs, and also for teachers with exceptional students in their classes.

- Regular classroom teachers need to work more closely with special education staff (and vice versa) in order to address issues of curriculum adaptation by drawing upon the expertise of both. Collaboration, teamwork and mutual support are referred to frequently as key features of successful partnerships between teachers, and between teachers, parents and other professionals.

- Classrooms where co-operative learning, group work and peer assistance are encouraged appear to offer most to students with special needs.

- Effective instruction which embodies clear modelling, explaining, practising and strategy training is important for *all* students.

- Teachers need, and benefit from, additional in-service training which gives them increased knowledge about curricular and instructional modifications, together with practical skills in adapting curriculum content and resource materials. If inclusive practices are to be the norm, teachers need to know how classroom instruction can be differentiated according to students' characteristics. Successful inclusion will depend very heavily upon teachers' skills in developing differentiated practices.

Differentiation defined

The term 'differentiation' is used in Britain and in North America to describe the various strategies teachers use to enable groups of students with diverse learning characteristics to participate in the mainstream programme (Good and Brophy 1994; Bearne 1996). According to Quicke (1995), the purpose of differentiation in teaching practices and in curriculum design is to ensure that all children maximize their potential and receive a curriculum through which they can experience success. The principle of differentiation in educational programming applies quite as much to addressing the characteristics and needs of gifted and talented students as it does to meeting the needs of students with disabilities.

In Australia, differentiated teaching of this type is often referred to 'adaptive education'. Adaptive education represents an approach which utilizes many different forms of teaching and classroom organization to accommodate differences among learners and to cater for students' special needs.

The notion of differentiation is fundamental to the concept of inclusion. If students with special needs are to be accommodated successfully in regular schools, the ways in which instruction is delivered will need to be flexible enough to respond to individual differences (Stainback, Stainback and Stefanich 1996). This flexibility comes in part from the rethinking of teaching approaches, the application of different grouping strategies in the classroom and the optimum use of whatever resources and support may be available (Sebba and Ainscow 1996). It is stated in the Code of Practice (Department for Education 1994: 11) that 'Differentiation of class work within a common curriculum framework will help the schoool to meet the learning needs of all children'.

DIFFERENTIATION IN ACTION

Adapting instruction

In Chapter 1 several suggestions were made to indicate how teachers can 'personalize' their approach within a whole class or group lesson. These are the first steps in differentiation. Such adaptations should result in improved success rates for lower-ability students. Some of the suggestions from Chapter 1 are summarized again here, together with other adaptations described by Lewis and Doorlag (1991), Cohen and Lynch (1991), Lewis (1992), Good and Brophy (1994), Wood (1996), Smith and Urquhart (1996) and Bearne (1996).

- *Short-term goals*: for some students, setting more easily attainable goals within the lesson will help to ensure progress.

- *Presentation*: varying the style and mode of presentation of content (explicit teaching, video, talks, texts, discussions, investigations, debates, etc.) will help to cater for different learning styles and capabilities. In general, making greater use of visual aids, using real materials and providing experiential learning all enhance understanding and increase interest.

- *Instructions*: clarifying, shortening and repeating instructions is often necessary. Having peers repeat or paraphrase instructions for partners can assist lower-achieving students.

- *Demonstration and modelling*: providing additional demonstrations for certain students, using a step-by-step approach is often helpful, as is re-teaching key points to some individuals or small groups.

- *Questioning*: asking many questions and asking questions that build confidence is important. Open-ended questioning allows more students to respond. Providing clues or hints will facilitate student responses. Using different levels of complexity when asking questions to different students ensures a higher response rate. At least 80 per cent of questions should focus on core concepts and information and should be answered easily by all students.

- *Wait time*: when questioning, allowing a few seconds longer for responses from certain students, prompting when necessary.

- *Core plus extension*: this involves planning topics in such a way that activities and materials covering the core content thoroughly are supplemented with resources and activities for extension work; also ensuring that materials covering the core provide additional examples and practice items for those students requiring extra experience.

- *Revision*: providing more frequent reviews and revision is essential for some students.

- *Practice*: it is necessary to give additional time to guided practice for some students, for example by setting more practice items requiring more responses in the time available, by scheduling extra time for guided practice within the lesson, or by using time outside the lesson for further practice and homework.

- *Assistance*: support may be given by more direct assistance and frequent feedback to some students during guided practice. It is important to be proactive in this respect by anticipating which students will need additional support.

- *Work output*: it is realistic to expect different quantity and quality of work from different students; but it is also important to work toward an increase in both over time for all individuals.

- *Activities*: one of the main ways in which differentiation occurs is by the provision of a wide range of activities planned around a central theme. Some activities may involve the application of literacy and numeracy skills, while others may be more practical in nature. All will represent tasks of different levels of complexity which challenge each student to the best of his or her ability. Some tasks will be individual assignments, while others will require collaboration and teamwork.

- *Texts and resources*: it is essential to select reading materials and other resources at different levels of complexity. Seek the assistance of teacher-librarians in locating a variety of materials to supplement topics being taught. Design your own alternative materials around a topic (see below).

- *Response mode*: do not rely solely on written responses from students, but use other modes too, such as drawing, selecting from multiple choice answers, tape recording, etc.

- *Seating*: to create a supportive work environment, make frequent use of group and partner activities requiring collaboration. Seat students together who are most likely to co-operate well and are least likely to antagonize or distract one another. Ensure that students with attention difficulties, or students with sensory impairments, are seated where they can see or hear the teacher and the other students clearly.

- *Peer mediation or peer assistance*: establish a classroom climate where students assisting each other with their work is encouraged and facilitated. Peer assistance can include such things as reading aloud an assignment for another student, helping the student write a response or locate a section of text, checking a partner's work, helping the partner to get started, etc.).

- *Student–teacher interaction*: teachers may need to interact more frequently and positively with lower-ability students. Research findings suggest that teachers tend, on average, to spend much less time with these students in whole class lessons.

- *Personal interests*: when possible, draw on personal interests and knowledge of students to provide curriculum content or points for discussion.

- *Praising*: for some students, it is necessary to use more frequent and more descriptive praise.

- *Rewards*: some students respond well to external rewards and it is useful to increase incentives for some students by using reward systems and charting of progress. Finding out what different students value as rewards is important.

Of the strategies listed above, the most commonly quoted in the literature on inclusion and differentiation are peer tutoring, co-operative group work, developing alternative resources and using thematic studies. These may well represent appropriate starting points for teachers wanting to move toward increased differentiation in their own classrooms.

No one suggests that adapting curricula and instruction to individual needs is easy. However, effective teaching within an inclusive setting does require teachers to recognize individual differences among students and to make adjustments for these where possible.

Modifying instructional materials

Often a simple modification to teaching materials (worksheets, texts, diagrams, audio-tapes, etc.) allows a student with mild disabilities to access the mainstream curriculum without further adaptations. When selecting or modifying materials consider alternative methods of presentation if reading and writing are major problem areas (e.g. use audio-tape, video-tape, computer program, pictorial recording).

Bearne (1996: 253) warns against the tendency to respond to the challenge of differentiation merely by providing worksheets at three levels of difficulty, from very easy to more challenging. She says, 'It is not difficult to imagine the messages this kind of practice gives to all the learners in the classroom'. While there is a place for providing assignments at different levels, the system should not perpetuate that notion that the least able students are too dumb to attempt interesting or challenging work. These students can participate fully if given interesting tasks and provided with support and encouragement.

When preparing print materials for students with learning difficulties, the following principles from Currie (1990), Meese (1992) and Lovitt and Horton (1994) may be helpful:

- simplify the language (use short sentences, substitute simple words for difficult terms);
- preteach any new vocabulary (if a difficult word cannot be simplified, ensure that it is looked at and discussed before students are expected to read it);
- provide clear illustrations or diagrams;
- use cues or prompts where responses are required (e.g. provide the initial letter of the answer; underline key terms in the text; provide answers to be matched to questions, rather than requiring recall from memory, etc.);
- make response items self-correcting where possible;
- improve legibility of print and layout;
- highlight critical features;
- reduce extraneous detail;
- if necessary, provide a tape-recorded version of the print material.

Task analysis

One of the most important aspects of differentiation is the ability to present learning tasks in easy steps for students who require such a degree of structure. Task analysis involves the process of breaking down something which is to be learned into teachable units. These teachable units are then ordered into the most effective sequence to facilitate learning.

Task analytic approaches have been used intuitively by teachers for many years. It is only with the rise of interest in more precise methods of instructional planning that the approach has received more overt attention. It is now recognized that the tasks and skills to be presented to students with learning difficulties need to be precisely analysed and taught in small, incremental steps. When teachers do modify tasks in this way children with learning difficulties experience greater success.

There is, of course, a limit to how far one can go with step-by-step reduction of the curriculum without creating separate learning tasks which, in themselves, are meaningless. For this reason task analysis is not regarded highly by some teachers. It looks too mechanistic to be appropriate for human learning and development. Some would argue quite rightly that we don't usually learn to do something by gradually learning all the separate 'bits' which can be identified in the total performance. We do tend to learn many things in rather holistic, all-embracing ways, not in the step-by-step sequential pattern suggested in task analysis schedules. As a general rule, the greater the degree of disability experienced by the student, the more valuable it is to analyse and carefully sequence tasks within the curriculum.

There are several steps involved in carrying out a task analysis. They may be summarized thus:

- the teacher personally performs the task several times to observe the steps involved;
- the teacher identifies any prerequisite knowledge or skills necessary for performing the task;
- the task should be analysed at a metacognitive level as well as practical performance level. (What do I need to think about at this stage? How will I know if I'm doing this well? Is this step going to be easy or difficult?);
- the task should be broken down into teachable units that are small enough to be mastered by the student;
- for some students it may be possible to chunk two or more of these steps together;
- if necessary, prepare a flow chart showing the sequence of steps and the prerequisite skills.

Example A: Domain = Self-help (dressing)

A skill is identified which the student needs to master: for example, putting on socks. The goal is stated: 'The child will be able to put on own socks without adult assistance when these are handed to him or her.' The actual task of putting on socks is then analysed. What are the identifiable steps or stages involved? These steps are listed in logical sequence:

1 child adopts suitable position with knee raised (on floor, on chair, edge of bed, etc.);
2 child picks up sock;
3 identifies open end of sock;
4 slides toes into open end while enlarging the opening with both hands;
5 pulls sock toward heel of foot;
6 pulls sock up to correct height.

The checklist of steps thus constructed is used to determine precisely how much of the task the child can do already (for example, he or she may achieve up to stage 5 but not beyond). A teaching objective is then stated for that child (usually based on the next step in the sequence).

The dressing example used above can also serve to illustrate the principle of 'back chaining'. In back chaining the child actually masters a skill step by step, working in reverse order. For example, perhaps he/she cannot put on a sock. At first the adult puts the sock on the child's foot and does everything apart from pulling it up (stage 6). The child does only the last action. When this is mastered, the child has to complete stages 5 and 6, then 4, 5, 6, etc.

until finally, after a period of time, the child does all the steps set out in the example and successfully puts on own socks.

Example B: Domain = Mathematics (TU subtraction)

$$
\begin{array}{r}
40 \\
-17 \\
\hline
\end{array}
$$

Steps involved in carrying out the procedure:

1 identify the problem as subtraction;
2 identify starting point;
3 recognize that 7 cannot be subtracted directly from 0;
4 regroup from tens column;
5 cross out 4 and write 3 tens;
6 place 1 ten before the zero (10);
7 subtract 7 from 10;
8 write 3;
9 subtract 1 from 3 in tens column;
10 write 2;
11 read answer correctly as 23;
12 check: 17 + 23 = 40.

Over to you: Task analysis

- Carry out a task analysis to identify the component steps involved in locating a specific word in a dictionary and writing down the definition.

- Identify the prerequisite skills required for using a dictionary efficiently.

- What prerequisite skills would be involved in each of the two examples of task analysis given above?

SELECTING CURRICULUM CONTENT

In inclusive settings, some characteristics of students with disabilities will significantly influence the priorities given to certain aspects of the curriculum. For example, students with hearing impairment will always need to have maximum attention devoted to vocabulary development and oral-aural communication skills. Students with intellectual disability will always need attention given to self-help and daily living skills, social skills and communication. Students with physical disabilities which severely restrict mobility and access to real-life learning experiences and social contact will need curriculum content which is designed to compensate for this deprivation of experience. Students with emotional disorders need a curriculum containing many success situations which consistently build confidence and self-esteem, develop self-management skills, and foster social and interpersonal communication.

In the context of special schools and special classes, Brennan (1985) suggested that some learning is so important that it should be regarded as 'core content' which must be mastered by all special needs students. Beyond this core there is a periphery of knowledge, skills, attitudes and values which it is desirable, but possibly not essential, for students to acquire. In recent years general education has also created the notion of a core curriculum (Print 1992), and students with special needs now to have to attempt to achieve within that mainstream core.

To help teachers select appropriate content for inclusion in the class curriculum or in individualized programmes Brennan (1985) proposed a '4R test'. To apply the test consider the proposed content under the following headings:

- Is it *real*? Does it figure in the student's experiences and can it be presented in real-life ways?
- Is it *relevant*? Will it be of value to the student to know this or to be able to do this?
- Is it *realistic*? Given this student's age, ability and aptitude, is the goal achievable at this time?
- Is it *rational*? Can the purpose of learning this be made clear to the student?

These questions are not unique to planning curricula for students with special needs. They are highly appropriate for selecting curriculum content for any students.

In order to evaluate curriculum content in this way it is first necessary to appraise the students in terms of their relevant characteristics. Ainscow and Muncey (1990) suggest that the following factors should be examined:

- *Previous experience*: what sorts of experience has the student had inside and out of school?
- *Current knowledge and skills*: what does the student understand and what is he or she able to do?
- *Interests*: what are the student's particular interests and enthusiasms?
- *Attitudes*: does the student have any positive or negative feelings which may influence learning?

At times it will be necessary to design special programmes which address the highly specific needs of some students with disabilities. These programmes may operate only at certain times in the day, possibly in a withdrawal setting, or they may be fully integrated into the mainstream curriculum

INDIVIDUALIZED EDUCATION PLANS

The 1970s saw the advent of individualized education plans (IEPs) in the United States of America, as a direct result of Public Law 94–142: The Education of All Handicapped Children Act. Without necessarily using the term individual education plan, several other countries have adopted a similar model (e.g. Australia, New Zealand). In Great Britain, under the 1993 Education Act, the 1994 Education (Special Educational Needs) Regulations, and the Code of Practice, the process of producing an official 'statement' indicating a student's special needs also leads to an individual education plan (Department for Education 1994).

An IEP is drawn up through a process of consultation and collaboration, usually involving class teacher, special education teacher, parents and school principal, with input from relevant specialists such as psychologists, speech pathologists, physiotherapists, disability advisers, etc. Taking into account the child's current strengths and weaknesses, long-term goals and short-term objectives are carefully prepared, and resource needs are identified. Time lines are established for the achievement of the goals and objectives. Procedures are put in place to ensure monitoring and regular review of progress. The roles and responsibilities of different personnel involved in implementing and monitoring the programme are specified.

Under the inclusive schooling policy, many students with IEPs are currently placed in regular school settings. The broad framework of the IEP should therefore serve as a basis for planning differentiated curriculum and teaching for them at classroom level. For example, the IEP should indicate what modifications, if any, are necessary to the learning objectives, the teaching methods, classroom groupings and resources required by the student for specific areas of study. Equally important, the IEP should help to identify areas of the curriculum where no modification is required and where the student can most easily be counted in with the general class.

Ideally, it should be possible within the mainstream curriculum to meet the goals and objectives set down in a student's IEP. To facilitate this, it is suggested that classroom teachers construct a matrix or grid in their curriculum planning documents, with the goals for the child listed on the left side and the key areas of the curriculum and specific curricular topics listed across the top (Williams and Fox 1996; LeRoy and Simpson 1996). Under each topic a tick is placed against a goal if that goal can be achieved through activities and experiences provided within the topic.

It may well be necessary to provide a student with additional teaching activities if certain goals in an IEP cannot be achieved within the general classroom programme. It may not be feasible to meet all the objectives for a

Example: Curriculum planning matrix

	Maths	English	PE	Art	Science, etc.
1 Child to increase frequency of asking questions	√	√	√	√	√
2 Child to master the spelling of phonetically regular words		√			
3 Child to master counting to 100	√		√		√
4 Child to improve gross motor co-ordination			√		

student (particularly those dealing with self-care, for example) simply through a differentiated mainstream curriculum (Moore 1992). Most students with significant learning problems will require a combination of differentiated instruction and individualized programming.

The underlying concepts of IEP development are philosophically and educationally sound. The IEP holds education service providers accountable, and offers the best possible chance for a student to receive an appropriate educational programme. It also allows parents to have some input into the process of setting priorities in the child's curriculum.

SUMMARY

This chapter has examined some of the basic principles of inclusive practice and has suggested that adapted and differentiated teaching is needed in order to accommodate the ever-increasing diversity among learners. Suggestions were made for selecting curriculum content for students with special needs and for adapting teaching and management procedures to cater for individual differences. The relationship between Individualized Education Plans and differentiated instruction was briefly discussed.

Discussion points

- What problems are likely to be encountered by teachers when required to implement a national or state compulsory curriculum with *all* students?

- When students are withdrawn from class to receive individual or small group tuition, what impact is this likely to have upon their contact with the regular class curriculum? What can be done to minimize these problems?

- What are the obstacles to the inclusion of students with severe and multiple disabilities in regular schools?

Further reading

Andrews, J. and Lupart, J. (1993) *The Inclusive Classroom*, Scarborough, Ontario: Nelson.

Ashdown, R., Carpenter, B. and Bovair, K. (1991) *The Curriculum Challenge: Access to the National Curriculum for Pupils with Learning Difficulties*, London: Falmer.

Bearne, E. (ed.) (1996) *Differentiation and Diversity in the Primary School*, London: Routledge.

Brennan, W.K. (1985) *Curriculum for Special Needs*, Milton Keynes: Open University Press.

Clark, C., Dyson, A. and Millward, A. (eds) *Towards Inclusive Schools?*, London: Fulton.

Falvey, M.A. (1995) *Inclusive and Heterogeneous Schooling*, Baltimore: Brookes.

Fiore, T. and Cook, R. (1994) 'Adapting textbooks and other instructional materials', *Remedial and Special Education* 15, 6: 333–47.

Hart, S. (ed.) (1996) *Differentiation and the Secondary Curriculum: Debates and Dilemmas*, London: Routledge.

Lewis, A. (1991) *Primary Special Needs and the National Curriculum*, London: Routledge.

McGrath, H. and Noble, B. (1993) *Different Kids, Same Classroom*, Melbourne: Longman Cheshire.

Putnam, J.W. (1993) *Cooperative Learning and Strategies for Inclusion*, Baltimore: Brookes.

Salend, S.J. (1994) *Effective Mainstreaming: Creating Inclusive Classrooms* (2nd edn), New York: Macmillan.

Udavari-Solner, A. (1996) 'Examining teacher thinking: constructing a process and to design curricular adaptions', *Remedial and Special Education*, 17, 4: 245–54.

Chapter 14

The changing nature of special education support

[In order to cater for students with special needs] individual schools will continue to make the best internal provision they deem suitable but will turn to the network when they require specialist resources, information or help. Clearly, they will not only be able to draw on such support but will also contribute to the group. The range of possibilities is enormous.

(Gains and Smith 1994: 95)

The quotation above illustrates a new situation that has evolved alongside the inclusive schooling movement during the 1990s. It is now argued that schools in each district, rather than working in total isolation from one another, should try to organize themselves in clusters in order to share resources and make better use of available expertise to serve students with special educational needs. This view has grown partly from a recognition that much professional expertise in schools had been left untapped in the past and could be better utilized to help schools meet their own needs, and partly from the economic reality that resources are finite and demand always outstrips supply.

CLUSTERS AND NETWORKS

In place of the older model of special education service delivery, in which schools immediately looked to outside 'experts' for assistance, it is now expected that schools will look first to their own resources and their own curricula before calling on external help. While support services will still be maintained within the options available to meet special educational needs, neighbourhood schools are being actively encouraged to establish mutual help networks in order to share resources, solve problems and develop a pool of expertise that can be of benefit to all teachers and students. The key word in service provision and resourcing in the 1990s is 'collaboration' (Lunt *et al.* 1994).

The emphasis in planning and responding to special educational needs has quite clearly moved to a 'whole school' approach . This trend toward a school-based, self-sufficient support system was evident even before the *Code of*

Practice on Identification and Assessment of Special Educational Needs (Department for Education 1994) was published in Britain; but the Code has served to highlight the need for whole school acceptance of responsibility for special education. The provision for students with special needs has to be seen as an integral part of the planning for all students.

To facilitate school-level responses to the needs of individual students and their teachers, one system which appears to operate well is the establishment of a school-based 'teacher assistance team' or 'special needs team' (Bradley and Roaf 1995). The 'team' is made up from school staff who have a broad knowledge of different teaching strategies and are conversant with flexible ways of managing classrooms. A teacher who has a student with learning or behaviour difficulties is encouraged to join the team, and through open discussion with colleagues, strategies are developed to meet the student's needs. By drawing upon the existing pool of knowledge and experience many classroom problems can be resolved and teacher-support structures put in place. Referral of a problem to a school-based special needs team usually brings far more rapid action and assistance than referral to outside agencies could ever achieve. The system is also said to help individual teachers to become more confident in sharing problems with colleagues, and eventually more self-sufficient in dealing with students' difficulties and differences.

Teachers' networks for mutual help can extend beyond the school itself. It is extremely helpful for staff with similar concerns across a number of different schools to be able to contact one another to discuss problems and possible solutions. Sometimes such networks become established informally; but it should be part of the role of a special needs co-ordinator or visiting special education adviser to help establish contact between teachers with similar professional needs.

THE COLLABORATIVE CONSULTATION MODEL

The 1990s have seen the emergence of the collaborative consultation model for school-based planning. This model is based on the premise that more is to be gained by classroom teachers working collaboratively with other professionals to reach solutions to their problems, rather than being presented with ready-made recipes from outside experts. Often such ready-made solutions do not work, given the complexities of the classroom situation, and teachers feel no particular commitment to them.

Collaboration in this special needs context implies that two or more individuals with useful knowledge will work together to devise appropriate strategies for school-level and classroom-level intervention. Implicit in the notion of collaboration is the sharing of expertise. Givner and Haager (1995) suggest that inclusion of students with special needs will be facilitated if special education teachers and regular class teachers increase their level of communication and learn from one another.

Also implicit in professional collaboration are feelings of shared commitment, responsibility and accountability for outcomes (Davis and Kemp 1995). By having significant input into the decision-making process, the teacher feels ownership for the plans that are made and can comment at once on the feasibility of any intervention strategies being suggested.

The 'consultant' in this process may well be a special education support teacher, the school's special educational needs co-ordinator or an adviser from a special services division, such as a speech pathologist, educational psychologist, physiotherapist or disability adviser. The role of such individuals is to contribute ideas and suggestions to a general plan of action, not to supply ready-made prescriptions. Davis and Kemp (1995: 22) have said, 'Consultants need the skills to provide facilitative assistance as well as prescriptive advice'. It is believed that, given the scarcity of human resources, support teachers and other specialists can achieve greater impact by working in a consultative role with teachers than by working directly with individual students with special needs (Fields 1994).

In the early stages, the collaborative consultation model met with some resistance from teachers. This was due to such factors as their reluctance to accept full responsibility for students who previously would have been handed over to the remedial teacher or special class teacher, and having to learn new ways of organizing their programmes and teaching. It is also clear that some regular class teachers find difficulty in communicating and sharing their problems and concerns with other professionals (Fields 1995). This is not something that their previous training or experience required them to do. While consultants should have effective skills in communication and collaborative planning, they need to recognize that some teachers do not have these skills well developed and do not find the consultation process easy.

There are also difficulties experienced by some consultants. When these specialists move from school to school it is difficult for them to feel part of any school staff (Bailey and Bailey 1993). It is hard to present oneself as highly credible in a particular field if there is little opportunity to demonstrate one's skills. While the current view is that consultants should work with teachers rather than students, the only way to establish one's credibility initially may well be through direct work with students.

What do regular class teachers want to know?

Some of the most common questions and issues raised by regular class teachers in collaborative consultation situations are listed below. Rather than an outside expert providing glib answers to these questions, the preferred approach allows for a support teacher or other appropriate professional to work with the teacher to plan solutions together.

Teachers who are including students with disabilities and difficulties in their classes usually want to know:

- how to establish appropriate objectives for the student with disabilities in both the academic and the social areas, and how to use these objectives as the basis for regular assessment of progress;
- how to teach diagnostically and adapt teaching procedures to match the characteristics and needs of different students (differentiation);
- how to provide learning situations which will enable the student to be 'counted in' as much as possible with the other students and make a contribution to the lessons (inclusive curriculum);
- how to implement individual education programmes when necessary to provide training in specific areas not covered in the regular classroom programme, but required by the individual student (individual programming);
- how to create situations where social skills and group-working skills are developed through interaction between the student and the peer group (social inclusion);
- how to train a student in self-management skills and how to encourage independence and initiative;
- how to liaise effectively with parents in order to establish a situation of mutual trust and mutual help;
- how to liaise with specialists where necessary (e.g. speech therapist; psychologist);
- how to make optimum use of available support (both material and human);
- how to apply the strategies and tactics which are associated with high-quality education for all students.

SPECIAL EDUCATIONAL NEEDS CO-ORDINATORS

In Britain, the Code of Practice (Department for Education 1994) has significantly raised the profile of special needs in all schools, and has increased the responsibilities attached to the role of 'special educational needs co-ordinator' (SENCO) in each school. A teacher with similar responsibilities is typically found in schools in other developed countries, although the exact title of the position may differ. When examining the responsibilities of SENCOs, Gains (1994: 102) has written, 'The role conceived for this group of teachers is breathtakingly broad, full of challenge and potential but equally fraught with problems and difficulties'.

The role description provided in the Code of Practice (para. 2.14) indicates that the SENCO is responsible for:

- the day-to-day operation of the school's special educational needs policy;
- liaising with and advising fellow teachers;

- co-ordinating provision for children with special educational needs;
- maintaining the school's special needs register and keeping records on the education and progress of all students with special needs;
- liaising with parents of children with special needs;
- contributing to the in-service training and development of staff;
- liaising with outside agencies.

From this list of responsibilities, Gains (1994) identifies eight key functions to be carried out by SENCOs:

- *administration and management*: for example, responsibility for organizing the support system in the school; implementing the school policy; maintaining records; attending meetings and case conferences, obtaining resources and preparing budgets, etc.;
- *assessment*: identifying students with special educational needs by drawing upon information from a variety of sources; monitoring students' progress;
- *prescription and planning*: preparing and processing IEPs; matching resources to needs, using assessment data to guide curriculum planning, etc.;
- *teaching and pastoral care*: directly supporting students with special needs; indirectly supporting students with special needs through team teaching and other forms of collaboration with staff; counselling individual students, etc.;
- *curriculum support*: helping colleagues adapt programmes, differentiate curricula and prepare resources, etc.;
- *liaison*: with parents, staff, outside agencies, other schools, etc.;
- *training and development*: assisting with professional development of colleagues through consultation, in-service workshops, resources, etc.;
- *collaboration*: working with other co-ordinators in other schools, and with other professionals to assist with IEPs, differentiated curricula and special services provision.

It has been suggested that in large schools the task confronting the SENCO is enormous (Dyson and Gains 1995). Given that up to 20 per cent of students in a school may have long-term or short-term special educational needs, the prospect of overseeing provision, keeping records and liaising with staff involved with up to two hundred individuals is daunting. However, judging from the very positive examples of well co-ordinated services being provided in schools, it seems that the role can be enacted effectively (Cade and Caffyn 1994; Harvey 1995; Wheal 1995).

In addition to the creation of a special educational needs co-ordinator's position and the establishment of teacher assistance teams, it is important to consider what other school-based arrangements can be made to cater for the needs of a diverse population of students.

HELPING STRATEGIES WITHIN THE CLASSROOM

One of the major problems faced by the teacher who has a student with a learning difficulty or disability in the regular class is how to organize in such a way that, if necessary, he or she can spend a little time with that student each day. This individual attention must not be achieved at the expense of other students in the group. The following options are worth consideration:

- peer tutoring;
- cross-age tutoring;
- teacher aides and paraprofessionals;
- parents;
- volunteer helpers;
- high-school, college and university students;
- team teaching;
- school principal or deputy principal;
- support teachers;
- computer-assisted instruction.

Peer tutoring and cross-age tutoring

The most readily available human resource in the classroom is the students. McCoy (1995) describes the creation of a system whereby students can help each other to learn. This should not always be seen as 'the more able helping the less able' but rather students working in the role of tutor and tutee and applying the principle 'One who teaches also learns'. The value of peer tutoring is well documented (Cole and Chan 1990).

All the advocates of peer tutoring or cross-age tutoring stress the importance of having preparation sessions for the tutors so that they adopt appropriate skills and techniques. In general, peer tutors seem to benefit from the following guidance:

- clear directions as to what they are to do and how they are to do it;
- a specific teaching task to undertake and appropriate instructional materials;
- a demonstration of effective tutoring behaviours;
- an opportunity to role play or practise tutoring, with feedback and correction.

Peer tutoring has the advantage of reducing the time a teacher needs to spend interacting with a whole class. It thus increases the amount of time he or she has available to work directly with students who have learning problems. Alternatively, a student with a problem, for example in mathematics, reading or writing, may well be helped very efficiently by a friend in the class or by a student from a higher grade. Many schools make use of older students to help younger children, to the benefit of both. It appears that the 'tutors' often use simple, direct language and demonstrate things more rapidly and effectively than do many teachers. Payne (1991) reports great success in using peer tutoring at secondary level, not only in language arts but also science and mathematics. Her system is so well accepted by the students that those with learning difficulties now take the initiative and ask for a tutor to assist them.

McCoy (1995) suggests that peer tutors can carry out two main types of teaching task:

- helping the tutee acquire a new skill or new information;
- providing the tutee with extra practice in an acquired skill to increase fluency.

When tutoring a student with learning difficulties, the peer tutor's role is often best confined to building the tutee's fluency in areas such as reading aloud, spelling, mathematics facts or the memorization of important information.

Teacher aides and paraprofessionals

An aide can either work individually with the student on material and activities planned by the teacher, or the aide could supervise in a general way the rest of class on work set by the teacher while the teacher works with the student. The aide should not be expected to determine what the student needs; that is clearly the teacher's responsibility.

Aides can fulfil the important role of 'trusted adults' who have time to listen to individual students' interests and worries. They are therefore instrumental in improving the students' communication skills while acting as counsellor and friend.

Parents

Many schools now involve parents in the educational programme. The parents usually require some degree of training and preparation by the teacher in order to be used to maximum advantage (e.g. how to talk with students and be encouraging; how to listen to students read; how to use the 'pause, prompt, praise' approach to reading; how to offer conference writing sessions; how to use particular word-building, spelling or number games, etc.). Parental involvement need not be confined to the reading programme. Hawkins (1991) reports very positive effects when using parents as tutors in mathematics.

The suggested training to be given to peer tutors described above applies equally to parent helpers. This structured use of parental involvement appears to yield the best results in terms of gains in student achievement (Topping 1991).

Parents are not necessarily natural teachers, particularly of their own children. Without some initial guidance on strategies for working with children, parents tend to require them to perform perfectly in tasks such as reading, writing and spelling, and when errors arise are too critical and negative, rather than encouraging in their feedback. In reading, they tend to have students focus attention too much on isolated words or letters, rather than helping them develop strategies for using context and reading for meaning (Builder 1991). Similarly, parents tend to want students to read for unreasonably long periods of time, particularly when tutoring the child at home. With guidance they can become much more effective in their supporting role.

The involvement of parents in schools can have some real benefits for the parents as well as the students with whom they work (Payne 1991). They develop an understanding of the aims of the school and of the methods being used. They learn new approaches they can use at home (e.g. in managing behaviour, encouraging reading). They can share interests and concerns with other parents, and if their own child has a learning difficulty they can often be relieved to discover that many other students have problems too. They grow in confidence as people and establish a much more positive relationship with the teachers.

Volunteer helpers

Volunteers are often used to excellent advantage in both special schools and regular classrooms. With unemployment running at a high level many volunteers could be found for such a role. Some retired people who wish to remain active have been used very successfully as tutors in high-school programmes and as mentors in gifted children's projects. The preparation they need is similar to that described for peer tutors and parents.

High-school and college students

Many high-school students are gaining experience from working with children in kindergartens and junior primary schools. This is usually as part of a work-experience or community involvement programme for senior students. If their presence is timetabled on a regular basis the teacher can make use of their services for group work or individual help.

Team teaching

If two or more teachers are prepared to work together for a least part of each day, the organizational options are at once increased. Quite large groups may be taken for certain activities (e.g. films, TV, story, etc.) by one teacher, so releasing the other to work with quite small groups of individuals. Team teaching also allows teachers to discuss and share their problems and to learn from one another. In may ways, differentiation of approach and collaborative planning are more easily facilitated if more than one adult is involved in delivering the programme.

Principal or deputy

The head teacher or deputy may take a regular time slot with the class, thus releasing the teacher for individual work with certain students.

Support teachers

Usually, when a student with a significant disability is integrated into the class, the services of a special education support teacher will be provided for at least a few hours each week. It is expected that initially the support teacher might work directly with the student, but gradually move toward providing more support to the teacher by assisting with modifications to curriculum content, developing alternative resources and setting up student-support networks in the class. Support teachers play a key role in helping teachers to differentiate programme content and teaching approach.

Computer-assisted instruction

The use of computers has been discussed in chapters on literacy and numeracy. In effect, a computer can act as an additional 'person' in the classroom, providing instruction and giving feedback. Students may work collaboratively in pairs at the computer, or parents or volunteers may elect to work with certain students. With some students receiving computer-assisted instruction there is at once the possibility to reduce the class size and allow for more individual contact from the teacher.

THE RESOURCE ROOM MODEL

Students with disabilities, including those with specific learning disabilities, integrated in regular classes may still need to receive additional help from personnel outside the classroom setting. The resource room model as a school-based support system still appears to meet some students' needs, particularly in high schools. Sceptics argue that the resource room is nothing more than the old 'remedial withdrawal room' given a more palatable name. On the other hand, advocates point out that the resource room operates in a much more flexible manner than the traditional remedial room and provides a base from which the support or resource teacher can operate. Students may go to the room for special help but it is equally likely that the teacher may go to the student's classroom to provide in-class support.

The resource room is often the focal point from which general classroom teachers can borrow materials and equipment to support their differentiated practices. For example, it is also seen as the collecting house for materials and ideas for the most able, as well as the least able students.

Sindelar and Deno (1978) reviewed seventeen studies concerned with the efficacy of resource programming. They conclude that in the academic domain, learning disabled and mildly disturbed students seem to benefit from resource room programmes which involve withdrawal from the regular classroom. It may not be possible to provide interventions with adequate intensity and precision for these students through in-class support alone. The resource room programme can meet that need.

Resource teachers can produce greater impact when they manage a support system involving other personnel than when they merely instruct small groups or individuals themselves. As well as supporting other teaching staff and some individual students, the resource teacher may also be involved in setting up such classroom-based strategies as peer tutoring, cross-age tutoring or learning assistance programmes using volunteers.

SCHOOL-BASED POLICIES FOR SPECIAL NEEDS

The ways in which a school can marshal its resources, both material and human, should be formalized through the establishment of a school policy created by, and genuinely 'owned' by, the whole school staff (Ashman and Elkins 1994). Bines (1989) has concluded that developing a whole-school policy document is a useful and important process. It is a method for clarifying beliefs, accepting responsibility at school level and making the best use of available expertise and resources.

The Code of Practice in Britain (Department for Education 1994) requires schools to produce a special educational needs policy, and indicates the three main types of information to be provided within it. These areas are:

- *information about the school's special education provisions*: objectives, co-ordination, admissions procedures, special facilities, range of options available at classroom level and at school level (e.g. in-class support, withdrawal, resource room, teacher assistance teams, team teaching, learning assistance programmes, etc.);
- *information about the school's procedures:* identification of special needs, assessment, allocation of resources, access to mainstream curriculum, review procedures, support systems, etc.;
- *information about staffing, and partnership with agencies and individuals outside the school*: arrangements for staff development and training, contacts with parents, support teachers, specialists, other schools, social services, health and welfare services, etc.

Other elements which may be integrated into a school policy include:

- *situational analysis*: a description of the school population, with particular reference to special educational needs and available personnel and resources;
- *belief statements*: a summary of the consensus of opinion and beliefs within the school staff concerning the most effective ways of meeting students' special needs in terms of instruction, management and placement; beliefs are usually linked with existing policies on social justice, equality of opportunity and inclusion;
- *staff roles and responsibilities*: an indication of who is directly responsible for identification, referral, decision-making and resource allocation for special educational needs.

THE ROLE OF THE SUPPORT TEACHER

In recent years, the role of the support teacher has changed from the direct teaching of students with special needs to supporting regular class teachers as they attempt to include students with disabilities within their classroom programmes (Lovey 1996). In particular, the support teacher engages much more in collaborative consultation with teachers and assists them with curriculum differentiation. Greenhalgh (1996) suggests that rather than referring to it as 'support' teaching, we should now call it 'partnership teaching', as that term more accurately describes the role as it has evolved.

The current emphasis upon school-based policy making, and the development of self-sufficiency in meeting special educational needs, has not rendered visiting support teachers redundant. Indeed, there is some indication that their role may become even more important in providing input into the planning and implementation of students' individual education plans, assisting with differentiated curriculum design, and providing staff training and development activities (Bines and Loxley 1995).

The following duties are still seen as part of the support teacher's role, but one which is now shared with the special educational needs co-ordinator in most schools:

- educational assessment and diagnosis, using formal and informal methods in conjunction with information available from other sources;
- regular evaluation of the progress made by students receiving direct support;
- collaboration with staff in the development and implementation of IEPs;
- assistance to staff in devising inclusive curricula and differentiation in classroom practice;
- provision or loan of resource materials to assist with differentiated curricula;
- teaching of individuals or small groups within the classroom or elsewhere;
- co-teaching with the regular class teacher;
- taking the class while the class teacher works with a small group;
- providing school-based and regional in-service sessions for teachers.

As many support teachers work across a region, they should be deployed where possible in such a way that ensures that they do not have too many schools or too many students and staff to service. Efficiency will be lessened if the service is spread too thinly. It is best that a thorough job be done intensively in a small number of schools or with a small number of students for a viable period. As class teachers gradually become more adaptive in their approach to all students, it should be possible to withdraw much of the direct help and contact which was required initially.

Over to you: *Special educational needs in the regular school*

- Your school may have a significant number of children with special educational needs. How might you determine the size of the problem in your school?

- Given an ideal situation how would you organize the timetable and deploy teaching staff and other available personnel to create a viable support system?

- Identify and list the main obstacles which would need to be overcome in order to implement such a programme in your school.

- If your school already has a support system established for children with special needs, evaluate its present positive and negative features. How might it be improved?

Regardless of whether a special education support teacher provides help to a regular class teacher via collaborative consultation, a resource room programme, co-teaching, the production of resources or through any combination of these, certain issues are important. Support teachers and SENCOs need to have 'change-agent skills'. They need to be able to relate appropriately to the teachers and principals with whom they work. This 'change-agent/support' role is a very difficult one. To be able to relate to and influence the behaviour of colleagues requires enormous tact and subtlety. One of the most obvious temptations for the support teacher in the consultant role is 'coming the expert'. From the first moment of contact with a teacher who has requested advice or help, the support teacher should establish the idea that he or she is there to work out possible solutions or strategies jointly with the teacher, and that there are no ready-made answers or panaceas, but that *together* they will try various solutions.

It is vital that the support teacher recognizes from the start that a teacher who seeks help has certain attitudes and expectations concerning the student with special needs. These attitudes and expectations may be very positive and very realistic, or they may be totally unrealistic. The teacher will also have certain expectations of the support teacher which may be unrealistic. Whatever the attitude and expectations are they will not be changed overnight. Establishing a working relationship with the teacher must involve mutual trust and gradual adaptation. Collaboration will only work successfully if the contributions of all parties are valued equally.

SUMMARY

This chapter has discussed some of the recent changes in the ways in which support is provided to students with special needs and their teachers. In particular, attention has been given to the current move toward making all schools more self-sufficient in meeting students' special needs. The positive features of the collaborative consultation approach were discussed, together with some of the minor problems associated with its implementation. The role and contribution of outside agencies, advisers, special educational needs co-ordinators and support teachers has been considered.

Discussion points

• Most research literature on problems involved in educational change (e.g. Fullan 1991) indicates that teachers are reluctant to change unless the benefits of doing so obviously outweigh the personal costs. Inclusion of students with disabilities frequently requires teachers to change in ways which they may perceive to be threatening and unreasonable. How might the problems involved in implementing inclusive practices be minimized?

• Given an ideal situation, what outside services and personnel do you feel are necessary for really effective educational support for students with disabilities in the mainstream?

• Discuss some of the interpersonal skills teachers, advisers and specialists need to develop in order to be effective participants in collaborative consultation.

Further reading

Baker, D. and Bovair, K. (eds) (1989) *Making the Special Schools Ordinary*, London: Falmer.

Bay, M., Bryan, T. and O'Connor, R. (1994) 'Teachers assisting teachers: a pre-referral model', *Teacher Education and Special Education* 17, 1: 10–21.

Davis, L. and Kemp, C. (1995) 'A collaborative consultation service delivery model for support teachers', *Special Education Perspectives* 4, 1: 17–28.

Friend, M. and Cook, L. (1992) *Interactions: Collaboration Skills for School Professionals*, New York: Longman.

Hornby, G., Taylor, G. and Davis, G. (1995) *The Special Educational Needs Co-ordinator's Handbook*, London: Routledge.

Jordan, A. (1994) *Skills in Collaborative Classroom Consultation*, London: Routledge.

Lovey, J. (1995) *Supporting Special Needs in Secondary Classrooms*, London: Fulton.

Morsink, C.V., Thomas, C.C. and Correa, V.I. (1991) *Interactive Teaming: Consultation and Collaboration in Special Programs*, New York: Macmillan.

Panter, S. (1995) *How to Survive as a SEN Co-ordinator*, Lichfield, Staffs.: QEd Publishing.

West, J.F. and Idol, L. (1990) 'Collaborative consultation in the education of mildly handicapped and at-risk students', *Remedial and Special Education* 11, 1: 22–31.

Wiederholt, J.L., Hammill, D. and Brown, V. (1993) *The Resource Program*, Austin: Pro-Ed.

References

Achilles, C.M. (1996) 'Students achieve more in smaller classes', *Educational Leadership* 53, 5: 76–7.

Adams, M.J. (1990) *Beginning to Read: Thinking and Learning about Print*, Cambridge, Mass.: MIT Press.

Adams, M.J. (1994) 'The progress of the whole-language debate', *Educational Psychologist* 29, 4: 217–22.

Adelman, H.S. and Taylor, L. (1987) *An Introduction to Learning Disability*, London: Scott Foresman.

Agudelo-Valderrama, A.C. (1996) 'Improving mathematics education in Colombian schools: mathematics for all', *International Journal of Educational Development* 16, 1: 15–29.

Ainscow, M. and Muncey, J. (1990) *Meeting Individual Needs*, London: Fulton.

American Guidance Service (1991) *Early Screening Profiles*, Circle Pines, Minn.: AGS.

American Psychiatric Association (1994) *Diagnostic and Statistical Manual of Mental Disorders* (DSM IV), Washington, DC: APA.

Anderson, J. (1990) 'Computers as learning tools in remedial teaching', *Australian Journal of Remedial Education* 22, 2: 8–12.

Andrews, J. and Lupart, J. (1993) *The Inclusive Classroom: Educating Exceptional Children*, Scarborough, Ontario: Nelson.

Ariel, A. (1992) *Education of Children and Adolescents with Learning Disabilities*, New York: Merrill.

Ashcraft, M.H. (1985) 'Is it farfetched that some of us remember our number facts?', *Journal for Research in Mathematics Education* 16, 2: 99–105.

Ashman, A. and Conway, R. (1989) *Cognitive Strategies for Special Education*, London: Routledge.

Ashman, A. and Elkins, J. (eds) (1994) *Educating Children with Special Needs* (2nd edn), New York: Prentice Hall.

Ashman, A.F., van Kraayenoord, C.E. and Elkins, J. (1992) 'Intervention research in Australia', in B.Y.Wong (ed.) *Contemporary Intervention Research in Learning Disabilities: International Perspectives*, New York: Springer Verlag.

Au, W.K. and Bruce, M. (1990) 'Using computers in special education', *Australian Journal of Remedial Education* 22, 1: 13–18.

Ayers, L. (1995) 'The efficacy of three training conditions on phonological awareness of kindergarten children and the longitudinal effect of each on later reading acquisition', *Reading Research Quarterly* 30, 4: 604–6.

Badian, N.A. (1988) 'Predicting dyslexia in a preschool population', in R.L. Masland

and M.W. Masland (eds) *Preschool Prevention of Reading Failure*, Parkton: York Press.

Badian, N.A. (1996) 'Dyslexia: a validation of the concept at two age levels', *Journal of Learning Disabilities* 29, 1: 102–12.

Bailey, J. and Bailey, R. (1993) 'Improving the morale of learning support teachers', *Australian Journal of Remedial Education* 25, 2: 7–10.

Baker, E.L., Herman, J.L. and Yeh, J.P. (1981) 'Fun and games; their contribution to basic skills instruction', *American Educational Research Journal* 18, 1: 83–92.

Ball, E.W. and Blachman, B.A. (1991) 'Does phonemic awareness training in kindergarten make a difference in early word recognition and developmental spelling?', *Reading Research Quarterly* 26, 1: 49–66.

Balson, M. (1992) *Understanding Classroom Behaviour* (3rd edn), Hawthorn: Australian Council for Educational Research.

Banerji, M. and Dailey, R.A. (1995) 'A study of the effects of an inclusion model on students with specific learning disabilities', *Journal of Learning Disabilities* 28, 8: 511–22.

Baroff, G.S. (1991) *Developmental Disabilities*, Austin: Pro-Ed.

Barry, A.L. (1995) 'Easing into inclusion classrooms', *Educational Leadership* 52, 4: 4–6.

Barton, L. (1995) 'The politics of education for all', *Support for Learning* 10, 4: 156–60.

Bearne, E. (1996) *Differentiation and Diversity in the Primary School*, London: Routledge.

Bechtol, W.M. and Sorenson, J.S. (1993) *Restructuring Schooling for Individual Students*, Boston: Allyn and Bacon.

Beck, I.L. and Juel, C. (1992) 'The role of decoding in learning to read', in S.J. Samuels and A.E. Farstrup (eds) *What Research has to Say about Reading Instruction* (2nd edn), Newark, NJ: International Reading Association.

Bendell, D., Tollefson, N. and Fine, M. (1980) 'Interaction of locus of control and the performance of learning disabled adolescents', *Journal of Learning Disabilities* 13, 2: 83–6.

Bennett, F. (1993) 'Early intervention: a paediatric perspective', *Special Education Perspectives* 2, 2: 73–7.

Bentley, D. (1990) *Teaching Spelling: Some Questions Answered*, Earley: University of Reading.

Biemiller, A. (1994) 'Some observations on beginning reading instruction', *Educational Psychologist* 29, 4: 203–9.

Bines, H. (1989) 'Whole school policies at primary level', *British Journal of Special Education* 16, 2: 80–2.

Bines, H. and Loxley, A., (1995) 'Implementing the Code of Practice for special educational needs', *Oxford Review of Education* 21, 4: 381–94.

Bishop, K.D. and Jubala, K.A. (1995) 'Positive behaviour support strategies', in M.A. Falvey (ed.) *Inclusive and Heterogeneous Schooling*, Baltimore: Brookes.

Blumenfeld, S.L. (1991) *Alpha-Phonics: A Primer for Beginning Readers*, Boise, Idaho: Paradigm.

Booth, T. (1996) 'A perspective on inclusion from England', *Cambridge Journal of Education* 26, 1: 87–99.

Bosch, K.A. and Bowers, R.S. (1992) 'Count me in too: math instruction strategies for the discouraged learner', *The Clearing House* 66, 2: 104–6.

Bourke, S. (1981) 'Community expectations of numeracy in schools', *SET Research Information for Teachers, No. 1*, Hawthorn: ACER.

Bowd, A. (1990) *Exceptional Children in Class* (2nd edn.), Melbourne: Hargreen.

Boyle, G. (1990) 'Time out: a remedial strategy', in S. Butler (ed.) *The Exceptional Child*, Sydney: Harcourt Brace Jovanovich.

Bradley, C. and Roaf, C. (1995) 'Meeting special educational needs in the secondary school: a team approach', *Support for Learning* 10, 2: 93–9.

Bradley, L. (1990) 'Rhyming connections in learning to read and spell', in P. Pumfrey and C. Elliott (eds) *Children's Difficulties in Reading, Spelling and Writing*. London: Falmer.

Bradshaw, K. (1995) 'Learning disabilities: a cautionary tale', *Australian Journal of Remedial Education*, 27, 4: 15–17.

Brandt, R.S. (1985) 'Success through adaptive education', *Educational Leadership* 43, 1: 3.

Branson, J. and Miller, D. (1991) 'Discipline and integration programmes: normalization through schooling', in M.N. Lovegrove and R. Lewis (eds) *Classroom Discipline*, Melbourne: Longman Cheshire.

Brennan, W.K. (1985) *Curriculum for Special Needs*, Milton Keynes: Open University Press.

Brock, A. (1995) 'Developmental dyslexia', *Australian Journal of Remedial Education* 27, 4: 20–5.

Brucker, P.O. (1995) 'The advantages of inclusion for students with learning disabilities', *Journal of Learning Disabilities* 27, 9: 581–2.

Bryant, P. and Bradley, L. (1985) *Children's Reading Problems*, Oxford: Blackwell.

Builder, P. (1991) *Exploring Reading: Empowering Readers with Special Needs*, Hawthorn: ACER.

Burton, G.M. (1985) *Towards a Good Beginning: Teaching Early Childhood Mathematics*, Menlo Park: Addison-Wesley.

Butler, D.L. (1995) 'Promoting strategic learning by post-secondary students with learning disabilities', *Journal of Learning Disabilities* 28, 3: 170–90.

Butler, S. (ed.) (1990) *The Exceptional Child*, Sydney: Harcourt Brace Jovanovich.

Cade, L. and Caffyn, R. (1994) 'The King Edward VI family: an example of clustering in Nottinghamshire', *Support for Learning* 9, 2: 83–8.

Calf, B. (1990) 'Educational implications', in S. Butler (ed.) *The Exceptional Child*, Sydney: Harcourt Brace Jovanovich.

Cambourne, B. (1988) *The Whole Story: Natural Learning and Literacy Acquisition*, Auckland: Ashton Scholastic.

Campbell, F.A. and Ramey, C.T. (1994) 'Effects of early intervention on intellectual and academic achievement', *Child Development* 65, 2: 684–98.

Campbell, P.F. and Stewart, E.L. (1993) 'Calculators and computers', in R.J. Jensen (ed.) *Research Ideas for the Classroom: Early Childhood Mathematics*, New York: Macmillan.

Carbo, M. (1996) 'Reading styles', *Educational Leadership* 53, 5: 8–13.

Carpenter, T.P. (1985) 'Research on the role of structure in thinking', *Arithmetic Teacher* 32, 6: 58–60.

Carroll, A. (1994) 'Current perspectives on attention deficit hyperactivity disorder: a review of literature', *Australasian Journal of Special Education* 18, 1: 15–24.

Casazza, M.E. (1992) 'Teaching summary writing to enhance comprehension', *Reading Today* 9, 4: 26.

Cashdan, A. and Wright, J. (1990) 'Intervention strategies for backward readers', in P. Pumfrey and C. Elliott (eds) *Children's Difficulties in Reading, Spelling and Writing*, London: Falmer.

Cawley, J.E., Baker-Kroczynski, S. and Urban, A. (1992) 'Seeking excellence in mathematics education for students with mild disabilities', *Teaching Exceptional Children* 24, 2: 40–3.

Chall, J. (1989) 'Learning to read: the great debate ten years later', *Phi Delta Kappan* 70, 7: 521–38.

Chan, L. (1991) 'Metacognition and remedial education', *Australian Journal of Remedial Education* 23, 1: 4–10.

Chapman, J.W and Tunmer, W.E. (1991) 'Recovering reading recovery', *Australian and New Zealand Journal of Developmental Disabilities* 17, 1: 59–71.

Chinn, S. and Ashcroft, J. (1993) *Mathematics for Dyslexics: A Teaching Handbook*, London: Whurr.

Choate, J.S. (1993) *Successful Mainstreaming*, Boston: Allyn and Bacon.

Choate, J.S. and Rakes, T.A, (1993)'Recognizing words: the tools for reading comprehension', in J.S. Choate, *Successful Mainstreaming*, Boston: Allyn and Bacon.

Church, J. and Langley, J. (1990) 'Behaviour disordered children', *SET Research Information for Teachers 2/90*, Hawthorn: Australian Council for Educational Research.

Clark, D.B. (1992) 'Beginning reading instruction for learning disabled and at-risk students', in S.A, Vogel (ed.) *Educational Alternatives for Students with Learning Disabilities*, New York: Springer Verlag.

Clark, G.M. (1994) 'Is a functional curriculum approach compatible with an inclusive education model?' *Teaching Exceptional Children* 26, 2: 36–9.

Clarke, D.J. (1992) 'Activating assessment alternatives in mathematics', *Arithmetic Teacher* 39, 6: 24–39.

Clay, M.M. (1985) *The Early Detection of Reading Difficulties* (3rd edn), Auckland: Heinemann.

Clay, M.M. (1990) 'The Reading Recovery Programme, 1984–1988', *New Zealand Journal of Educational Studies* 25, 1: 61–70.

Clerehugh, J. (1991) *Early Years Easy Screen (EYES)*, Windsor: NFER-Nelson.

Cohen, N.J. and Minde, K. (1983) 'The hyperactive syndrome in kindergarten children', *Journal of Child Psychology and Psychiatry* 24, 3: 443–55.

Cohen, S.B. and Lynch, D.K. (1991) 'An instructional modification process', *Teaching Exceptional Children* 23, 4: 12–18.

Cole, P. (1995) 'Motivation and learning', in F. Maltby, N. Gage and D. Berliner (eds) *Educational Psychology: An Australian and New Zealand Perspective*, Brisbane: Wiley.

Cole, P. and Chan, L. (1990) *Methods and Strategies for Special Education*, New York: Prentice Hall.

Conners, F.A. (1992) 'Reading instruction for students with moderate mental retardation: review and analysis of research', *American Journal on Mental Retardation* 96, 6: 577–97.

Connor, M. (1994) 'Specific learning difficulty (dyslexia) and interventions', *Support for Learning* 9, 3: 114–19.

Conway, R. (1990) 'Behaviour disorders', in A. Ashman and J. Elkins (eds) *Educating Children with Special Needs*, New York: Prentice Hall.

Conway, R. and Gow, L. (1990) 'Moderate to mild disability: teaching and learning strategies', in S. Butler (ed.) *The Exceptional Child*, Sydney: Harcourt Brace Jovanovich.

Cooper, C.S. and McEvoy, M.A. (1996) 'Group friendship activities', *Teaching Exceptional Children* 28, 3: 67–9.

Cornoldi, C. (1990) 'Metacognitive control processes', *Learning Disability Quarterly* 13, 4: 245–55.

Creemers, B. (1994) *The Effective Classroom*, London: Cassell.

Cripps, C. (1978) *Catchwords: Ideas for Teaching Spelling*, Sydney: Harcourt Brace Jovanovich.

Cripps, C. (1983) 'A report of an experiment to see whether young children can be taught to write from memory', *Remedial Education* 18, 1: 19–24.

Cripps, C. (1990) 'Teaching joined writing to children on school entry as an agent for catching spelling', *Australian Journal of Remedial Education* 22, 3: 13–15.

Crittenden, B. (1991) 'Three approaches to classroom discipline: philosophical perspectives', in M.N. Lovegrove and R. Lewis (eds) *Classroom Discipline*, Melbourne: Longman Cheshire.

Crux, S.C. (1991) 'HELP: a whole language literacy strategy that works', *Education Canada* 31, 2: 16–21.

Csapo, M. (1983) 'Effectiveness of coaching socially withdrawn and isolated children in specific social skills', *Educational Psychology* 3, 1: 31–42.

Currie, H. (1990) 'Making texts more readable', *British Journal of Special Education* 17, 4: 137–9.

Darch, C., Carnine, D. and Gersten, R. (1984) 'Explicit instruction in mathematics problem solving', *Journal of Educational Research* 77, 6: 351–9.

Davidson and associates (1991) *'Spell It Plus': Computer Program*, Torrance, Calif.: Davidson.

Davis, L. and Kemp, C. (1995) 'A collaborative consultation service model for suppport teachers', *Special Education Perspectives* 4, 1: 17–28.

DeFord, D.E. (1991) 'Fluency in initial reading instruction: Reading Recovery', *Theory into Practice* 30, 3: 201–10.

de Hirsch, K., Jansky, J.J. and Langford, W.S. (1966) *Predicting Reading Failure*, New York: Harper and Row.

Dempster, F.N. (1991) 'Synthesis of research on reviews and tests', *Educational Leadership* 48, 7: 71–6.

Department for Education (1994) *Code of Practice on the Identification and Assessment of Special Educational Needs*, London: HMSO.

DeVries, R. and Zan, B. (1995) 'Creating a constructivist classroom atmosphere', *Young Children* 51, 1: 4–13.

Dohrn, E. and Tanis, B. (1994) 'Attribution instruction', *Teaching Exceptional Children* 26, 4: 61–3.

Dole, J., Duffy, G., Roehler, L.R. and Pearson, P.D. (1991) 'Moving from the old to the new: research in reading comprehension', *Review of Educational Research* 61, 2: 239–64.

Dole, J.A., Brown, K.J. and Trathen, W. (1996) 'The effects of strategy instruction on the comprehension performance of at-risk students', *Reading Research Quarterly* 31, 1: 62–88.

Dougherty, B.J. and Scott, L. (1993) 'Curriculum: a vision for early childhood mathematics', in R.J. Jensen (ed.) *Research Ideas for the Classroom: Early Childhood Mathematics*, New York: Macmillan.

Downing, J. (1966) 'Reading readiness re-examined', in J. Downing (ed.) *The First International Reading Symposium*, London: Cassell.

Downing, J., Schaefer, B. and Ayers, J.D. (1993) *LARR Test of Emergent Literacy*, Windsor: NFER-Nelson.

Drosdeck, C.C. (1995) 'Promoting calculator use in elementary classrooms', *Teaching Children Mathematics* 1, 5: 300–5.

Dyer, C. (1991) 'An end to the slow lane: a critique of the term "slow learner"', *Support for Learning* 6, 2: 66–70.

Dyson, A. (1994) 'Towards a collaborative learning model for responding to student diversity', *Support for Learning* 9, 2: 53–60.

Dyson, A. and Gains, C. (1995) 'The role of the special needs co-ordinator: poisoned chalice or crock of gold?', *Support for Learning* 10, 2: 50–6.

Eldredge, J.L. (1990) 'Increasing the performance of poor readers in the Third Grade with a group-assisted strategy', *Journal of Educational Research* 84, 2: 69–76.

Elliott, P. and Garnett, C. (1994) 'Mathematics power for all', in C.A.Thornton and N.S. Bley (eds) *Windows of Opportunity: Mathematics for Students with Special Needs*, Reston: National Council of Teachers of Mathematics.

Ellis, E.S. (1993) 'Integrative strategy instruction: a potential model for teaching content area subjects to adolescents with learning disabilities', *Journal of Learning Disabilities* 26, 6: 358–83, 398.

Emblem, B. and Conti-Ramsden, G. (1990) 'Towards Level 1 – Reality or illusion?', *British Journal of Special Education* 17, 3: 88–90.

English, K., Goldstein, H., Kaczmarek, L. and Shafer, K. (1996) 'Buddy skills for preschoolers', *Teaching Exceptional Children* 28, 3: 62–6.

Enright, B.E. and Choate, J.S. (1993) 'Arithmetic computation: from concrete to abstract', in J.S.Choate (ed.) *Successful Mainstreaming*, Boston: Allyn and Bacon.

ERIC Digest #E540 (1996) 'Beginning reading and phonological awareness for students with learning disabilities', *Teaching Exceptional Children* 28, 3: 78–9.

Ernest, P. (1996) 'The negative influence of progressive ideas on school mathematics', *Mathematics in School* 25, 2: 6–7.

Evans, D. (1995) 'Human diversity and schools: children with special needs', in F. Maltby, N. Gage and D. Berliner (eds) *Educational Psychology: An Australian and New Zealand Perspective*, Brisbane: Wiley.

Falvey, M.A. and Rosenberg, R.L. (1995) 'Developing and fostering friendships', in M.A. Falvey (ed.) *Inclusive and Heterogeneous Schooling*, Baltimore: Brookes.

Farlow, L. (1996) 'A quartet of success stories: how to make inclusion work', *Educational Leadership* 53, 5: 51–5.

Farmer, T.W. and Farmer, E.M. (1996) 'Social relationships of students with exceptionalities in mainstream classrooms: social networks and homophily', *Exceptional Children*, 62, 5: 431–50.

Felton, R. (1992) 'Early identification of children at risk for reading disabilities', *Topics in Early Childhood Special Education* 12, 2: 212–29.

Fenwick, G. (1988) *USSR: Uninterrupted Sustained Silent Reading*, Reading: University of Reading.

Fielding, L.G. and Pearson, P.D. (1994) 'Reading comprehension: what works?', *Educational Leadership* 51, 5: 62–8.

Fields, B. (1994) 'Consultation models: a comparison of the preferences of primary teachers and support teachers', *Australian Journal of Remedial Education* 26, 1: 21–3.

Fields, B. (1995) 'Teacher resistance: a barrier to special and remedial education support services', *Australian Journal of Remedial Education* 27, 2: 13–18.

Fisher, J.B., Schumaker, J.B. and Deshler, D.D. (1995) 'Searching for validated inclusive practices: a review of the literature', *Focus on Exceptional Children* 28, 4: 1–20.

Flynn, J.M., Deering, W., Goldstein, M. and Mohammad, H.R. (1992) 'Electrophysiological correlates of dyslexic subtypes', *Journal of Learning Disabilities* 25, 2: 133–41.

Franco, D., Christoff, K., Crimmins, D. and Kelly, J. (1983) 'Social skills training for an extremely shy adolescent', *Behaviour Therapy* 14: 568–575.

Frank, A.R. and Brown, D. (1992) 'Self-monitoring strategies in arithmetic', *Teaching Exceptional Children* 24, 2: 52–3.

Franklyn, B. (ed.) (1987) *Learning Disability: Dissenting Essays*, London: Falmer.

Frost, J.A. and Emery, M.J. (1996) 'Academic interventions for children with dyslexia who have phonological core deficits', *Teaching Exceptional Children* 28, 3: 80–3.

Froyen, L.A. (1993) *Classroom Management: The Reflective Teacher-Leader*, New York: Merrill.

Fuchs, D. and Fuchs, L.S. (1994) 'Inclusive schools movement and the radicalization of special education reform', *Exceptional Children* 60, 4: 294–309.

Fuchs, D. and Fuchs, L.S. (1995) 'What's special about special education?', *Phi Delta Kappan* 76, 7: 522–30.

Fullan, M. (1991) *The New Meaning of Educational Change*, London: Cassell.

Fuson, K.C. and Fuson, A.M. (1992) 'Instruction supporting children's counting on and counting up', *Journal for Research in Mathematics Education* 23, 1: 72–8.

Gagne, R., Briggs, L. and Wager, W. (1992) *Principles of Instructional Design* (4th edn), Chicago: Holt Rinehart and Winston.

Gains, C. and Smith, C.J. (1994) 'Cluster models', *Support for Learning* 9, 2: 94–8.

Gains, C.W. (1994) 'New roles for SENCOs', *Support for Learning* 9, 3: 102.

Gaskins, R.W., Gaskins, I.W., Anderson, R.C. and Schommer, M. (1995) 'The reciprocal relationship between research and development: an example involving a decoding strand for poor readers', *Journal of Reading Behaviour* 27, 3: 337–77.

Giangreco, M.F. (1996) 'What do I do now? A teacher's guide to including students with disabilities', *Educational Leadership* 53, 5: 56–9.

Gillet, S. and Bernard, M.E. (1989) *Reading Rescue* (2nd edn), Hawthorn: ACER.

Gillingham, A. and Stillman, B.W. (1960) *Remedial Training for Children with Specific Disability in Reading, Writing and Penmanship*, Cambridge, Mass.: Educators Publishing Service.

Ginsburg, H. and Baroody, A. (1983) *TEMA: Test of Early Mathematics Ability*, Austin: Pro-Ed.

Givner, C.C. and Haager, D. (1995) 'Strategies for effective collaboration', in M.A. Falvey (ed.) *Inclusive and Heterogeneous Schooling*, Baltimore: Brookes.

Goddard, A. (1995) 'From product to process in curriculum planning: a view from Britain, *Journal of Learning Disabilities* 28, 5: 258–63.

Good, T. and Brophy, J. (1994) *Looking in Classrooms* (6th edn), New York: Harper Collins.

Good, T., Mulryan, C. and McCaslin, M. (1992) 'Group instruction in mathematics', in D.A. Grouws (ed.) *Handbook of Research on Mathematics Teaching and Learning*, New York: Macmillan.

Goodman, K. (1967) 'Reading: a psycholinguistic guessing game', *Journal of the Reading Specialist* 6: 126–35.

Goodman, K.S. (1986) *What's Whole in Whole Language?*, Portsmouth: Heinemann.

Goodman, K.S. (1989) 'Whole language is whole: a response to Heymsfeld', *Educational Leadership* 46, 6: 69–70.

Goodman, K.S. (1994a) 'Whole language debate continues: a response to Nicholson', *The Reading Teacher* 47, 8: 599.

Goodman, K.S. (1994b) 'Deconstructing the rhetoric of Moorman, Blanton and McLaughlin', *Reading Research Quarterly* 29, 4: 340–6.

Goswami, U. (1992) 'Phonological factors in spelling development', *Journal of Child Psychology and Psychiatry* 33: 967–75.

Gow, L. and Ward, J. (1991) 'Progress towards integration: impressions from a national review', *Australian Disability Review* 4–91: 8–19.

Graham, S. and Harris K.R. (1994) 'Implications of constructivism for teaching writing to students with special needs', *Journal of Special Education* 28: 275–89.

Graham, S., Harris, K.R. and Loynachan, C. (1996) 'The Directed Spelling Thinking Activity: application with high-frequency words', *Learning Disabilities Research and Practice* 11, 1: 34–40.

Graham, S. Harris, K.R. and Sawyer, R. (1987) 'Composition instruction with learning disabled students: self-instructional strategy training', *Focus on Exceptional Children* 20, 4: 1–11.

Graves, A. and Hauge, R. (1993) 'Using cues and prompts to improve story writing', *Teaching Exceptional Children* 25, 4: 38–40.

Graves, D.H. (1983) *Writing: Teachers and Children at Work*, Exeter, NH: Heinemann.

Green, J. (1993) 'Constructivist strategies for the mathematics teacher', in J.A. Malone and P.C. Taylor (eds) *Constructivist Interpretations of Teaching and Learning Mathematics*, Perth: Curtin University of Technology.

Greenhalgh, P. (1996) 'Behaviour: roles, responsibilities and referrals in the shadow of the Code of Practice', *Support for Learning* 11, 1: 17–24.

Grenot-Scheyer, M., Abernathy, P.A., Williamson, D., Jubala, K. and Coots, J.J. (1995) 'Elementary curriculum and instruction', in M.A. Falvey (ed.) *Inclusive and Heterogeneous Schooling*, Baltimore: Brookes.

Gresham, F.M. (1982) 'Social skills instruction for exceptional children', *Theory into Practice* 21, 2: 129–33.

Gross, H. and Gipps, C. (1987) *Supporting Warnock's Eighteen Percent*, London: Falmer.

Gross, J. (1993) *Special Educational Needs in the Primary School*, London: Open University Press.

Grossman, H. (1995) *Classroom Behaviour Management in a Diverse Society* (2nd edn), Mountain View: Mayfield.

Grossman, H.J. (1983) *Classification in Mental Retardation*, Washington, DC: American Association on Mental Deficiency.

Gulliford, R. (1969) *Backwardness and Educational Failure*, Slough: NFER.

Gunning, T.G. (1995) 'Word building: a strategic approach to the teaching of phonics', *The Reading Teacher* 48, 6: 484–8.

Gurry, D. (1990) 'The physician and the politics of learning difficulties', in S. Butler (ed.) *The Exceptional Child*, Sydney: Harcourt Brace Jovanovich.

Haigh, G. (1977) *Teaching Slow Learners*, London: Temple Smith.

Hallahan, D.P. and Kauffman, J.M. (1986) *Exceptional Children* (3rd edn), Englewood Cliffs: Prentice Hall.

Hallahan, D.P. and Kauffman, J.M. (1991) *Exceptional Children* (5th edn), Englewood Cliffs: Prentice Hall.

Hallahan, D.P. and Kauffman, J.M. (1994) *Exceptional Children* (6th edn), Boston: Allyn and Bacon.

Hannavy, S. (1993) *Middle Infant Screening Test (MIST)*, Windsor: NFER-Nelson.

Hanson, R.A. and Farrell, D. (1995) 'The long-term effects on high school seniors of learning to read in kindergarten', *Reading Research Quarterly* 30, 3: 908–33.

Harris, K.R. and Graham, S. (1996) 'Memo to constructivists: skills count too', *Educational Leadership* 53, 5: 26–9.

Harris, K.R. and Pressley, M. (1991) 'The nature of cognitive instruction', *Exceptional Children* 57, 5: 392–403.

Harrison, B., Zollner, J. and Magill, B. (1996) 'The hole in whole language', *Australian Journal of Remedial Education* 27, 5: 6–18.

Harvey, J. (1995) 'The role of the special educational needs co-ordinator at Marton Grove Primary School', *Support for Learning* 10, 2: 79–82.

Hasselbring, T.S. and Goin, L.I. (1989) 'Enhancing learning through microcomputer technology', in E.A. Polloway and T.R. Patton, *Strategies for Teaching Learners with Special Needs* (5th edn), Columbus: Merrill.

Hasselbring, T.S., Goin, L. and Bransford, J. (1988) 'Developing math automaticity in learning handicapped children: the role of computerized drill and practice', *Focus on Exceptional Children* 20, 6: 1–7.

Hastings, N. and Schwieso, J. (1995) 'Tasks and tables: the effects of seating arrangements in primary classrooms', *Educational Research* 37, 3: 279–91.

Hatcher, P.J., Hulme, C. and Ellis, A.W. (1994) 'Ameliorating early reading failure by integrating the teaching of reading and phonological skills: the phonological linkage hypothesis', *Child Development* 65, 1: 41–57.

Hawkins, W. (1991) 'Parents as tutors of mathematics', *Australian Journal of Remedial Education* 23, 4: 16–19.

Heilman, A.W. (1993) *Phonics in Proper Perspective* (7th edn), Columbus: Merrill.

Henk, W.A., and Melnick, S.A. (1995) 'The Reader's Self-Perception Scale (RSPS): a new tool for measuring how children feel about themselves as readers', *The Reading Teacher* 48, 6: 470–82.

Heymsfeld, C.R. (1989) 'Filling the hole in whole language', *Educational Leadership* 46, 6: 65–9.

Hickerson, B. (1992) 'Reading and thinking with content area texts', *Reading Today* 9, 3: 32.

Hickson, F. (1990) 'The socialisation process', in S. Butler (ed.) *The Exceptional Child*, Sydney: Harcourt Brace Jovanovich.

Hiebert, E.H. and Taylor, B.M. (1994) *Getting Reading Right from the Start*, Boston: Allyn and Bacon.

Holdaway, D. (1982) 'Shared book experience: teaching reading using favourite books', *Theory into Practice* 21, 4: 293–300.

Holdaway, D. (1990) *Independence in Reading* (3rd edn), Sydney: Ashton Scholastic.

Hollowood, T., Salisbury, C., Rainforth, B. and Palombaro, M. (1995) 'Use of instructional time in classrooms serving students with and without severe disabilities', *Exceptional Children* 61, 3: 242–53.

Holmes, E.E. (1990) 'Motivation: an essential component of mathematics instruction', in T.T. Cooney and C.R. Hirsch (eds) *Teaching and Learning Mathematics in the 1990s*, Reston: National Council of Teachers of Mathematics.

Honig, A.S. and Wittmer, D.S. (1996) 'Helping children become more prosocial: ideas for classrooms, families, schools and communities', *Young Children* 51, 2: 62–74.

Horn, W.F. and Packard, T. (1985) 'Early identification of learning problems: a meta analysis', *Journal of Educational Psychology* 77, 5: 597–607.

Howell, K.W., Fox, S.L. and Morehead, M.K. (1993) *Curriculum-based Evaluation: Teaching and Decision Making* (2nd edn), Pacific Grove: Brooks Cole.

Howell, S.C. and Barnhart, R.S. (1992) 'Teaching word problem solving at primary level', *Teaching Exceptional Children* 24, 2: 44–6.

Hughes, C.A., Korinek, L. and Gorman, J. (1991) 'Self-managment for students with mental retardation in public school settings: a research review', *Education and Training in Mental Retardation* 26, 3: 271–91.

Humes, A. (1983) 'Putting writing research into practice' *Elementary School Journal* 84, 1: 3–17.

Hunting, R.P. (1996) 'Does it matter if Mary can read but can't add up?', *Education Australia* 33: 16–19.

Ilg, F.L. and Ames, L.B. (1964) *School Readiness*, New York: Harper and Row.

Isaacson, S.L. (1987) 'Effective instruction in written language', *Focus on Exceptional Children* 19, 6: 1–12.

Iversen, S. and Tunmer, W.E. (1993) 'Phonological processing skills and the Reading Recovery Program', *Journal of Educational Psychology* 85, 1: 112–26.

Jackson, M. (1972) *Reading Disability: Experiment, Innovation and Individual Therapy*, Sydney: Angus and Robertson.

Jackson, M.S. (1987) 'The treatment of severe reading disability: dyslexia', *Australian Journal of Remedial Education* 19, 2: 10–16.

Jackson, M.S. (1991) *Discipline: An Approach for Teachers and Parents*, Melbourne: Longman Cheshire.

Jansky, J. (1978) 'A critical review of some developmental and predictive precursors of reading disabilities', in A. Benton and D. Pearl (eds) *Dyslexia: An Appraisal of Current Knowledge*, New York: Oxford University Press.

Jansky, J. and de Hirsch, K. (1972) *Preventing Reading Failure*, New York: Harper and Row.

Johns, J. (1986) *Handbook for Remediation of Reading Difficulties*, Englewood Cliffs: Prentice Hall.

Johnson, D.W., Johnson, R.T. and Holubec, E. (1990) *Circles of Learning* (3rd edn), Edina, Minn.: Interaction Books.

Johnson, R.T. and Johnson, D.W. (1991) 'Cooperative learning: the best of the one-room schoolhouse', *The Teacher Educator* 27, 1: 6–13.

Jolly, C. (1992) *Jolly Phonics Handbook*, Chigwell: Jolly Learning Ltd.

Jongsma, K.S. (1990) 'Reading–spelling links', *The Reading Teacher*, 43: 608–10.

Jorgensen, C.M. (1995) 'Essential questions: inclusive answers', *Educational Leadership* 52, 4: 52–5.

Jorm, A.F. (1983) *The Psychology of Reading and Spelling Disability*, London: Routledge.

Kameenui, E.J. (1993) 'Diverse learners and the tyranny of time', *The Reading Teacher* 46, 5: 376–83.

Kauffman, J.M., Lloyd, J., Baker, J. and Riedel, T.M. (1995) 'Inclusion of all students with emotional or behavioural disorders? Let's think again', *Phi Delta Kappan* 76, 7: 542–6.

Kavale, K., Forness, S. and Lorsbach, T. (1991) 'Definition for definitions of learning disability', *Learning Disability Quarterly* 14, 4: 257–66.

Keith, R.W. and Engineer, P. (1991) 'Effects of methylphenidate on the auditory processing abilities of children with Attention Deficit-Hyperactivity Disorder', *Journal of Learning Disabilities* 24, 10: 630–40.

Kemp, C. (1992) 'Distinctive features of early childhood intervention services within early childhood education', *Special Education Perspectives* 1, 1: 3–14.

Kemp, M. (1987) *Watching Children Read and Write*, Melbourne: Nelson.

Kerin, M. (1990) 'The writing process with a computer', *Australian Journal of Remedial Education* 22, 1: 25–6.

Kindsvatter, R., Wilen, W. and Ishler, M. (1992) *Dynamics of Effective Teaching* (2nd edn), New York: Longman.

King, L. (1995) 'Classroom teaching', in F. Maltby, N. Gage and D. Berliner (eds) *Educational Psychology: An Australian and New Zealand Perspective*, Brisbane: Wiley.

Knight, B.A. (1992) 'The development of a locus of control measure designed to assess intellectually disabled students' beliefs in adaptive behaviour situations', *Australasian Journal of Special Education* 16, 2: 13–21.

Knight, B.A. (1994) 'The effects of a teaching perspective of guided internality on intellectually disabled students' locus of control orientation', *Educational Psychology* 14, 2: 155–65.

Knight, G., Arnold, G., Carter, M., Kelly, P. and Thornley, G. (1995) 'The mathematical needs of school leavers', *The Best of SET: Mathematics*, Camberwell: Australian Council for Educational Research.

Koop, T. and Minchinton, J. (1995) 'Inclusive curriculum: making it happen for students with disabilities', *Curriculum Perspectives* 15, 3: 1–8.

Kouba, V.L. and Franklin, K. (1993) 'Multiplication and division: sense making and meaning', in R.J. Jensen (ed.) *Research Ideas for the Classroom: Early Childhood Mathematics*, New York: Macmillan.

Lawrence, E.A. and Winschel, J.F. (1975) 'Locus of control: implications for special education', *Exceptional Children* 41, 7: 483–9.

LeGere, A. (1991) 'Collaboration and writing in the mathematics classroom', *Mathematics Teacher* 84, 3: 166–71.

LeRoy, B. and Simpson, C. (1996) 'Improving student outcomes through inclusive education', *Support for Learning* 11, 1: 32–6.

Lewis, A. (1992) 'From planning to practice', *British Journal of Special Education* 19, 1: 24–7.

Lewis, R. and Doorlag, D.H. (1991) *Teaching Special Students in the Mainstream* (3rd edn), New York: Merrill.

Lindsley, O.R. (1992) 'Precision teaching: discoveries and effects', *Journal of Applied Behaviour Analysis* 25, 1: 51–7.

Lingard, T. (1996) 'Literacy acceleration: enabling secondary-age students to become literate', *Support for Learning* 11, 1: 25–31.

Lipsky, D. and Gartner, A. (1989) *Beyond a Separate Education: Quality Education for All*, Baltimore: Brookes.

Lloyd, J.W. (1988) 'Direct academic interventions in learning disabilities', in M.C. Wang, M.C. Reynolds and H.J. Walberg (eds) *Handbook of Special Education: Research and Practice 2*, Oxford: Pergamon.

Lloyd, J.W. and Keller, C.E. (1989) 'Effective mathematics instruction: development, instruction and programs', *Focus on Exceptional Children* 21, 7: 1–10.

Loughrey, D. (1991) 'Hands on computer experience and the child with special educational needs', *Support for Learning* 6, 3: 124–6.

Lovey, J. (1996) 'Concepts in identifying effective classroom support', *Support for Learning* 11, 1: 9–12.

Lovitt, T.C. (1991) *Preventing School Dropouts*, Austin: Pro-Ed.

Lovitt, T.C. and Horton, S.V. (1994) 'Strategies for adapting science textbooks for youth with learning disabilities', *Remedial and Special Education* 15, 2: 105–16.

Lowenthal, B. (1996) 'Teaching social skills to preschoolers with special needs', *Childhood Education* 72, 3: 137–40.

Lunt, I., Evans, J., Norwich, B. and Wedell, K. (1994) 'Collaborating to meet special educational needs: effective clusters', *Support for Learning* 9, 2: 73 – 8.

Lyle, S. (1996) 'An analysis of collaborative group work in the primary school and factors relevant to its success', *Language and Education* 10, 1: 13–31.

Lyndon, H. (1989) 'I did it my way: an introduction to "Old Way: New Way"' *Australasian Journal of Special Education* 13, 1: 32–7.

McCormick, W. (1979) 'Teachers can learn to teach more effectively', *Educational Leadership* 37, 1: 59–60.

McCoy, K.M. (1995) *Teaching Special Learners in the General Classroom* (2nd edn), Denver: Love.

McGuiness, D., McGuiness, C. and Donohue, J. (1995) 'Phonological training and the alphabet principle: evidence for reciprocal causality', *Reading Research Quarterly* 30, 4: 830–52.

MacInnis, C. and Hemming, H. (1995) 'Linking the needs of students with learning disabilities to a whole language curriculum', *Journal of Learning Disabilities* 28, 9: 535–44.

McIntosh, M.E. and Draper, R.J. (1995) 'Applying the question-answer relationship strategy in mathematics', *Journal of Adolescent and Adult Literacy* 39, 2: 120–31.

McKinney, J.D. (1988) 'Research on conceptually and empirically derived sub-types of specific learning disability', in M.C. Wang, M. Reynolds and H.J. Walberg (eds) *Handbook of Special Education, Vol 2*, Oxford: Pergamon.

Maclellan, E. (1993) 'The significance of counting', *Education 3–13* 21, 3: 18–22.

McLeod, D.B. (1992) 'Research on affect in mathematics education', in D.A.Grouws (ed.) *Handbook of Research on Mathematics Teaching and Learning*, New York: Macmillan.

McManus, M. (1989) *Troublesome Behaviour in the Classroom*, London: Routledge.

McNally, J. and Murray, W. (1968) *Key Words to Literacy* (2nd edn), London: Schoolmaster Publishing Company.

Majsterek, D.J. and Ellenwood, A.E. (1995) 'Phonological awareness and beginning reading: evaluation of a school-based screening procedure', *Journal of Learning Disabilities* 28, 7: 449–56.

Malone, L.D., and Mastropieri, M.A. (1992) 'Reading comprehension instruction: summarization and self-monitoring', *Exceptional Children* 58, 3: 270–9.

Mann, V.A. (1993) 'Phonemic awareness and future reading ability', *Journal of Learning Disabilities* 26, 4: 259–69.

Mantzicopoulos, P. and Morrison, D. (1994) 'Early prediction of reading achievement', *Remedial and Special Education* 15, 4: 244–51.

Margalit, M. (1995) 'Effects of social skills training for students with an intellectual disability', *International Journal of Disability, Development and Education* 42, 1: 75–85.

Marsh, L.G. and Cooke, N.L. (1996) 'The effects of using manipulatives in teaching math problem solving to students with learning disabilities', *Learning Disabilities Research and Practice* 11, 1: 58–65.

Martin, K.F. and Manno, C. (1995) 'Use of a check-off system to improve middle school students' story compositions', *Journal of Learning Disabilities* 28, 3: 139–49.

Mather, N. (1992) 'Whole language reading instruction for students with learning disabilities: caught in the crossfire', *Learning Disabilities Research and Practice* 7: 87–95.

Mauer, D.M. and Kamhi, A.G. (1996) 'Factors that influence phoneme-grapheme correspondence learning', *Journal of Learning Disabilities* 29, 3: 259–70.

Meese, R.L. (1992) 'Adapting textbooks for children with learning disabilities', *Teaching Exceptional Children* 24, 3: 49–51.

Merrett, F. and Wheldall, K. (1984) 'Classroom behaviour problems which junior school teachers find most troublesome', *Educational Studies* 10, 2: 87–92.

Merry, R. and Peutrill, I. (1994) 'Improving word recognition for children with reading difficulties', *British Journal of Special Education* 21, 3: 121–3.

Milem, M. and Garcia, M. (1996) 'Student critics, teacher models: introducing process writing to high school students with learning disabilities', *Teaching Exceptional Children* 28, 3: 46–7.

Monroe, M. (1935) *Reading Aptitude Tests*, Boston: Houghton Mifflin.

Montague, M. and Fonseca, F. (1993) 'Using computers to improve story writing', *Teaching Exceptional Children* 25, 4: 46–9.

Moore, J. (1992) 'Good planning is the key', *British Journal of Special Education* 19, 1: 16–19.

Moustafa, M. (1993) 'Recoding in whole language reading instruction', *Language Arts* 70, 6: 483–7.

Murray-Seegert, C. (1992) 'Integration in Germany', *Remedial and Special Education* 13, 1: 34–43.

National Health and Medical Research Council (1990) *Learning Difficulties in Children and Adolescents*, Canberra: Australian Government Publishing Service.

Neale, M.D. (1988) *Neale Analysis of Reading Ability* (2nd edn), Hawthorn: ACER.

Neale, M.D. (1989) *Neale Analysis of Reading Ability (revised British edition)*, Windsor: NFER-Helson.

Newman, J.M. and Church, S.M. (1990) 'Myths of whole language', *Reading Teacher* 44, 1: 20–6.

Nichols, R. (1985) *Helping Your Child Spell*, Earley: University of Reading.

North, C. and Parker, M. (1994) 'Teaching phonolgical awareness', *Child Language Teaching and Therapy* 10, 3: 247–57.

O'Brien, D. (1992) *Writing in The Primary School*, Melbourne: Longman Cheshire

O'Neil, J. (1995) 'Can inclusion work? A conversation with Jim Kauffman and Mara Sapon-Shevin', *Educational Leadership* 52, 4: 4–6.

Olson, M.W. (1990) 'Phonemic awareness and reading achievement', *Reading Psychology* 11: 347–53.

Olssen, K., Adams, G., Grace, N. and Anderson, P. (1994) *Using the Mathematics Profile*, Melbourne: Curriculum Corporation.

Orton, A. (1992) *Learning Mathematics: Issues, Theory and Classroom Practice* (2nd edn), London: Cassell.

Paris, S.G. and Winograd, P. (1990) 'Promoting metacognition and motivation in exceptional children', *Remedial and Special Education* 11, 6: 7–15.

Parmar, R.S. and Cawley, J.F. (1994) 'Structuring word problems for diagnostic teaching', *Teaching Exceptional Children* 26, 4: 16–21.

Parmar, R.S., Cawley, J.F. and Frazita, R.R. (1996) 'Word-problem solving by students with and without mild disabilities', *Exceptional Children* 62, 5: 415–29.

Payne, E. (1991) 'Parents at work in special education in a middle school', *Australian Journal of Remedial Education* 23, 3: 27–9.

Perfetti, C.A., (1992) 'The representation problem in reading acquisition', in P.B. Gough, L.C. Ehri and R. Treiman (eds) *Reading Acquisition*, Hillsdale, NJ: Erlbaum.

Peters, M.L. (1985) *Spelling Caught or Taught: A New Look* (2nd edn), London: Routledge.

Peters, M.L. and Smith, B. (1993) *Spelling in Context*, Windsor: NFER-Nelson.

Phillips, N.B., Fuchs, L., Fuchs, D. and Hamlett, C. (1996) 'Instruction variables affecting student achievement: case studies of two contrasting teachers', *Learning Disabilities: Research and Practice* 11, 1: 24–33.

Phillips, V. and McCullough, L. (1990) 'Consultation-based programming: instituting a collaborative ethic in schools', *Exceptional Children* 45, 4: 291–304.

Pikulski, J.J. (1994) 'Preventing reading failure: a review of five effective programs', *The Reading Teacher* 48, 1: 30–9.

Pinnell, G.S. and associates (1994) 'Comparing instructional models for the literacy education of high-risk first graders', *Reading Research Quarterly* 29, 1: 9–39.

Polloway, E.A. and Patton, J.R. (1993) *Strategies for Teaching Learners with Special Needs* (5th edn), New York: Merrill.

Preen, B. and Barker, D. (1987) *Literacy Development*, Sydney: Harcourt Brace Jovanovich.

Pressley, M. (1994) 'State-of-the-science primary grade reading instruction or whole language?' *Educational Psychologist* 29, 4: 211–15.

Pressley, M., Brown, R., VanMeter, P. and Schuder, T. (1995) 'Transactional strategies', *Educational Leadership* 52, 8: 81.

Pressley, M. and McCormick, C.B. (1995) *Advanced Educational Psychology*, New York: Harper Collins.

Pressley, M. and Rankin, J. (1994) 'More about whole language methods of reading instruction for students at risk for early reading failure', *Learning Disabilities: Research and Practice* 9, 3: 157–68.

Print, M. (1992) *Curriculum Development and Design*, Sydney: Allen and Unwin.

Pumfrey, P. (1991) *Improving Children's Reading in the Junior School*, London: Cassell.

Putnam, J.W., Spiegel, A.N. and Bruininks, R.H. (1995) 'Future directions in education and inclusion of students with disabilities', *Exceptional Children* 61, 6: 553–76.

Quicke, J. (1995) 'Differentiation: a contested concept', *Cambridge Journal of Education* 25, 2: 213–24.

Rees, R. and Young, B. (1995) 'Bored witless', *Children Australia* 20, 4: 29–31.

Reetz, L.J. and Hoover, J.H. (1992) 'The acceptability and utility of five reading approaches as judged by middle school LD students', *Learning Disabilities Research and Practice* 7: 11–15.

Reisman, F.K. (1982) *A Guide to the Diagnostic Teaching of Arithmetic*, Columbus: Merrill.

Reynolds, M. and Dallas, S. (1991) *Reading Success*, Sydney: Prince of Wales Hospital.

Richardson, S.O. (1992) 'Historical perspectives on dyslexia', *Journal of Learning Disabilities* 25, 1: 40–7.

Rickleman, R. and Henk, W.A. (1991) 'Parents and computers: partners in helping children learn to read', *Reading Teacher* 44, 7: 508–9.

Roach, V. (1995) 'Supporting inclusion: beyond the rhetoric', *Phi Delta Kappan* 77, 4: 275–99.

Roberts, R. and Mather, N. (1995) 'The return of students with learning disabilities to regular classrooms: a sell out?', *Learning Disabilities: Research and Practice* 10, 1: 46–58.

Robinson, G.E. and Bartlett, K.T. (1995) 'Assessing mathematical learning', *Teaching Children Mathematics* 2, 1: 24–7.

Rogers, G. (1982) *Truckin' with Kenny*, Berri: South Australian Education Department.

Rogers, H. and Saklofske, D.H. (1985) 'Self-concept, locus of control and performance expectations of learning disabled children', *Journal of Learning Disabilities* 18, 5: 273–8.

Rogers, W. (1989a) *Decisive Discipline*, Geelong: Institute of Educational Administration.

Rogers, W. (1989b) *Making a Discipline Plan*, Melbourne: Nelson.

Rogers, W. (1995) *Behaviour Management: A Whole School Approach*, Sydney: Ashton Scholastic.

Rosenshine, B. (1986) 'Classroom instruction', in N.L. Gage (ed.), *The Psychology of Teaching Methods*, Chicago: NSSE.

Rosenshine, B. (1995) 'Advances in research on instruction', *Journal of Educational Research* 88, 5: 262–8.

Rowe, M.B. (1986) 'Wait time: slowing down may be a way of speeding up', *Journal of Teacher Education* 37, 1: 43–50.

Ruthven, K. (1995) 'Pupils views of number work and calculators', *Educational Research* 37, 3: 229–37.

Sacks, S.Z., Kekelis, L.S. and Gaylord-Ross, R.J. (1992) *The Development of Social Skills by Blind and Visually Impaired Students*, New York: American Foundation for the Blind.

Sale, P. and Carey, D.M. (1995) 'The sociometric status of students with disabilities in a full-inclusion school', *Exceptional Children* 62, 1: 6–19.

Salend, S.J. (1994) *Effective Mainstreaming: Creating Inclusive Classrooms* (2nd edn), New York: Macmillan.

Salisbury, C.L., Gallucci, C., Palombaro, M. and Peck, C.A. (1995) 'Strategies that promote social relations among elementary students with and without disabilities in inclusive schools', *Exceptional Children* 62, 2: 125–37.

Salmon, B. (1990) 'The role of games in the primary curriculum', *Teaching Mathematics* 15, 2: 24.

Salvesen, K.A. and Undheim, J.O. (1994) 'Screening for learning disabilities with teacher rating scales', *Journal of Learning Disabilities* 27, 1: 60–6.

Salvia, J. and Hughes, C. (1990) *Curriculum-based Assessment*, New York: Macmillan.

Satz, P. and Friel, J. (1974) 'Some predictive antecedents of specific reading disability: a preliminary two-year follow-up', *Journal of Learning Disabilities* 7, 7: 437–44.

Satz, P., Taylor, H.G., Friel, J. and Fletcher, J. (1978) 'Some developmental and predictive precursors of reading disability: a six year follow-up', in A.L. Benton and D.P. Pearl (eds) *Dyslexia: An Appraisal of Current Knowledge*, New York: Oxford University Press.

Sawyer, D.J. and Fox, B.J. (1991) *Phonological Awareness in Reading*, New York: Springer Verlag.

Schunk, D.H. (1989) 'Self-efficacy and cognitive achievement', *Journal of Learning Disabilities* 22, 1: 14–22.

Schwartz, S.L. and Curcio, F.R. (1995) 'Learning mathematics in meaningful contexts: an action-based approach in the primary grades', in P.A. House and A.F. Coxford (eds) *Connecting Mathematics Across the Curriculum*, Reston: National Council of Teachers of Mathematics.

Sears, H.C. and Johnson, D.M. (1986) 'The effects of visual imagery on spelling performance', *Journal of Educational Research* 79, 4: 230–3.

Sebba, J. and Ainscow, M. (1996) 'International development in inclusive schooling', *Cambridge Journal of Education* 26, 1: 5–18.

Secada, W.G. (1992) 'Race, ethnicity, social class, language, and achievement in mathematics', in D.A. Grouws (ed.) *Handbook of Research on Mathematics Teaching and Learning*, New York: Macmillan.

Serna, L. (1993) 'Social skills instruction', in E.A. Polloway and J.R. Patton (eds) *Strategies for Teaching Learners with Special Needs* (5th edn), New York: Merrill.

Shanahan, T. and Barr, R. (1995) 'Reading Recovery: an independent evaluation of the effects of an early instructional intervention for at-risk learners', *Reading Research Quarterly* 30, 4: 958–96.

Shaw, S., Cullen, J., McGuire, J. and Brinckerhoff, L. (1995) 'Operationalizing a definition of learning disabilities', *Journal of Learning Disabilities* 28, 9: 586–97.

Silver, A.A. (1978) 'Prevention', in A.L. Benton and D. Pearl (eds) *Dyslexia: An Appraisal of Current Knowledge*, New York: Oxford University Press.

Sindelar, P. and Deno, S.L. (1978) 'The effectiveness of resource programming', *Journal of Special Education* 12, 1: 17–28.

Skemp, R. (1976) 'Relational understanding and instrumental understanding', *Mathematics Teaching* 77: 20–6.

Slavin, R.E. (1991) 'Synthesis of research on cooperative learning', *Educational Leadership* 48, 5: 71–82.

Slavin, R.E. (1996) 'Neverstreaming: preventing learning disabilities', *Educational Leadership* 53, 5: 4–7.

Smelter, R.W., Rasch, B. and Yudewitz, G. (1994) 'Thinking of inclusion for all special needs students? Better think again', *Phi Delta Kappan* 76, 1: 35–8.

Smith, F. (1978) *Reading without Nonsense*, New York: Teachers College Press.

Smith, F. (1992) 'Learning to read: the never ending debate', *Phi Delta Kappan* 73, 6: 432–41.

Smith, N.B. (1969) 'The many faces of reading comprehension', *Reading Teacher* 23, 3: 249–59.

Smith, R. and Urquhart, I. (1996) 'Science and special educational needs', in E. Bearne (ed.) *Differentiation and Diversity in the Primary School*, London: Routledge.

Snider, V.E. (1992) 'Learning styles and learning to read: a critique', *Remedial and Special Education* 13, 1: 6–18.

Sparzo, F.J. and Poteet, J.A. (1993) 'Managing classroom behaviour to enhance teaching and learning', in J.S. Choate (ed.) *Successful Mainstreaming*, Boston: Allyn and Bacon.

Stahl, S.A. (1992) 'Saying the "p" word: nine guidelines for exemplary phonics instruction', *The Reading Teacher* 45, 6: 618–25.

Stainback, S., Stainback, W., East, K. and Sapon-Shevin, M. (1994) 'A commentary on inclusion and the development of a positive self-identity by people with disabilities', *Exceptional Children* 60, 6: 486–90.

Stainback, W., Stainback, S. and Stefanich, G. (1996) 'Learning together in inclusive classrooms', *Teaching Exceptional Children* 28, 3: 14–19.

Stainback, W., Stainback, S. and Wilkinson, A. (1992) 'Encouraging peer support and friendships', *Teaching Exceptional Children* 24, 2: 6–11.

Stanovich, K.E. (1986) 'Matthew Effects in reading: some consequences of individual differences in the acquisition of literacy', *Reading Research Quarterly* 21, 4: 360–407.

Staub, D. and Peck, C.A. (1995) 'What are the outcomes for nondisabled students?', *Educational Leadership* 52, 4: 36–40.

Stoessiger, R. and Wilkinson, M. (1991) 'Emergent Mathematics', *Education 3–13* 19, 1: 3–11.

Stott, D.H. (1978) *Helping Children with Learning Difficulties*, London: Ward Lock.

Stott, D.H., Green, L., and Francis, J. (1983) 'Learning style and school attainment', *Human Learning* 2: 61–75.

Stuart, M. (1995) 'Prediction and qualitative assessment of five- and six-year old children's reading: a longitudinal study', *British Journal of Educational Psychology* 65: 287–96.

Sullivan, G.S., Mastropieri, M.A. and Scruggs, T.E. (1995) 'Reasoning and remembering: coaching students with learning disabilities to think', *Journal of Special Education* 29, 3: 310–22.

Sutton, G. (1992) 'Cooperative learning works in mathematics', *Mathematics Teacher* 85, 1: 63–6.

Swicegood, P.R. and Linehan, S.L. (1995) 'Literacy and academic learning for students with behavioral disorders: a constructivist view', *Education and Treatment of Children* 18, 3: 335–47.

Taffe, R. and Smith, I.D. (1993) 'Behavioural and cognitive approaches to social skills training with young children', *Australasian Journal of Special Education* 18, 1: 26–35.

Talay-Ongan, A. (1994) 'Preventive intervention: preschoolers at-risk for learning difficulties', *Australasian Journal of Special Education* 18, 2: 11–20.

Templeton, S. (1992) 'New trends in an historical perspective: old story, new resolution, – sound and meaning in spelling', *Language Arts* 69: 454–63.

Tester, B. and Horoch, S. (1995) *Whole Language Phonics*, Melbourne: Longman.

Thompson, R., White, K. and Morgan, D. (1982) 'Teacher–student interaction patterns in classrooms with mainstreamed mildly handicapped students', *American Educational Research Journal* 19, 2: 220–36.

Thornton, C. and Bley, N. (eds) (1994) *Windows on Opportunity: Mathematics for Students with Special Needs*, Reston: National Council of Teachers of Mathematics.

Thornton, C. and Jones, G. (1994) 'Computational sense', in C.A. Thortnton and N. Bleys (eds) *Windows of Opportunity: Mathematics for Students with Special Needs*, Reston, National Council of Teachers of Mathematics.

Threlfall, J. (1996) 'The role of practical apparatus in the teaching and learning of arithmetic', *Educational Review* 48, 1: 3–12.

Thurman, S.K. and Widerstrom, A.H. (1990) *Infants and Young Children with Special Needs* (2nd edn), Baltimore: Brookes.

Topping, K. (1991) 'Achieving more with less: raising reading standards via parental involvement and peer tutoring', *Support for Learning* 6, 3: 112–15.

Torgesen, J.K., Wagner, R.K. and Rashotte, C.A. (1994) 'Longitudinal studies of phonological processing and reading', *Journal of Learning Disabilities* 27, 5: 276–86.

Trethowan, V., Harvey, D. and Fraser, C. (1996) 'Reading Recovery: comparison between its efficacy and normal classroom instruction', *Australian Journal of Language and Literacy* 19, 1: 29–37.

Vallecorsa, A., Ledford, R. and Parnell, G. (1991) 'Strategies for teaching composing skills', *Teaching Exceptional Children* 23, 2: 52–5.

Vandervelden, M.C. and Siegel, L.S. (1995) 'Phonological recoding and phoneme awareness in early literacy: a developmental approach', *Reading Research Quarterly* 30, 4: 854–75.

Van Kraayenoord, C. and Elkins, J. (1994) 'Learning difficulties in regular classrooms', in A. Ashman and J. Elkins (eds) *Educating Children with Special Needs* (2nd edn), New York: Prentice Hall.

Varnhagen, C.K. and Das, J.P. (1992) 'Analysis of cognitive processing and spelling errors of average and reading disabled children', *Reading Psychology* 13: 217–39.

Vaughn, S. and Schumm, J.S. (1995) 'Responsible inclusion for students with learning disabilities', *Journal of Learning Disabilities* 28, 5: 264–70, 290.

Vincent, L.J. (1995) 'Preschool curriculum and instruction', in M.A. Falvey (ed.) *Inclusive and Heterogeneous Schooling*, Baltimore: Brookes.

Wales, M.L. (1994) 'A language experience approach (LEA) in adult immigrant literacy programs in Australia', *Journal of Reading* 38, 3: 200–8.

Walker, D., Greenwood, C., Hart, B. and Carta, J. (1994) 'Prediction of school outcomes based on early language production and socio-economic factors', *Child Development* 65, 2: 606–21.

Wallace, G. and Kauffman, J.M. (1986) *Teaching Students with Learning and Behaviour Problems* (3rd edn), Columbus: Merrill.

Wang, M.C. (1981) 'Mainstreaming exceptional children: some instructional design and implementation considerations', *Elementary School Journal* 81, 4: 195–221.

Wang, M.C. and Stiles, B. (1976) 'An investigation of children's concept of self-responsibility for their school learning', *American Educational Research Journal* 13, 3: 159–79.

Wang, M.C. and Zollers, N.J. (1990) 'Adaptive instruction: an alternative service delivery approach', *Remedial and Special Education* 11, 1: 7–21.

Warger, C.L. and Pugach, M.C. (1996) 'Forming partnerships around curriculum', *Educational Leadership* 53, 5: 62–5.

Warren, J.S. and Flynt, S.W. (1995) 'Children with Attention Deficit Disorder: diagnosis and prescription of reading skill deficits', *Reading Improvement* 32, 2: 105–10.

Wasik, B.A. and Karweit, N.L. (1994) 'Off to a good start: effects of birth to three interventions on early school success', in R.E. Slavin, N.L. Karweit and B.A. Wasik (eds) *Preventing Early School Failure*, Boston: Allyn and Bacon.

Wasik, B.A. and Slavin, R.E. (1993) 'Preventing early reading failure with one-to-one tutoring: a review of five programs', *Reading Research Quarterly* 28, 2: 179–200.

Weckert, C. (1989) *Spelling Companion for Teachers*, Sydney: Martin.

Weimer, W. and Weimer, A. (1977) *Arithmetic Readiness Inventory*, Columbus: Merrill.

Weinstein, C.E., Ridley, D.S., Dahl, T. and Weber, E.S. (1989) 'Helping students develop strategies for effective learning', *Educational Leadership* 46, 4: 17–19.

Weisberg, P. and Savard, C.F. (1993) 'Teaching preschoolers to read: don't stop between the sounds when segmenting words', *Education and Treatment of Children* 16, 1: 1–18.

Wendon, L. (1992) *Letterland* (5th edn), Barton, Cambridge: Letterland Publications.

Wepner, S.B. (1991) 'Linking technology to genre-based reading', *Reading Teacher* 45, 1: 68–9.

Westwood, P.S. (1994) 'Reading and writing in the special school', *Australian Journal of Remedial Education* 26, 1: 28–32.

Westwood, P.S. (1995a) 'Learner and teacher: perhaps the most important partnership of all', *The Australasian Journal of Special Education* 19, 1: 5–16.

Westwood, P.S. (1995b) 'Teachers' beliefs and expectations concerning students with learning difficulties', *Australian Journal of Remedial Education* 27, 2: 19–21.

Wheal, R. (1995) 'Unleashing individual potential: a team approach', *Support Learning* 10, 2: 83–7.

Wheldall, K. (1995) 'Helping readers who are behind', *Education Monitor* 6, 1: 23–5.

Wheldall, K., Center, Y. and Freeman, L. (1993) 'Reading recovery in Sydney primary schools', *Australasian Journal of Special Education* 17, 2: 51–63.

Whitin, D.J. (1995) 'Connecting literature and mathematics', in P.A. House and A.F. Coxford (eds) *Connecting Mathematics Across the Curriculum*, Reston: National Council of Teachers of Mathematics.

Williams, W. and Fox, T.J. (1996) 'Planning for inclusion: a practical process', *Teaching Exceptional Children* 28, 3: 6–13.

Wilson, C.L. and Sindelar, P.T. (1991) 'Direct instruction in Math Word problems: students with learning disabilities', *Exceptional Children* 57, 6: 512–19.

Wimmer, H. (1996) 'The nonword reading deficit in developmental dyslexia: evidence from children learning to read German', *Journal of Experimental Child Psychology*, 61, 1: 80–90.

Wolf, A. and Fine, E. (1996) 'The Sharing Tree', *Teaching Exceptional Children* 28, 3: 76–7.

Wong, B., Butler, D.L., Ficzere, S.A. and Kuperis, S. (1996) 'Teaching low achievers and students with learning disabilities to plan, write, and revise opinion essays', *Journal of Learning Disabilities* 29, 2: 197–212.

Wong, B.Y. (1986) 'A cognitive approach to teaching spelling', *Exceptional Children* 53, 2: 169–73.

Wood, A. (1996) 'Differentiation in primary mathematics', in E. Bearne (ed.) *Differentiation and Diversity in the Primary School*, London: Routledge.

Wragg, J. (1989) *Talk Sense to Yourself*, Hawthorn: ACER.

Wray, D. and Medwell, J. (1989) 'Using desk-top publishing to develop literacy', *Reading* 23, 2: 62–8.

Young, B. and Rees, R. (1995) 'Born to fail: children at risk for severe learning difficulties', *Children Australia* 20, 4: 31–2.

Zalud, G.G., Hoag, C.C. and Wood, R.W. (1995) 'Combining the best aspects of different positions in reading instruction', *Reading Improvement* 32, 2: 121–3.

Zimmerman, B. and Schunk, D. (1989) *Self-regulated Learning and Academic Achievement*, New York: Springer Verlag.

Zipprich, M.A. (1995) 'Teaching web making as a guided planning tool to improve student narrative writing', *Remedial and Special Education* 16, 1: 3–15, 52.

Index